VOGUE

DICTIONARY OF
CROCHET STITCHES

Anne Matthews

DAVID & CHARLES
Newton Abbot   London

Published originally in Vogue Knitting, Butterick Company, instructions: page 164.

British Library Cataloguing in Publication Data

Matthews, Anne
   Vogue dictionary of crochet
   1. Crocheting
   I. Title
   746.43'4042   TT820

ISBN 0-7153-9010-4

Typeset by Typesetters (Birmingham) Ltd
Smethwick, West Midlands
Printed in West Germany
by Mohndruck
for David & Charles (Publishers) plc
Brunel House   Newton Abbot   Devon

Contents

Introduction

It isn't so many years ago that children were taught to crochet as well as to knit as a matter of course yet in recent years its use seems to have declined while the interest in knitting has increased. A pity, for crochet is as simple as knitting – both rely on a few basic stitches from which many patterns can be made.

Knitting patterns became much more interesting once designers understood the possibilities offered by the various stitches and how these could change according to the choice of yarn used to work them. The same is equally true for crochet. There are many interesting stitches each giving a different handle, a different look to the finished work, all well suited to the making of good looking, fashionable clothes. As it isn't always easy to find stylish crochet patterns, a section of this book shows how to adapt suitable knitting patterns or use crochet's ability to make firm 'fabric' like material to use in conjunction with commercial paper patterns.

The history of crochet is not well documented but it is thought to be as old as that of knitting. Discoveries of hooked needles have been dated as being from Biblical times and it has been suggested that the form of crochet known as Tunisian crochet was the link between knitting and crochet, worked as it is on a single long needle with a knob at one end and a hook at the other. Most writers about crochet agree that, in Europe at least, crochet developed from the form of embroidery known as tambour embroidery where the pattern was worked by taking the thread through the fabric using a hooked stick. In France the hooked stick was known as a "croc" and when the hook began to be used to make stitches in their own right, "crochet en air", both the hook and the art became generally known as crochet. By Victorian times crochet was used extensively for clothes and household furnishings, even to the crochet pantaloons used to cover piano legs, and Weldon and Company published a weekly Practical Crochet Magazine at 2d. or 2s 6d for a year's subscription.

Although crochet is international, two important differences should be noted. The stitches remain constant but there is a difference between American and European stitch terms. American crochet terms for the same stitch are one term behind that used in Europe and so, throughout this book, the crochet terms are given in both British and American terminology, ie **tr/dc**. It is exactly the same stitch, only the words are different; the important thing is to keep to the same side of the / while working a pattern. The other change was the move to standard hook sizes some years back. This rationalised hook sizes and modern patterns will quote these sizes. Anyone fortunate enough to find earlier crochet patterns should consult the hook chart guide on page 191.

Attractive crochet designs can be found in a number of foreign magazines and so a glossary of crochet terms in French, German and Italian is to be found at the back of the book. As there is also a trend towards using symbols rather than words for crochet instructions, these symbols are shown on page 190.

This book would not have been possible without the generous help of many. My thanks go to Mrs. Baker, Mrs. Haswell and Mrs. Nunn who worked many of the patterns, to Susan Wallace for her researches into the various aspects of crochet. My thanks must go too to J & P Coats, Vogue Knitting International and Pingouin for their kind permission to use material from their publications, to Alex Kroll for his guidance throughout, to Heather Johns for the layout and design of the pages and to Polly Sellar for her line drawings.

Facing page: sweater originally published in Vogue Knitting/Butterick instructions: see page 165

The Basic Stitches

*The four most used stitches in crochet.
How to work them is shown in detail
on page 149. They can be used on their own
as here or worked in combination
as shown in the following chapters.*

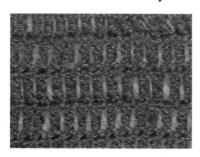

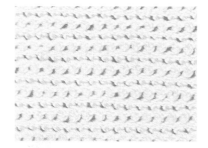

Double Treble/Treble Crochet (d.tr/tr)
any number of stitches, 4 turning ch

base row: work 1 d.tr/tr in fifth ch from hook and all subsequent ch to end of row, 4 turning ch.
row 1: miss first st, 1 d.tr/tr in every st to end of row ending with 1 d.tr/tr in turning ch, 4 turning ch.
repeat row 1

Double/Single Crochet (dc/sc)
any number of stitches, 1 turning ch

base row: work 1 dc/sc in second ch from hook and all subsequent ch to end of row, 1 turning ch.
row 1: 1 dc/sc in every st to end of row, 1 turning ch.
repeat row 1

Half Treble/Half Double Crochet (h.tr/h.dc)
any number of stitches, 2 turning ch

base row: work 1 h.tr/h.dc in third ch from hook and all subsequent ch to end of row, 2 turning ch.
row 1: miss first st, 1 h.tr/h.dc in every st to end of row ending with 1 h.tr/h.dc in turning ch, 2 turning ch.
repeat row 1

Treble/Double Crochet (tr/dc)
any number of stitches, 3 turning ch

base row: work 1 tr/dc in fourth ch from hook and all subsequent ch to end of row, 3 turning ch.
row 1: miss first st, 1 tr/dc in every st to end of row ending with 1 tr/dc in turning ch, 3 turning ch.
repeat row 1

Published originally in Vogue Knitting, Butterick Company, instructions: page 167.

Simple Patterns

Simple designs using a combination of basic stitches and chains to form interesting and effective patterns

multiple of 4+3, 1 turning ch

base row: work 1 dc/sc in second ch from hook, 1 dc/sc in next ch, * 3 ch, miss 3 ch, 1 dc/sc in next ch; repeat from * to end of row ending with 1 dc/sc in last ch, 1 turning ch.
row 1: 1 dc/sc in each first 2 sts, * 3 ch, miss 3 ch, 1 dc/sc in next st; repeat from * to end of row, 1 dc/sc in last st, 1 turning ch.
repeat row 1

multiple of 5, 5 turning ch

base row: work 1 dc/sc in sixth ch from hook, * 2 ch, miss 2 ch, 1 dc/sc in next ch, 4 ch, miss 2 ch, 1 dc/sc in next ch; repeat from * to end of row ending with 2 ch, 1 dc/sc in last st, 3 turning ch.
row 1: 1 tr/dc in first st, * 4 tr/dc in 2 ch space, 1 dc/sc in 4 ch loop; repeat from * to end of row ending with 1 tr/dc in turning ch, 5 turning ch.

row 2: miss first st, * 1 dc/sc in first tr/dc, 2 ch, 1 dc/sc in last tr/dc of 4 tr/dc group, 4 ch; repeat from * to end of row ending with 2 ch, 1 dc/sc in turning ch, 3 turning ch.
repeat rows 1–2

multiple of 2+1, 3 turning ch

base row: work 1 tr/dc in fourth ch from hook and all subsequent ch to end of row, 1 turning ch.
row 1: 1 dc/sc in first st, * 2 ch, miss 1 st, 1 dc/sc between next 2 sts; repeat from * to end of row ending with 1 dc/sc in turning ch, 3 turning ch.
row 2: 2 dc/sc in every 2 ch space to end of row, 1 dc/sc in turning ch, 3 turning ch.
row 3: miss first st, 1 tr/dc in every st to end of row, 1 tr/dc in turning ch, 1 turning ch.
repeat rows 1–3

Published originally in Vogue Knitting, Butterick Company, instructions: page 169

SIMPLE PATTERNS

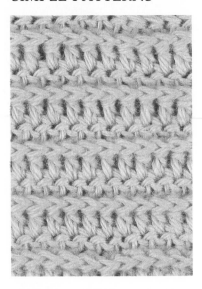

any number of stitches, 3 turning ch.

base row: work 1 tr/dc in fourth ch from hook and all subsequent ch to end of work, 2 turning ch.
row 1: * yoh, put hook horizontally behind the bar between first and second sts of previous row and bring it through space between second and third sts of previous row, yoh and work a tr/dc st; repeat from * to end of row, 2 turning ch.
row 2: miss first st, work 1 tr/dc in each st ending with 1 tr/dc into top of turning ch, 2 turning ch.
repeat rows 1–2

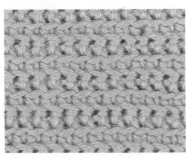

any number of stitches, 2 turning ch

base row: work 1 dc/sc in third ch from hook and all subsequent ch to end of row, 2 turning ch.
row 1: work 1 dc/sc into each st but into a single front loop only, 2 turning ch.
row 2: work 1 dc/sc into each st but into a single back loop only, 2 turning ch.
repeat rows 1–2

multiple of 2, 3 turning ch

base row: put hook in fourth ch, from hook, yoh, draw loop through, miss 1 ch, hook in next ch, yoh, draw loop through, yoh and draw loop through all 3 loops on hook, 1 ch, * hook into st just worked, yoh, draw loop through, miss 1 ch, hook into next ch, yoh, draw loop through, yoh and draw loop through all 3 loops, 1 ch; repeat from * ending with 1 dc/sc in last ch, 2 turning ch.
row 1: put hook under the 1 ch of previous row, yoh, draw loop through, hook under next 1 ch, yoh, draw loop through, yoh and draw through all 3 loops, 1 ch, * put hook under 1 ch just worked, yoh, draw loop through, hook into next 1 ch, yoh and draw loop through all 3 loops on hook, 1 ch; repeat from * ending with 1 dc/sc, 2 turning ch.
repeat row 1

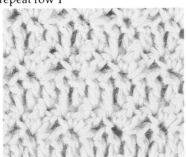

multiple of 3+1, 3 turning ch

base row: work 1 tr/dc in fourth ch from hook and all subsequent ch to end of row, 3 turning ch.
row 1: 2 tr/dc in first st, * miss 2 sts, (1 dc/sc, 2 tr/dc) in next st; repeat from * to end of row ending with 1 tr/dc in last st, 3 turning ch.
row 2: miss first st, 1 tr/dc in each next st to end of row, 1 tr/dc in turning ch.
repeat rows 1–2

multiple of 2+1, 2 turning ch

base row: work 1 tr/dc in third ch from hook and all subsequent ch to end of row, 2 turning ch.
row 1: miss first 2 sts, 1 tr/dc in third st, 1 tr/dc in second st, * miss next st, 1 tr/dc in next st, 1 tr/dc in missed st; repeat from * to end of row, 2 turning ch.
repeat row 1

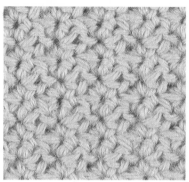

multiple of 3+2, 2 turning ch

base row: work 3 dc/sc in third ch from hook, * miss 2 ch, 3 dc/sc in next ch; repeat from * to end of row ending with 1 dc/sc in last ch, 1 turning ch.
row 1: work 3 dc/sc in second dc/sc of each group to end of row, ending with 1 dc/sc in last st, 1 turning ch.
repeat row 1

multiple of 3+1, 1 turning ch

base row: work (1 dc/sc, 1 h.tr/h.dc, 1 tr/dc) in second ch from hook, * miss 2 ch, (1 dc/sc. 1 h.tr/h.dc, 1 tr/dc) in next ch; repeat from * to end of row ending with 2 dc/sc in last ch, 1 turning ch.
row 1: (1 dc/sc 1 h.tr/h.dc, 1 tr/dc) in the dc/sc of each group of previous row, 1 turning ch.
repeat row 1

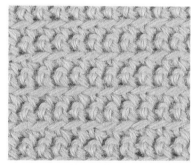

any number of stitches, 1 turning ch

base row: work 1 dc/sc in second ch from hook and all subsequent ch to end of row, 1 turning ch.
row 1: work 1 dc/sc in each st but into front loop only to end of row, 1 turning ch.

SIMPLE PATTERNS

multiple of 2+1, 2 turning ch

base row: work 1 dc/sc in third ch
from hook and all subsequent ch to
end of row, 1 turning ch.
row 1: miss first st, * 1 dc/sc into
next st, 1 dc/sc into base of next dc/
sc of previous row; repeat from * to
end of row ending with last st in
turning ch, 1 turning ch.
repeat row 1

any number of sts, 3 turning ch

base row: work 1 tr/dc in fourth ch
from hook and all subsequent ch to
end of row, 1 turning ch.
row 1: miss first st, 1 dc/sc in each
tr/dc to end of row ending with 1
dc/sc in turning ch, 3 turning ch.
row 2: miss first st, 1 tr/dc in each
dc/sc to end of row ending with 1
tr/dc in turning ch, 1 turning ch.
repeat rows 1–2

multiple of 5, 4 turning ch

base row: work 2 tr/dc in fifth ch
from hook, 2 tr/dc in next ch, miss 2
ch, 1 dc/sc in next ch, * 2 tr/dc in
next ch, 2 tr/dc in next ch, miss 2
ch, 1 dc/sc in next ch; repeat from *
to end of row, 3 turning ch.
row 1: * 1 dc/sc on last of the 4 tr/dc
sts, 2 ch, 4 tr/dc under 2 ch space;
repeat from * to end of row, 3
turning ch.
repeat row 1
NOTE this stitch needs a longer
chain foundation than actually
required as it tends to contract.

multiple of 3+1, 2 turning ch

row 1: work 1 tr/dc in third st from hook and all subsequent sts to end of row, 1 turning ch.
row 2: * (1 dc/sc, 2 tr/dc) in first st, miss 2 sts; repeat from * to end of row ending with 1 dc/sc in last st, 2 turning ch.
repeat rows 1–2

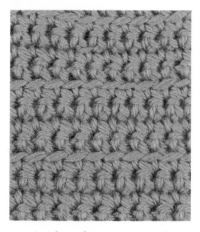

any number of sts, 1 turning ch

base row: work 1 dc/sc in second ch from hook and all subsequent ch to end of row, 1 turning ch.
row 1: 1 dc/sc in every st to end of row, 1 turning ch.
row 2: work 1 dc/sc in each st but into front loop only, to end of row, 1 turning ch.
rows 3, 4 and 5: as row 1.
row 6: as row 2.
repeat from row 3

multiple of 6+4, 3 turning ch

base row: work 2 tr/dc in fourth ch from hook, * miss 2 ch, 1 dc/sc in next ch, miss 2 ch, 5 tr/dc in next ch; repeat from * to end of row ending with miss 2 ch, 1 dc/sc in last ch, 3 turning ch.
row 1: 2 tr/dc into dc/sc, * 1 dc/sc in centre of tr/dc group, 5 tr/dc in dc/sc; repeat from * to end of row ending with 1 dc/sc into top of turning ch, 3 turning ch.
repeat row 1

any number of sts, 1 turning ch

base row: work 1 dc/sc in second ch from hook and all subsequent ch to end of row, 1 turning ch.
row 1: put hook into back horizontal loop only and work 1 dc/sc in each st, 1 turning ch.
repeat row 1

SIMPLE PATTERNS

multiple of 2, 1 turning ch

base row: work 1 dc/sc in second ch from hook, * 1 tr/dc in next ch, 1 dc/sc in next ch; repeat from * to end of row, ending with 1 tr/dc in last ch, 1 turning ch.
row 1: * 1 dc/sc in first st, 1 tr/dc in next st; repeat from * to end of row, 1 turning ch.
repeat row 1

multiple of 2+1, 1 turning ch

base row: work 1 dc/sc in second ch from hook and all subsequent ch to end of row, 1 turning ch.
row 1: * 1 dc/sc in first st, 1 h.tr/h.dc in next st; repeat from * to end of row ending with 1 dc/sc in last st, 1 turning ch.
row 2: work 1 dc/sc in every st to end of row, 1 turning ch.
repeat rows 1–2

multiple of 2+1, 2 turning ch

base row: work 1 tr/dc in third ch from hook, * miss 1 ch, 2 tr/dc in next ch; repeat from * to end of row ending with 1 tr/dc in last ch, 1 turning ch.
row 1: 1 dc/sc in first st, * 1 ch, 1 dc/sc between each group of 2 tr/dc; repeat from * to end of row, 3 turning ch.
row 2: miss first st and ch, * 2 tr/dc in next st, miss 1 ch; repeat from * to end of row ending with 1 tr/dc in last st, 1 turning ch.
repeat rows 1–2

multiple of 2+1, 2 turning ch

base row: work 1 tr/dc in third ch from hook, * miss 1 ch, 2 tr/dc in next ch; repeat from * to end of row ending with 1 tr/dc in last ch, 2 turning ch.
row 1: work 2 tr/dc between first 2 tr/dc and then 2 tr/dc between each next 2 sts ending with 1 tr/dc between last 2 sts, 2 turning ch.
repeat row 1

multiple of 8+4, 1 turning ch

base row: work 1 dc/sc in second ch from hook, 1 dc/sc in each next 3 ch, * 1 tr/dc in each next 4 ch, 1 dc/sc in each next 4 ch; repeat from * to end of row, 2 turning ch.
row 1: * 1 tr/dc in each first 4 sts, 1 dc/sc in each next 4 sts; repeat from * to end of row, 2 turning ch.
row 2: work 1 dc/sc in each tr/dc, 1 tr/dc in each dc/sc to end of row, 2 turning ch.
repeat rows 1–2

multiple of 6+1, 1 turning ch

base row: * work 1 dc/sc in second ch from hook and all subsequent ch to end of row, 1 turning ch.
row 1: * 1 dc/sc in first st, 1 h.tr/h.dc in next st, 1 tr/dc in next st, 1 d.tr/tr in next st, 1 tr/dc in next st, 1 h.tr/h.dc in next st; repeat from * to end of row, 3 turning ch.
row 2: * 1 d.tr/tr in first st, 1 tr/dc in next st, 1 h.tr/h.dc in next st, 1 dc/sc in next st, 1 h.tr/h.dc in next st, 1 tr/dc in next st; repeat from * to end of row, ending with 1 d.tr/tr in last st, 1 turning ch.
repeat rows 1–2

multiple of 6+4, 4 turning ch

base row: work 1 tr/dc in fifth ch from hook, * 1 ch, miss 1 ch, 1 tr/dc in each next 5 ch; repeat from * to end of row ending with 1 tr/dc in each last 2 ch, 3 turning ch.
row 1: 1 tr/dc in second st, * 1 d.tr/tr in missed 1 ch of previous row, 1 tr/dc in each next 2 sts, 1 ch, miss 1 st, 1 tr/dc in each next 2 sts; repeat from * to end of row ending with 1 tr/dc in last st, 1 tr/dc in turning ch, 3 turning ch.
row 2: 1 tr/dc in second st, * 1 ch, miss 1 st, 1 tr/dc in each next 2 sts, 1 d.tr/tr in missed 1 ch of previous row, 1 tr/dc in each next 2 sts; repeat from * to end of row ending with 1 tr/dc in last st, 1 tr/dc in turning ch, 3 turning ch.
repeat rows 1–2

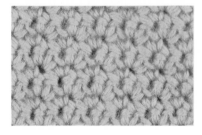

multiple of 2+1, 3 turning ch

base row: work 2 dc/sc in fourth ch from hook, * miss 1 ch, 2 dc/sc in next ch; repeat from * to end of row, 2 turning ch.
row 1: 2 dc/sc in second st, * miss 1 st, 2 dc/sc in next st; repeat from * to end of row, 2 turning ch.
row 2: miss 1 st, * 2 dc/sc in second st, miss 1 st; repeat from * to end of row, 2 turning ch.
repeat rows 1–2

SIMPLE PATTERNS

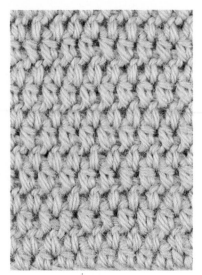

multiple of 2, 1 turning ch

base row: work 1 h.tr/h.dc in second ch from hook and all subsequent ch to end of row, 1 turning ch.
row 1: yoh, put hook between first 2 h.tr/h.dc and work 1 h.tr, * work 1 h.tr/h.dc between next 2 sts; repeat from * to end of row, 2 turning ch.
repeat row 1

multiple of 2, 2 turning ch

base row: with hook in third ch from hook, * yoh, draw through a loop, yoh, hook into next ch, yoh, draw through a loop, yoh and draw through the 5 loops, 1 ch, hook into next ch; repeat from * to end of row, 2 turning ch.
row 1: * yoh, hook into first st, yoh, draw through a loop, yoh, hook into next st, yoh, draw through the 5 loops, 1 ch; repeat from * to end of row, 2 turning ch.
repeat row 1

any number of sts, 2 turning ch.

base row: work 1 dc/sc in third ch from hook and in all subsequent ch to end of row, 2 turning ch.
row 1: * (yoh, hook into first st, yoh, draw up a loop, yoh, draw through 2 loops) twice in same st, yoh, draw loop through all 3 loops on hook; repeat from * to end of row, 2 turning ch.
repeat row 1

multiple of 4, 4 turning ch

base row: work 2 tr/dc in fifth ch from hook, 2 tr/dc in next ch, * miss 2 ch, 2 tr/dc in next ch, 2 tr/dc in next ch; repeat from * to end of row ending with 1 tr/dc in last ch, 3 turning ch.
row 1: miss first st * 2 tr/dc in second tr/dc, 2 tr/dc in third tr/dc; repeat from * to end of row ending with 1 tr/dc in turning ch, 3 turning ch.
repeat row 1

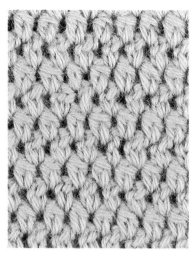

any number of sts, 2 turning ch

base row: * yoh, put hook in third ch from hook, yoh, draw up a loop, yoh, draw through 2 loops, yoh, put hook into the same ch, yoh, draw up a loop, yoh, draw through the four loops on hook; repeat from * working each ch thus to end of row ending with 1 h.tr/h.dc in last st, 2 turning ch.
row 1: * yoh, hook into space between first group of sts, yoh, draw up a loop, yoh, draw through 2 loops, yoh, hook into same space, yoh, draw up a loop, yoh, draw through the four loops on hook; repeat from * to end of row ending with 1 h.tr/h.dc, 2 turning ch.
repeat row 1

multiple of 3+1, 1 turning ch

base row: work (1 dc/sc, 1 ch, 1 dc/sc) in second ch from hook, * miss 2 ch, (1 dc/sc, 1 ch, 1 dc/sc) in next ch; repeat from * to end of row, 1 turning ch.
row 1: * (1 dc/sc, 1 ch, 1 dc/sc) in next 1 ch space; repeat from * to end of row, 1 turning ch.
repeat row 1

multiple of 3+1, 3 turning ch

base row: work (1 tr/dc, 2 ch, 1 dc/sc) in fourth ch from hook, * miss 2 ch, (2 tr/dc, 2 ch, 1 dc/sc) in next ch; repeat from * to end of row, 2 turning ch.
row 1: (1 tr/dc, 2 ch, 1 dc/sc) in first 2 ch space, * (2 tr/dc, 2 ch, 1 dc/sc) in next 2 ch space; repeat from * to end of row, 2 turning ch.
repeat row 1

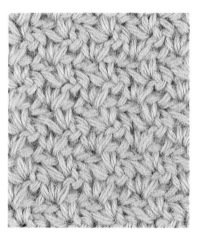

multiple of 3, 2 turning ch

base row: work 1 h.tr/h.dc in third ch from hook, miss 1 ch, * (1 dc/sc, 1 ch, 1 tr/dc) in next ch, miss 2 ch; repeat from * to end of row ending with 1 dc/sc in last ch, 3 turning ch.
row 1: * (1 dc/sc, 1 ch, 1 tr/dc) in 1 ch space; repeat from * to end of row ending with 1 dc/sc in turning ch, 3 turning ch.
repeat row 1

SIMPLE PATTERNS

multiple of 2+1, 2 turning ch

base row: put hook in third ch from hook and half work a tr/dc leaving 2 loops on hook, * miss 1 ch, work 1 tr/dc in next ch (3 loops on hook), yoh and draw through these loops, 1 ch, work 1 tr/dc in same st to 2 loops on hook; repeat from * to last 2 ch, miss 1 ch, work 1 tr/dc (3 loops on hook) yoh, draw through these loops, 3 turning ch.
row 1: work 1 tr/dc in first st to 2 loops, * miss 1 ch, work 1 tr/dc in next st (3 loops on hook) yoh and draw through these loops, 1 ch, work 1 tr/dc in same st to 2 loops on hook; repeat from * to end of row, 3 turning ch.
repeat row 1

multiple of 2+1 sts, 2 turning ch

base row: work 1 dc/sc in third ch from hook and all subsequent ch to end of row, 1 turning ch.
row 1: miss first st, * 1 dc/sc into back loop only of next st, 1 dc/sc into front loop only of next st; repeat from * to end of row, 1 turning ch.
repeat row 1

any number of sts, 4 turning ch

base row: work 1 d.tr/tr in fifth ch from hook and all subsequent ch to end of row, 2 turning ch.
row 1: miss first st, 1 h.tr/h.dc in each st to end of row ending with 1 h.tr/h.dc in turning ch, 4 turning ch.
row 2: miss first st, 1 d.tr/tr in back loop of each st to end of row, ending with d.tr/tr in turning ch, 2 turning ch.
repeat rows 1–2

multiple of 8+4, 2 turning ch

base row: work 1 dc/sc in third ch from hook, 1 dc/sc in each next 3 ch, * 1 tr/dc in each next 4 ch, 1 dc/sc in each next 4 ch; repeat from * to end of row, 2 turning ch.
row 1: * 1 tr/dc in back loop of each next 4 sts, 1 dc/sc in front loop each next 4 sts; repeat from * to end of row, 2 turning ch.
row 2: * 1 dc/sc in back loop of each next 4 sts, 1 tr/dc in front loop each next 4 sts; repeat from * to end of row, 2 turning ch.
repeat rows 1–2

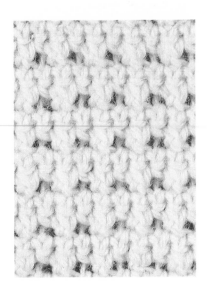

multiple of 2, 2 turning ch

base row: miss 2 ch, * put hook in next ch, draw through a loop, hook in next ch, draw through a loop, yoh and draw through first 2 loops, yoh and draw through last 2 loops, 1 ch; repeat from * to end of row, 1 turning ch.
row 1: 1 dc/sc in each st to end of row ending with 1 dc/sc in turning ch, 2 turning ch.
row 2: miss first st, * yoh, draw a loop through each of the next 2 sts, yoh, draw through 2 loops, yoh and draw through last 2 loops, 1 ch; repeat from * to end of row, 2 turning ch.
repeat rows 1–2

multiple of 3+1, 2 turning ch

base row: work 2 tr/dc in third ch from hook, miss 2 ch, * (1 dc/sc, 2 tr/dc) in next st, miss 2 ch; repeat from * to end of row ending with 1 dc/sc in last ch, 2 turning ch.
row 1: 2 tr/dc in first tr/dc, * (1 dc/sc, 2 tr/dc) in each dc/sc; repeat from * to end of row, ending with 1 dc/sc in turning ch, 2 turning ch.
repeat row 1

multiple of 2+1, 2 turning ch

base row: work 1 dc/sc in third ch from hook, * 1 ch, miss 1 ch, 1 dc/sc in next ch; repeat from * to end of row, 3 turning ch.
row 1: miss 2 sts, * 1 dc/sc in next dc/sc, 1 ch; repeat from * to end of row ending with 1 dc/sc in second st of turning ch, 3 turning ch.
repeat row 1

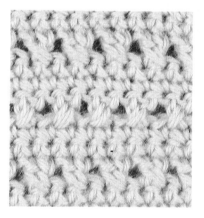

multiple of 2+1, 1 turning ch

row 1: work 1 dc/sc in second ch from hook and all subsequent sts to end of row, 1 turning ch.
row 2: work a dc/sc into each st to end of row, 2 turning ch.
row 3: miss first 2 sts, 1 tr/dc in third st, 1 tr/dc in second st, * miss next st, 1 tr/dc in second st, 1 tr/dc in missed st; repeat from * to end of row, 1 turning ch.
repeat rows 1–3

SIMPLE PATTERNS

any number of sts, 2 turning ch

base row: work 1 tr/dc in third ch from hook and all subsequent ch to end of row, 2 turning ch.
row 1: miss first st, 1 h.tr/h.dc in each st of previous row ending with 1 h.tr/h.dc in top of turning ch, 3 turning ch.
row 2: miss first st, 1 tr/dc in back loop of each st to end of row ending with 1 tr/dc in top of turning ch, 2 turning ch.
repeat rows 1–2

multiple of 2+1, 2 turning ch

base row: work (1 dc/sc, 1 ch, 1 dc/sc) in third ch from hook, miss 1 ch, * (1 dc/sc, 1 ch, 1 dc/sc) in next ch, miss 1 ch; repeat from * to end of row ending with (1 dc/sc, 1 ch, 1 dc/sc) in last st, 2 turning ch.
row 1: * work (1 dc/sc, 1 ch, 1 dc/sc) in 1 ch space; repeat from * to end of row ending with 1 dc/sc in last st, 2 turning ch.
repeat row 1

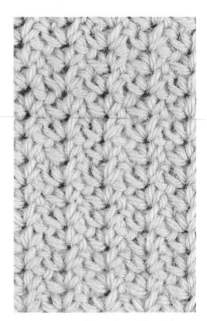

any even number of sts, 1 turning ch

base row: work (1 dc/sc, 2 ch, 1 dc/sc) in second ch from hook, * miss 1 ch, (1 dc/sc, 2 ch, 1 dc/sc) in next ch; repeat from * to end of row, 1 turning ch.
row 1: * (1 dc/sc, 2 ch, 1 dc/sc) in each 2 ch space; repeat from * to end of row, 1 turning ch.
repeat row 1

any number of sts, 3 turning ch

base row: put hook in fourth ch and work 1 hb.tr/hb.dc (yoh, hook in ch, yoh, draw through st and first loop, yoh, draw through 1 loop, yoh, draw through both loops on hook) in this and all subsequent ch to end of row, 3 turning ch.
row 1: miss first st, 1 hb.tr/hb.dc into each st and in turning ch to end of row, 3 turning ch.
repeat row 1

multiple of 2+1, 2 turning ch

base row: work 1 tr/dc in third ch from hook and all subsequent ch to end of row, 2 turning ch.
row 1: * 1 tr/dc into front loop of first st, 1 tr/dc into back loop of next st; repeat from * to end of row, 2 turning ch.
repeat row 1

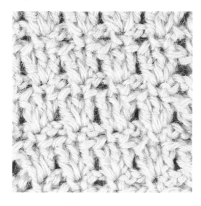

multiple of 3+1, 1 turning ch

base row: work 1 dc/sc in second ch from hook, * 2 ch, miss 2 ch, 1 dc/sc in next ch; repeat from * to end of row, 3 turning ch.
row 1: 1 tr/dc in first st, * 3 tr/dc in next dc/sc; repeat from * to end of row ending with 2 tr/dc in last dc/sc, 1 turning ch.
row 2: 1 dc/sc in first st, *2 ch, 1 dc/sc in centre tr/dc; repeat from * to end of row ending with 1 dc/sc in turning ch, 3 turning ch.
repeat rows 1–2

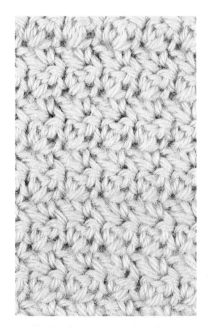

multiple of 2+1, 2 turning ch

base row: work (1 dc/sc, 1 tr/dc) in third ch from hook. * miss 1 ch, (1 dc/sc, 1 tr/dc) in next ch; repeat from * to end of row, ending with 1 tr/dc in last st, 2 turning ch.
row 1: (1 dc/sc, 1 tr/dc) in each second st to end of row ending with 1 tr/dc in turning ch, 2 turning ch.
repeat row 1

any number of sts, 2 turning ch

base row: put hook in third ch from hook, * yoh, draw yarn through, yoh, draw through 1 loop, yoh, draw through 2 loops hook into next ch; repeat from * in each ch to end of row, 2 turning ch.
row 1: * yoh in first st, draw yarn through, yoh, draw through 1 loop, yoh, draw through 2 loops hook into next st, repeat from * in each st to end of row, 2 turning ch.
repeat row 1

SIMPLE PATTERNS

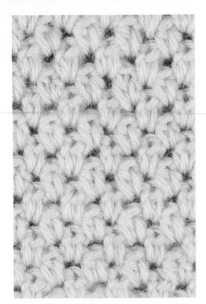

any uneven number of stitches

base row: work 2 h.tr/h.dc in third ch from hook, * miss 1 ch, 2 h.tr/h.dc in next ch; repeat from * to end of row, 2 turning ch.
row 1: miss two sts, * 2 h.tr/h.dc between next 2 h.tr/h.dc; repeat from * to end of row, 2 turning ch.
repeat row 1

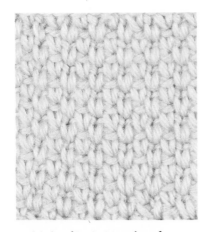

multiple of 2+1, 1 turning ch

base row: work 1 dc/sc in second ch from hook, * 1 ch, miss 1 ch, 1 dc/sc in next ch; repeat from * to end of row, 1 turning ch.
row 1: * 1 dc/sc in 1 ch space, 1 ch; repeat from * to end of row, 1 dc/sc in turning ch, 1 turning ch.
repeat row 1

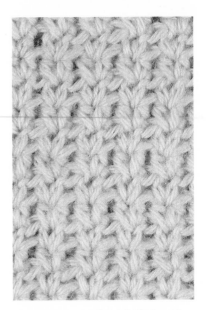

any uneven number of stitches, 2 turning ch

base row: work 1 h.tr/h.dc in third ch from hook, * miss 1 ch, 2 h.tr/h.dc in next ch; repeat from * to end of row, 3 turning ch.
row 1: 1 h.tr/h.dc between first 2 h.tr/h.dc of previous row, * 2 h.tr/h.dc between each 2 h.tr/h.dc group; repeat from * to end of row ending with 2 h.tr/h.dc between the last h.tr/h.dc and turning ch, 3 turning ch.
repeat row 1

multiple of 2, 2 turning ch

base row: work 1 tr/dc in third ch from hook and all subsequent ch to end of row, 2 turning ch.
row 1: * 1 tr/dc into gap between tr/dc sts of previous row; repeat from * to end of row, 2 turning ch.
repeat row 1

multiple of 2+1, 1 turning ch

base row: work 1 h.tr/h.dc in
second ch from hook and all
subsequent ch to end of row, 2
turning ch.
row 1: * 1 h.tr/h.dc in first st in back
loop only, 1 h.tr/h.dc in next st in
front loop only; repeat from * to last
st, 1 h.tr/h.dc in back loop, 2
turning ch.
repeat row 1

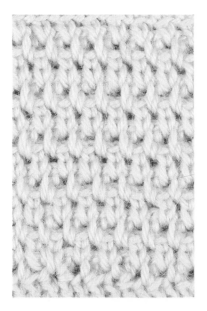

multiple of 2+1, 2 turning ch

base row: work 1 d.dc/d.sc in third
ch from hook, * 1 ch, miss 1 ch, 1
d.dc/d.sc in next ch; repeat from *
to end of row, 2 turning ch.
row 1: * 1 d.dc/d.sc into ch 1 space,
1 ch, miss 1 st; repeat from * to end
of row, 2 turning ch.
repeat row 1

multiple of 4+3, 3 turning ch

base row: work 2 tr/dc in fourth ch
from hook, * miss 1 ch, 1 dc/sc in
next ch, miss 1 ch, 3 tr/dc in next st;
repeat from * to end of row ending
with 1 dc/sc in last ch, 3 turning ch.
row 1: 2 tr/dc in first dc/sc, * 1 dc/sc
between first and second tr/dc of 3
tr/dc group of previous row, 3 tr/dc
in dc/sc; repeat from * to end of
row ending with 1 dc/sc in turning
ch, 3 turning ch.
repeat row 1

multiple of 3+1, 3 turning ch

base row: work (1 tr/dc, 2 ch, 1 dc/
sc) in fourth ch from hook, * miss 2
ch, (2 tr/dc, 2 ch, 1 dc/sc) in next ch;
repeat from * to end of row, 2
turning ch.
row 1: * (2 tr/dc, 2 ch, 1 dc/sc) in 2
ch space; repeat from * to end of
row, 2 turning ch.
repeat row 1

Textured Patterns

*A family of stitch designs
in widely different patterns with strong
surface and textural interest*

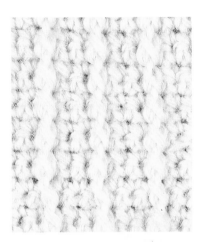 

multiple of 3, 1 turning ch

base row 1: work 1 dc/sc in second
ch from hook and all subsequent ch
to end of row, 1 turning ch.
base row 2: 1 dc/sc in every st to end
of row, 1 turning ch.
row 1: * 1 dc/sc in each first 2 sts,
hook from back to front of third st
two rows below, yoh and draw
loop through to level of row being
worked and complete as a dc/sc;
repeat from * to end of row, 1
turning ch.
row 2: 1 dc/sc in every st to end of
row, 1 turning ch.
repeat rows 1–2
NOTE: make sure that the ridge st
is always over the previously
lengthened st.

multiple of 15+2, 3 turning ch

base row: work 1 tr/dc in fourth ch
from hook 1 tr/dc in next ch, * 1 tr/
dc in each next 4 ch, (1 ch, miss 1
ch, 1 tr/dc in next st) three times, 1
tr/dc in each next 3 ch; repeat from
* to end of row ending with 1 tr/dc
in each last 2 sts, 1 turning ch.
row 1: 1 dc/sc in each next 6 sts, * tr/

dc5tog in 1 ch space, 1 dc/sc in each
next st, ch and st, tr/dc5tog in next
1 ch space, 1 dc/sc in each last 4 sts;
repeat from * to end of row ending
with 1 dc/sc in each last 2 sts, 3
turning ch.
row 2: 1 tr/dc in each first 2 sts, * 1
r.f.d.tr/tr in next st 2 rows below, 1
tr/dc in next st, 1 r.f.d.tr/tr in next
st 2 rows below, (1 ch, miss 1 st, 1
tr/dc in next st) three times, 1 ch, 1
r.f.d.tr/dc in next st 2 rows below, 1
tr/dc in next st, 1 r.f.d.tr/dc in next
st 2 rows below; repeat from * to
end of row ending with 1 tr/dc in
each last 2 sts, 1 turning ch.
row 3: 1 dc/sc in each next 2 sts, * 1
dc/sc in each next 6 sts and ch, 1 tr/
dc5tog in next st, 1 dc/sc in each
next 6 sts and ch; repeat from * to
end of row ending with 1 dc/sc in
each last 2 sts, 3 turning ch.
row 4: 1 tr/dc in each first 2 sts, * (1
r.f.d.tr/dc in equivalent st 2 rows
below, 1 tr/dc in next st) twice, (1
ch, miss 1 st, 1 tr/dc in next st) three
times, 1 r.f.d.tr/dc in equivalent st 2
rows below, 1 tr/dc in next st, 1
r.f.d.tr/dc in equivalent st 2 rows
below; repeat from * to end of row
ending with 1 tr/dc in each last 2
sts, 1 turning ch.
repeat rows 1–4

Published originally in Vogue Knitting, Butterick Company, instructions: page 170.

TEXTURED PATTERNS

multiple of 8+5, 2 turning ch.

base row: work 1 dc/sc in third ch
from hook, * 1 dc/sc in each next 3
sts, (1 dc/sc in next st, 3 ch, 1 dc/sc
in next st) twice, 1 dc/sc in next st;
repeat from * to end of row ending
with 1 dc/sc in each last 4 sts, 2
turning ch.
row 1: miss first st, 1 dc/sc in next
and all subsequent sts to end of
row ending with 1 dc/sc in turning
ch, 2 turning ch.
row 2: miss first st, * 1 dc/sc in each
next 4 sts, (1 dc/sc in next st, 3 ch, 1
dc/sc in next st) twice; repeat from
* to end of row ending with 1 dc/sc
in turning ch, 2 turning ch.
row 3: as row 1.
row 4: miss first st, (1 dc/sc in next
st, 3 ch, 1 dc/sc in next st) twice, 1
dc/sc in each next 4 sts; repeat from
* to end of row ending with 1 dc/sc
in turning ch, 2 turning ch.
row 5: as row 1.
row 6: as row 4.
row 7: as row 1.
row 8: as row 2.
repeat rows 1–8

multiple of 6+4, 1 turning ch

base row: work 1 dc/sc in second ch
from hook and all subsequent ch to
end of row, 1 turning ch.
row 1: miss first st, 1 dc/sc in all
subsequent st to end of row, 1 dc/
sc in turning ch, 1 turning ch.
row 2: miss first st, 1 dc/sc in next
st, * 3 ch bobble in next st, 1 dc/sc
in each next 5 sts; repeat from * to
end of row ending with 1 dc/sc in
turning ch, 1 turning ch.
row 3: as row 1.

row 4: miss first st, * 1 dc/sc in each
next 4 sts, 3 ch bobble in next st, 1
dc/sc in next st; repeat from * to
end of row ending with 1 dc/sc in
turning ch, 1 turning ch.
repeat rows 1–4

multiple of 4, 3 turning ch

base row: work 1 tr/dc in fourth ch
from hook and all subsequent ch to
end of row, 1 turning ch.
row 1: 1 dc/sc in each first 2 sts, 1
bobble (half work 5 tr/dc then
finish all sts together), * 1 dc/sc in
each next 3 sts, 1 bobble; repeat
from * to end of row ending with 1
dc/sc in last st, 1 dc/sc in turning
ch, 3 turning ch.
row 2: miss first st, * 1 tr/dc in each
st to end of row, 1 turning ch.
row 3: 1 dc/sc in each first 4 sts, * 1
bobble, 1 dc/sc in each next 3 sts;
repeat from * to end of row ending
with 1 dc/sc in turning ch, 3
turning ch.
row 4: as row 2.
repeat rows 1–4

multiple of 2+1, 2 turning ch

base row: work 1 dc/sc in third ch from hook and all subsequent ch to end of row, 3 turning ch.
row 1: 1 bobble into first st, (yarn over hook, draw through a loop, [yarn over hook, hook in same st, draw through a loop] twice, yarn over hook and draw through all 7 loops), * 1 dc/sc in next st, 1 bobble in next st; repeat from * to end of row, 2 turning ch.
row 2: 1 dc/sc in each st to end of row, 2 turning ch.
row 3: * 1 dc/sc in first st, 1 bobble in next st; repeat from * to end of row ending with 1 dc/sc in last st, 2 turning ch.
row 4: as row 2 but with 3 turning ch.
repeat rows 1–4

multiple of 6+2, 3 turning ch

base row: half work 4 tr/dc cluster in fourth ch from hook then finish the 4 sts together, * 1 tr/dc in each next 5 sts, 1 cluster in next st; repeat from * to end of row ending with 1 tr/dc in last st, 3 turning ch.
row 1: miss first st, 1 tr/dc in all subsequent sts to end of row ending with 1 tr/dc in turning ch, 3 turning ch.
row 2: miss first st, * 1 tr/dc in next st, 1 cluster in next st, 1 tr/dc in each next 4 sts; repeat from * to end of row ending with 1 tr/dc in last st, 1 tr/dc in turning ch, 3 turning ch.
row 3: as row 1.
row 4: miss first st, * 1 tr/dc in each next 2 sts, 1 cluster in next st, 1 tr/dc in each next 3 sts; repeat from * to end of row ending with 1 tr/dc in last st, 1 tr/dc in turning ch, 3 turning ch.

row 5: as row 1.
row 6: miss first st, 1 tr/dc in each next 3 sts, 1 cluster in next st, 1 tr/dc in each next 2 sts; repeat from * to end of row ending with 1 tr/dc in last st, 1 tr/dc in turning ch, 3 turning ch.
row 7: as row 1.
row 8: miss first st, * 1 tr/dc in each next 4 sts, 1 cluster in next st, 1 tr/dc in next st; repeat from * ending with 1 tr/dc in last st, 1 tr/dc in turning ch, 3 turning ch.
row 9: as row 1.
row 10: miss first st, * 1 tr/dc in each next 5 sts, 1 cluster in next st; repeat from * to end of row ending with 1 tr/dc in last st, 1 tr/dc in turning ch.
row 11: as row 1.
row 12: miss first st, * 1 cluster in next st, 1 tr/dc in each next 5 sts; repeat from * to end of row ending with 1 cluster in last st, 1 tr/dc in turning ch.
repeat rows 1–12

TEXTURED PATTERNS

multiple of 4, 3 turning ch

base row: work 1 tr/dc in fourth ch
from hook and each subsequent ch
to end of row, 2 turning ch.
row 1: miss first st, * 1 f.r.tr/dc
round each next 3 sts, 1 b.r.tr/dc
round next st; repeat from * to end
of row ending with 1 f.r.tr/dc
round each last three sts, 1 h.tr/h.dc
in turning ch, 2 turning ch.
row 2: miss first st, * 1 b.r.tr/dc
round each next 3 sts, 1 f.r.tr/dc
round next st; repeat from * to end
of row ending with 1 b.r.tr/dc
round each last 3 sts, 1 h.tr/h.dc in
turning ch. 2 turning ch.
repeat rows 1–2

multiple of 4+1, 3 turning ch

base row: work 1 tr/dc in fourth ch
from hook and all subsequent ch to
end of row, 2 turning ch.
row 1: miss first st, * 1 f.r.tr/dc
round each next 2 sts, 1 b.r.tr/dc
round each next 2 sts; repeat from *
to end of row ending with 1 tr/dc in
turning ch, 2 turning ch.
row 2: miss first st, * 1 b.r.tr/dc
round next st, 1 f.tr/dc round each
next 2 sts, 1 b.r.tr/dc round next st;
repeat from * to end of row, ending
with 1 tr/dc in turning ch, 2 turning
ch.
row 3: miss first st, * 1 b.r.tr/dc
round each next 2 sts, 1 f.r.tr/dc
round each next 2 sts; repeat from *
to end of row ending with 1 tr/dc in
turning ch, 2 turning ch.
row 4: miss first st, * 1 f.r.tr/dc
round next st, 1 b.r.tr/dc round
each next 2 sts, 1 f.r.tr/dc round

next st; repeat from * to end of row
ending with 1 tr/dc in turning ch, 2
turning ch.
row 5: as row 3.
row 6: as row 2.
row 7: as row 1.
row 8: as row 4.
repeat rows 1–8

multiple of 2+1, 2 turning ch.

base row: work 1 tr/dc in third ch
from hook and all subsequent ch to
end of row, 2 turning ch.
row 1: miss first st, * 1 f.r.tr/dc
round next st, 1 b.r.tr/dc round
next st; repeat from * to end of row,
1 tr/dc in turning ch, 2 turning ch.
repeat row 1

multiple of 8, 5 turning ch

base row: work 1 tr/dc in sixth ch from hook, * 1 ch, miss 1 ch, 1 tr/dc in next ch; repeat from * to end of row ending with 1 tr/dc in last ch, 2 turning ch.
row 1: miss first st, * (1 b.r.tr/dc round next st, 1 ch) twice, (1 f.r.tr/dc round next st, 1 ch) twice; repeat from * to end of row ending with 1 h.tr/h.dc in turning ch, 3 turning ch.
row 2: as row 1.
row 3: miss first st, * (1 f.r.tr/dc round next st, 1 ch) twice, (1 b.r.tr/dc round next st, 1 ch) twice; repeat from * to end of row ending with 1 h.tr/h.dc in turning ch, 3 turning ch.
row 4: as row 3.
repeat rows 1–4

multiple of 6+2, 2 turning ch

base row: work 1 tr/dc in third ch from hook and all subsequent ch to end of row, 2 turning ch.
row 1: miss first st, * 1 b.r.tr/dc round each next 3 sts, 1 f.r.tr/dc round each next 3 sts; repeat from * to end of row ending with 1 tr/dc in turning ch, 2 turning ch.
row 2: miss first st, * 1 f.r.tr/dc round next st, 1 b.r.tr/dc round each next 3 tr/dc. 1 f.r.tr/dc round each next 2 sts; repeat from * to end of row ending with 1 tr/dc in turning ch, 2 turning ch.
row 3: miss first st, * 1 b.r.tr/dc round next st, 1 f.r.tr/dc in each next 3 sts, 1 b.r.tr/dc in each next 2 sts; repeat from * to end of row ending with 1 tr/dc in turning ch, 2 turning ch.
row 4: miss first st, * 1 f.r.tr/dc in each next 3 sts, 1 b.r.tr/dc in each next 3 sts; repeat from * to end of row ending with 1 tr/dc in turning

ch, 2 turning ch.
row 5: miss first st, * 1 f.r.tr/dc in each next 2 sts, 1 b.r.tr/dc in each next 3 sts, 1 f.r.tr/dc in next st; repeat from * to end of row ending with 1 tr/dc in turning ch, 2 turning ch.
row 6: miss first st, * 1 b.r.tr/dc in each next 2 sts, 1 f.r.tr/dc in each next 3 sts, 1 b.r.tr/dc in next st; repeat from * to end of row ending with 1 tr/dc in turning ch, 2 turning ch.
repeat rows 1–6

multiple of 8+1, 2 turning ch

base row: work 1 tr/dc in third ch from hook and all subsequent ch to end of row, 2 turning ch.
row 1: miss first st, * 1 f.r.tr/dc in each next 4 sts, 1 b.r.tr/dc in each next 4 sts; repeat from * to end of row ending with 1 tr/dc in last st, 1 tr/dc in turning ch, 2 turning ch.
row 2: as row 1 ending with 1 tr/dc in turning ch, 2 turning ch.
rows 3 & 4: as row 2
row 5: miss first st, * 1 b.r.tr/dc in each next 4 sts, 1 f.r.tr/dc in each next 4 sts; repeat from * to end of row ending with 1 tr/dc in turning ch, 2 turning ch.
rows 6, 7 & 8: as row 5
repeat rows 1–8

TEXTURED PATTERNS

multiple of 8+1, 3 turning ch.

base row: work 1 tr/dc in fourth ch
from hook and all subsequent ch to
end of row, 3 turning ch.
row 1: miss first st, * 1 b.r.tr/dc in
each next 4 sts, 1 f.r.tr/dc in each
next 4 sts; repeat from * to end of
row, 3 turning ch.
row 2: as row 1 ending with 1 tr/dc
in turning ch, 3 turning ch.
row 3: miss first st, 1 b.r.tr/dc in
each next 2 sts, * 1 f.r.tr/dc in each
next 4 sts, 1 b.r.tr/dc in each next 4
sts; repeat from * to end of row
ending with 1 b.r.tr/dc in last st, 1
tr/dc in turning ch, 3 turning ch.
row 4: miss first st, 2 f.r.tr/dc in
each next 2 sts, * 1 b.r.tr/dc in each
next 4 sts, 1 f.r.tr/dc in each next 4
sts; repeat from * to end of row
ending with 1 f.r.tr/dc in last st, 1
tr/dc in turning ch, 3 turning ch.
row 5: miss first st, * 1 f.r.tr/dc in
each next 4 sts, 1 b.r.tr/dc in each
next 4 sts; repeat from * to end of
row ending with 1 b.r.tr/dc in each
last 3 sts, 1 tr/dc in turning ch, 3
turning ch.
row 6: as row 5
row 7: as row 4
row 8: as row 3
repeat rows 1–8

multiple of 10+9, 2 turning ch

base row: work 1 dc/sc in third ch
from hook and all subsequent ch to
end of row, 3 turning ch.
row 1: miss first st, 1 tr/dc in each
next 3 sts, * (1 ch, [yoh, hook round
stem of previous tr, draw up loop 7
times] miss next 2 sts, hook into
next st, yoh and draw through all
15 loops on hook, 1 ch), 1 tr/dc in
each next 7 sts; repeat from * to end
of row ending with 1 tr/dc in last 2
sts, 1 tr/dc in turning ch, 1
turning ch.
row 2: miss first st, * 1 dc/sc in each
next 3 sts, 3 dc/sc in top loop of
cluster, 1 dc/sc in each next 4 sts;
repeat from * to end of row ending
with 1 dc/sc in turning ch, 3
turning ch.
repeat rows 1–2

multiple of 3+3, 1 turning ch

base row: work 1 dc/sc in second ch
from hook and all subsequent ch to
end of row, 1 turning ch.
row 1: miss first st, 1 dc/sc in next
st, * 1 ch, 1 pineapple st, ([yoh,
hook into side of st just worked,
yoh and draw up a loop approx 1
cm] 4 times, miss next 2 sts, hook
into next st, yoh and draw through
all 9 loops on hook), 1 ch; repeat
from * to end of row ending with 1
dc/sc in last st, 3 turning ch.
row 2: miss first st, * 3 tr/dc in top
loop of pineapple st; repeat from *
to end of row ending with 1 tr/dc in
last st, 1 turning ch.
repeat rows 1–2

multiple of 5+1, 2 turning ch

base row: work 1 dc/sc in third ch
from hook and all subsequent ch to
end of row, 3 turning ch.
row 1: miss first st, * 1 tr/dc in next
st, (1 ch, yoh, hook round stem of
previous tr/dc, [yoh and draw up a
loop 7 times], miss 2 sts, hook into
next st, yoh and draw through all
15 loops on hook, 1 ch), 1 tr/dc in
next st; repeat from * to end of row
ending with 1 tr/dc in turning ch, 3
turning ch.
row 2: miss first st, * 1 tr/dc in next
st, 3 tr/dc in top loop of cluster, 1 tr/
dc in next st; repeat from * to end of
row ending with 1 tr/dc in turning

ch, 3 turning ch.
repeat rows 1–2

multiple of 6, 2 turning ch

base row: work 1 tr/dc in third ch
from hook and all subsequent ch to
end of row, 2 turning ch.
row 1: * 1 b.r.tr/dc in each next 3
sts, 1 f.r.tr/dc in each next 3 sts;
repeat from * to end of row, 2
turning ch.
rows 2 & 3: as row 1.
row 4: * 1 f.r.tr/dc in each next 3 sts,
1 b.r.tr/dc in each next 3 sts; repeat
from * to end of row, 2 turning ch.
rows 5 & 6: as row 4
repeat rows 1–6

TEXTURED PATTERNS

loops, 1 dc/sc in each next 3 sts; repeat from * to end of row ending with 1 dc/sc in turning ch, 1 turning ch.
repeat rows 1–4

multiple of 5, 1 turning ch

base row: work 1 dc/sc in second ch from hook and all subsequent ch to end of row, 1 turning ch.
row 1: 1 dc/sc in every st to end of row, 1 turning ch.
rows 2 & 3: as row 1
row 4: 1 dc/sc, hook into fourth st of second row, draw up a loop and finish as a dc/sc, * 1 dc/sc in each next 4 sts, hook into fifth st of row 2, draw up a loop and finish as a dc/sc; repeat from * to end of row ending with 1 dc/sc in each last 3 sts, 1 turning ch.
repeat rows 1–4

multiple of 4+3, 1 turning ch

base row 1: work 1 dc/sc in second ch from hook and all subsequent ch to end of row, 1 turning ch.
row 1: miss first st, 1 dc/sc in every st ending with 1 dc/sc in turning ch, 1 turning ch.
row 2: miss first st, * 1 dc/sc in each next 3 sts, hook into equivalent next st of 2 rows before, yoh and draw up a loop, yoh and draw through 2 loops; repeat from * to end of row ending with 1 dc/sc in last 2 sts, 1 turning ch.
row 3: as row 1
row 4: miss first st, 1 dc/sc in next st, * hook into equivalent next st 2 rows below, yoh and draw up a loop, yoh and draw through 2

multiple of 2, 2 turning ch

base row: work 1 dc/sc in third ch from hook and all subsequent ch to end of row, 1 turning ch.
row 1: miss first st, * 1 dc/sc in next st, hook into equivalent next st of previous row, yoh, pull up a loop, yoh and draw through both loops; repeat from * to end of row ending with 1 dc/sc in last st, 1 dc/sc in turning ch, 1 turning ch.
row 2: miss first st, 1 dc/sc in every st to end of row, 1 dc/sc in turning ch, 1 turning ch.
repeat rows 1–2

multiple of 4+1, 2 turning ch

base row: work 1 dc/sc in third ch from hook and all subsequent ch to end of row, 2 turning ch.
row 1: miss first st, 1 dc/sc in every st to end of row, 1 dc/sc in turning ch, 2 turning ch.
rows 2 & 3: as row 1
row 4: 1 dc/sc in first st, hook in fourth st of row 1, draw up a loop and finish as a dc/sc, * 1 dc/sc in each next three sts, hook in same st of row one, draw up a loop and finish as a dc/sc, 1 dc/sc in next st, hook into sixth st of row 1, draw up a loop and finish as a dc/sc; repeat from * to end of row, 1 turning ch.
repeat rows 1–4

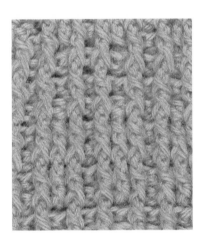

multiple of 4+1, 2 turning ch

base row: work 1 tr/dc in third ch from hook and all subsequent ch to end of row, 2 turning ch.
row 1: miss first st, * 1 f.r.tr/dc in next st, 1 b.r.tr/dc in next st; repeat from * to end of row ending with 1 tr/dc in turning ch, 2 turning ch.
rows 2, 3 & 4: as row 1
row 5: miss first st, * 1 f.r.tr/dc in each next 3 sts, 1 b.r.tr/dc in next st; repeat from * to end of row ending with 1 tr/dc in turning ch, 2 turning ch.
row 6: miss first st, * 1 f.r.tr/dc in next st, 1 b.r.tr/dc in each next 3 sts; repeat from * to end of row ending with 1 tr/dc in turning ch, 2 turning ch.
row 7: as row 5
row 8: as row 6
repeat rows 1–8

TEXTURED PATTERNS

multiple of 7+6, 1 turning ch

base row: work 1 dc/sc in second ch
from hook and all subsequent ch to
end of row, 1 turning ch
row 1: 1 dc/sc in every st to end of
row, 1 turning ch.
row 2: as row 1
row 3: as row 1
row 4: 1 dc/sc in each first 4 sts, 1
tr.tr/d.tr in first st of row 1, * miss 3
sts, 4 d.tr/tr in next st of row 1
working first 2 loops of each only,
yoh and draw through 4 loops (3
loops on hook), miss 2 sts, 1 tr.tr/
d.tr in next st of row 1, yoh and
draw through 4 loops on hook,
miss first st at back of work, 1 dc/sc
in each next 6 sts, 1 tr.tr/d.tr in last
tr.tr/d.tr worked; repeat from * to
end of row ending with 1 dc/sc in
last st, 1 turning ch.
row 5: as row 1
row 6: as row 1
row 7: as row 1
row 8: 1 dc/sc, * 1 tr.tr/d.tr in loop
of raised sts from row 4, 1 dc/sc in
each next 6 sts, 1 tr.tr/d.tr in same
loop of raised sts, miss 3 sts, 4 d.tr/
tr in next st of row 5 working first 2
loops of each only, yoh and draw
through 4 loops (3 loops on hook),
miss 2 sts; repeat from * to end of
row ending with 1 tr.tr/d.tr in last
raised loop of row 5, 1 dc/sc in last
4 sts, 1 turning ch.
repeat rows 1–8

multiple of 2, 3 turning ch

base row: work 1 tr/dc in fourth ch
from hook and all subsequent ch to
end of row, 1 turning ch.
row 1: 1 dc/sc in every st to end of
row, 1 dc/sc in turning ch, 3
turning ch.
row 2: miss first st, * 1 f.r.d.tr/tr
round tr/dc st of row below, 1 tr/dc
in next st; repeat from * to end of
row, 1 tr/dc in turning ch, 1 turning
ch.
row 3: as row 1.
row 4: miss first st, * 1 tr/dc in next
st, 1 f.r.d.tr/dc round tr/dc of row
below; repeat from * to end of row,
1 tr/dc in turning ch, 1 turning ch.
repeat rows 1–4

multiple of 6, 1 turning ch.

base row: work 1 dc/sc in second ch from hook and all subsequent ch to end of row, 1 turning ch.
row 1: 1 dc/sc in every st to end of row, 1 turning ch.
rows 2 & 3: as row 1
row 4: 1 dc/sc in next st, yoh, hook round first st of first row, pull up a loop ½ in (1.2 cm) then work the loop as a tr/dc [a long tr/dc], * miss next 4 sts of first row, 1 long tr/dc in next st, miss next 2 sts of third row, 1 dc/sc in each next 4 sts, 1 long tr/dc in st next to last long tr/dc; repeat from * to last 4 sts, 1 long tr/dc in last st, miss next 2 sts in third row, 1 dc/sc in each last 2 sts, 1 turning ch.
rows 5 & 6: as row 1
row 7: as row 1 but omitting the 1 turning ch.
row 8: 1 long tr/dc in third st of fifth row, miss first st in seventh row, 1 dc/sc in each next 4 sts, 1 long tr/dc in st in fifth row next to the last long tr/dc, * miss next 4 sts in fifth row, 1 long tr/dc in next st, miss next 2 sts in seventh row, 1 dc/sc in each next 4 sts; repeat from * to end of row ending with 1 long tr/dc in st next to last long tr/dc in fifth row, 1 dc/sc in last st, 1 turning ch.
repeat rows 1–8

multiple of 8+3, 1 turning ch.

base row: work 1 dc/sc in third ch from hook and all subsequent ch to end of row, 1 turning ch.

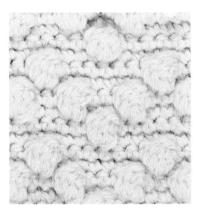

row 1: 1 dc/sc in first st, 1 berry st in next st (half work 4 tr.dc in st and then finish sts together), * 1 dc/sc in each next 7 sts, 1 berry in next st; repeat from * ending with 1 dc/sc in last st, 1 turning ch.
row 2: 1 dc/sc in all sts to end of row, 1 turning ch.
row 3: 1 dc/sc in first st, 1 dc/sc in each next 2 sts, * 1 berry in next st, 1 dc/sc in each next 3 sts; repeat from * to end of row, 1 turning ch.
rows 4 and 6: as row 2
row 5: 1 dc/sc in first st, * 1 dc/sc in each next 4 sts, 1 berry in next st, 1 dc/sc in each next 3 sts; repeat from * to end of row ending with 1 dc/sc in each last 2 sts, 1 turning ch.
repeat rows 1–6

multiple of 3+2, 3 turning ch

base row: work 1 tr/dc in fourth ch from hook and all subsequent ch to end of row, 3 turning ch.
row 1: miss first two sts, 1 tr/dc in each next two sts, 1 f.r.d.tr/tr in second missed st, * miss 1 st, 1 tr/dc in each next 2 sts, 1 f.r.d.tr/tr in missed st; repeat from * to end of row ending with 1 tr/dc in turning ch, 3 turning ch.
row 2: miss first st, 1 tr/dc in each st to end of row ending with 1 tr/dc in turning ch, 3 turning ch.
repeat rows 1–2

TEXTURED PATTERNS

multiple of 10, 2 turning ch

base row: work 1 dc/sc in third ch
from hook, 1 dc/sc in each next
three sts, * begin 1 thistle in next st
(1 dc/sc, [10 ch, 1 dc/sc] three
times), 1 dc/sc in each next 9 sts;
repeat from * to end of row ending
with 1 dc/sc in each last 5 sts, 1
turning ch.
row 1: miss first st, * 1 dc/sc in each
next 4 sts, miss first dc/sc, hook
into centre 2 dc/sc of thistle base,
yoh and draw loop through, miss
next st, 1 dc/sc in each next 9 sts;
repeat from * to end of row ending
with 1 dc/sc in each last 4 sts, 1 dc/
sc in turning ch, 1 turning ch.
row 2: miss first st, 1 dc/sc in every
st to end of row, 1 dc/sc in turning
ch, 1 turning ch.
row 3: miss first st, * 1 dc/sc in next
st, hook into next st and first loop
of thistle, yoh and draw loop
through, 1 dc/sc in each next 5 sts,
hook into next st and third loop of
thistle, yoh and draw loop through,
1 dc/sc in each next 2 sts; repeat
from * to end of row ending with 1
dc/sc in last st, 1 dc/sc in turning
ch, 1 turning ch.
row 4: as row 2
row 5: miss first st, * 1 dc/sc in each
next 4 sts, yoh, hook into next st
and centre loop and work 6 tr/dc, 1
dc/sc in each next 5 sts; repeat from
* to end of row ending with 1 dc/sc
in turning ch, 1 turning ch.
row 6: miss first st, * 1 dc/sc in each
next 4 sts, 1 ch, miss 6 tr/dc, 1 dc/sc
in each next 4 sts, begin a thistle in
next st; repeat from * to end of row
ending with 1 dc/sc in turning ch, 1
turning ch.
row 7: miss first st, * 1 dc/sc in each
next 9 sts, hook into centre 2 sts of

base, yoh and pull loop through;
repeat from * to end of row ending
with 1 dc/sc in turning ch, 1
turning ch.
row 8: as row 2
row 9: miss first st, 1 dc/sc in each
next 6 sts, * hook into next st and
first loop, yoh and draw loop
through, 1 dc/sc in each 5 sts, hook
into next st and third loop, yoh and
draw loop through, 1 dc/sc in each
next 3 sts; repeat from * to end of
row ending with 1 dc/sc in last 3
sts, 1 dc/sc in turning ch, 1 turning
ch.
row 10: as row 2
row 11: miss first st, * 1 dc/sc in
each next 9 sts, yoh, hook in next st
and central loop and work 6 tr/dc;
repeat from * to end of row ending
with 1 dc/sc in turning ch.
row 12: miss first st, 1 dc/sc in each
next 4 sts, * begin a thistle in next
st,
1 dc/sc in each next 4 sts, 1 ch,
miss 6 tr/dc. 1 dc/sc in each next 4
sts; repeat from * to end of row
ending with 1 dc/sc in turning ch,
1 turning ch.
repeat rows 1–12

multiple of 4, 1 turning ch

base row: work 1 dc/sc in second ch
from hook and all subsequent ch to
end of row, 1 turning ch.
row 1: 1 dc/sc in every st to end of
row, 3 turning ch.
row 2: miss first st, 1 tr/dc in next
st, * miss next 3 sts, 1 d.tr/tr in next
st, working behind this st, work 1
tr/dc in each of the 3 missed sts;
repeat from * to end of row ending
with 1 tr/dc in each last 2 dc/sc, 3

turning ch.

row 3: miss first tr/dc, 1 tr/dc in next tr/dc, * miss 3 sts, 1 d.tr/tr in the d.tr/tr working in front of this st, 1 tr/dc in each of the 3 missed sts; repeat from * to end of row ending with 1 tr/dc in last st, 1 tr/dc in turning ch, 1 turning ch.

row 4: 1 dc/sc in every tr/dc to end of row, 1 tr/dc in turning ch, 1 turning ch.

repeat rows 1–4

every st to end of row, 3 turning ch.

row 3: miss first two sts, 1 tr/dc in each next two sts, 1 f.r.d.tr/tr in last missed st, * miss 2 sts, 1 f.r.d.tr/tr in next st, 1 tr/dc in each 2 missed sts, miss 1 st, 1 tr/dc in each next 2 sts, 1 f.r.d.tr/tr in missed st; repeat from * to end of row ending with 1 tr/dc in turning ch, 3 turning ch.

repeat rows 1–4

multiple of 4+1, 1 turning ch

base row 1: work 1 dc/sc in second ch from hook and all subsequent ch to end of row, 3 turning ch.

base row 2: miss first st, * miss next st, 1 tr/dc in each next 2 sts, 1 tr/dc in missed st worked in front of previous 2 sts, 1 tr/dc in next st; repeat from * to end of row, 3 turning ch.

row 1: miss first st, * miss next st, 1 tr/dc in each next 2 sts, 1 tr/dc in missed st worked behind previous 2 sts, 1 b.r.tr/dc in next st; repeat from * to end of row ending with 1 tr/dc in turning ch, 3 turning ch.

row 2: miss first st, * miss next st, 1 tr/dc in each next 2 sts, 1 tr/dc in missed st worked in front of previous 2 sts, 1 f.r.tr/dc in next st; repeat from * to end of row ending with 1 tr/dc in turning ch, 3 turning ch.

repeat rows 1–2

multiple of 6+2, 3 turning ch

base row: work 1 tr/dc in fourth ch from hook, 1 tr/dc in all subsequent ch to end of row, 3 turning ch.

row 1: miss first three sts, 1 f.r.d.tr/tr in next st, 1 tr/dc in each of missed 2 sts, * miss next st, 1 tr/dc in next 2 sts, 1 f.r.d.tr/tr in missed st, miss 2 sts, 1 f.r.d.tr/tr in next st, 1 tr/dc in each 2 missed sts; repeat from * to end of row ending with 1 tr/dc in turning ch, 3 turning ch.

rows 2 & 4: miss first st, 1 tr/dc in

TEXTURED PATTERNS

multiple of 8+1, 2 turning ch

row 1: work 1 tr/dc in third ch from hook, * 4 tr/dc in fifth st, 3 ch, 4 tr/dc in prev third st, 1 tr/dc in third st; repeat from * to end of row, 3 turning ch.
row 2: 3 tr/dc in first st, * 1 dc/sc in 3 ch loop, 4 tr/dc in centre st of 2nd tr/dc group, 3 ch, 4 tr/dc in centre st of prev tr/dc group; repeat from * to end of row, 4 tr/dc in turning ch, 3 turning ch.
repeat rows 1–2 alternating the groups of crossed stitches.

multiple of 4+1, 3 turning ch

base row: work 1 tr/dc in fourth ch from hook and all subsequent ch to end of row, 3 turning ch.
row 1: miss first st, * (1 f.r.tr/dc in next st) twice, (1 b.r.tr/dc in next st) twice; repeat from * to end of row ending with 1 tr/dc in turning ch, 3 turning ch.
repeat row 1

any number of sts, 3 turning ch.

base row: work 1 tr/dc in fourth ch from hook and all subsequent ch to end of row. DO NOT TURN.
row 1: * 7 ch, sl.st to front loop of next tr/dc to right of work; repeat from * to end of row ending with 7 ch, sl.st to top of turning ch. DO NOT TURN.
row 2: 3 ch, 1 tr/dc in back loop only of every st of last but one row to end of work. DO NOT TURN.
repeat rows 1–2

multiple of 3, 3 turning ch

base row: work 1 tr/dc in fourth ch from hook and all subsequent ch to end of row, 2 turning ch.
row 1: miss first st, * 1 f.r.tr/dc in each next 2 sts, 1 tr/dc in next st; repeat from * ending with 1 tr/dc in turning ch, 2 turning ch.
row 2: miss first st, * 1 tr/dc in each next 2 sts, 1 f.r.tr/dc in next st; repeat from * to end of row ending with 1 tr/dc in turning ch
repeat rows 1–2

multiple of 6+5, 1 turning ch

base row: work 1 dc/sc in second ch from hook and all subsequent ch to end of row, 1 turning ch.
row 1: 1 dc/sc in every st to end of row, 1 turning ch.
rows 2 & 3: as row 1
row 4: 1 dc/sc in each of first four sts, * (yoh, hook into next equivalent st of first row, yoh, draw up a loop, hook into next st, yoh, draw through a loop, yoh and draw through all loops on hook) three times, 1 dc/sc in each next 3 sts; repeat from * to end of row ending with 1 dc/sc in last st, 1 turning ch.
rows 5, 6 & 7: as row 1
row 8: 1 dc/sc in first st, * (yoh, hook into next equivalent st of fifth row, yoh, draw up a loop, hook into next st, yoh, draw through a loop, yoh and draw through all loops on hook) three times, 1 dc/sc in each next 3 sts; repeat from * to end of row ending with 1 dc/sc in last st, 1 turning ch.
repeat rows 1–8

any number of sts, 1 turning ch.

base row: work 1 dc/sc in second ch from hook and all subsequent ch to end of row, 1 turning ch.
row 1: miss first st, * hook into next st, yarn over hook then round fore finger of left hand, yarn under and round the hook, draw the 2 loops on hook through the st, yoh and draw through all loops, slip loop off finger; repeat from * to end of row, 1 turning ch.
row 2: 1 dc/sc in every st to end of row, 1 turning ch.
repeat rows 1–2

any number of sts, 1 turning ch

worked as previous pattern but when finished cut through all loops for a different effect.

Multi-colour Patterns

Using several colours to give tweed effects, checks and plaids, stripes and simple two colour effects

multiple of 11+9+3 turning ch

base row: (A) work 1 tr/dc in fourth ch from hook, 1 tr/dc in each next 2 ch, * 1 ch, miss 1 ch, 1 tr/dc in each next 2 ch, 1 ch, miss 1 ch, 1 tr/dc in each next 7 ch; repeat from * to end of row ending with 1 tr/dc in last 3 ch, 3 turning ch.
row 1: miss first st, 1 tr/dc in each next 2 sts, * 1 ch, miss 1 ch, 1 tr/dc in each next 2 sts, 1 ch, miss 1 ch, 1 tr/dc in each next 7 sts; repeat from * to end of row ending with 1 tr/dc in turning ch, 3 turning ch.
rows 2–4: as row 1
Do not turn work
row 5: (with B) 1 dc/sc in every st and 1 ch over 1 ch space to end of row. Fasten off.
rows 6 and 7: (with C) 1 tr/dc in every st and 1 ch over 1 ch space to end of row. Fasten off.
repeat rows 1–7

on this base with a crochet hook work sl.st stripes in 1 ch spaces using colours B and C alternately.

multiple of 9+4, 3 turning ch.

base row: (with A) work 1 tr/dc in fourth ch from hook, * 1 ch, miss 1 ch, 1 tr/dc in each next 8 ch; repeat from * to end of row ending with 1 tr/dc in last 2 ch, 3 turning ch. 2 ch, 3 turning ch.
row 1: miss first st, 1 tr/dc in next st, * 1 ch, miss 1 ch, 1 tr/dc in each next 8 sts; repeat from * to end of row ending with 1 tr/dc in turning ch, 3 turning ch.
rows 2–4: as row 1 but omitting the turning ch on row 4
row 5: with (B) 1 dc/sc in every st to end of row. Fasten off.
row 6: (with C) sl.st to first st, 3 ch, miss first st, 1 tr/dc in next st, * 1 ch, miss 1 ch, 1 tr/dc in next 8 sts; repeat from * to end of row ending with 1 tr/dc in turning ch, 3 turning ch.
rows 7–9: as row 6
row 10: as row 5
repeat rows 1–10
on this base and using a crochet hook work a sl.st up the vertical 1 ch spaces

Published originally in Vogue Knitting, Butterick Company, instructions: page 173.

MULTI-COLOUR PATTERNS

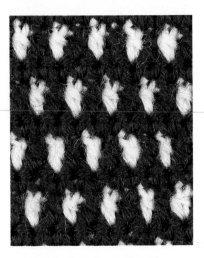

multiple of 2+1, 3 turning ch.

base row: (with A) work 1 tr/dc in fourth ch from hook and all subsequent ch to end of row, 3 turning ch.

row 1: * (with A) 1 tr/dc in first st, (with B) 1 tr/dc in next st; repeat from * to end of row, 1 turning ch. Fasten off col B.

row 2: (with A) 1 dc/sc in every st to end of row.

row 3: * (with B) 1 tr/dc in first st, (with A) 1 tr/dc in next st; repeat from * to end of row, 1 turning ch. Fasten off col B.

row 4: as row 2 but 3 turning ch. repeat rows 1–4

multiple of 4, 3 turning ch.

base row: (with A) work 1 tr/dc in fourth ch from the hook and all subsequent ch to end of row, 1 turning ch.

row 1: (with A) 1 dc/sc in every st to end of row.

row 2: (with B) sl.st to first st, 3 ch (forms first st), 1 tr/dc in next st, * 1 r.f.tr/dc in next st 2 rows down, 1 tr/dc in each next 3 sts; repeat from * to end of row ending with 1 tr/dc in last st, 1 turning ch.

row 3: (with B) 1 dc/sc in every st to end of row ending with 1 dc/sc in last ch.

row 4: (with A) sl.st to first st, 3 ch (forms first st), * 1 tr/dc in each next 3 sts, 1 r.f.tr/dc in next st 2 rows below; repeat from * to end of row ending with 1 turning ch. repeat rows 1–4

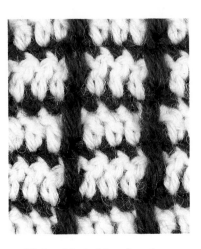

multiple of 4+1, 1 turning ch

base row: (with A) work 1 dc/sc in second ch from hook and all subsequent ch to end of row. Fasten off col A.

row 1: (with B) 1 tr/dc in first st, * 1 ch, miss 1 st, 1 tr/dc in each next 3 sts; repeat from * to end of row ending with 1 tr/dc in each last 2 sts. Fasten off col B.

row 2: (with A) 1 dc/sc in each first 2 sts, * hook into dc/sc 2 rows below, yoh, draw up a loop and finish as a dc/sc, 1 dc/sc in each next 3 sts; repeat from * to end of row. Fasten off col A. repeat rows 1–2

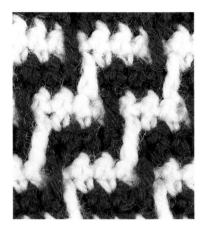

multiple of 4, 1 turning ch

base row: (with A) work 1 dc/sc in second ch from hook and all subsequent ch to end of row, 1 turning ch.
row 1: (with A) 1 dc/sc in every st to end of row ending with 1 dc/sc in last st.
row 2: (with B) 1 dc/sc in first st, 1 dc/sc in next and all subsequent sts to end of row, 1 turning ch.
row 3: (with B) 1 dc/sc in every st to end of row ending with 1 dc/sc in last st.
row 4: (with A) 1 dc/sc in first st, * 1 r.f.tr/dc in next st of row 1, 1 dc/sc in each next 3 sts; repeat from * to end of row ending with 1 dc/sc in last st, 1 turning ch.
row 5: (with A) 1 dc/sc in every st to end of row ending with 1 dc/sc in last st.
row 6: (with B) 1 dc/sc in first st, 1 dc/sc in next st, * 1 r.f.tr/dc in next st of row 3, 1 dc/sc in each next 3 sts; repeat from * to end of row ending with 1 dc/sc in last st, 1 turning ch.
row 7: (with B) 1 dc/sc in every st to end of row.
row 8: (with A) 1 dc/sc in first st, 1 dc/sc in each next 2 sts, * 1 r.f.tr/dc in next st of row 5, 1 dc/sc in each next 3 sts; repeat from * to end of row ending with 1 dc/sc in last st, 1 turning ch.
row 9: as row 5.
row 10: (with B) 1 dc/sc in first st, * 1 dc/sc in each next 3 sts, 1 r.f.tr/dc in next st of row 7; repeat from * to end of row ending with 1 dc/sc in last st, 1 turning ch.
row 11: as row 7
repeat rows 4–11

multiple of 2+1, 2 turning ch

base row: (with A) work 1 dc/sc in third ch from hook, * 1 ch, miss 1 ch, 1 dc/sc in next ch; repeat from * to end of row, 1 turning ch.
row 1: (with A) miss first st, * 1 dc/sc in 1 ch space, 1 ch, miss 1 st; repeat from * to end of row ending with 1 dc/sc in last st, 1 turning ch.
row 2: (with B) * 1 dc/sc in first st, 1 ch, miss 1 st; repeat from * to end of row, 1 dc/sc in last ch, 1 turning ch.
row 3: (with B), miss first st, * 1 dc/sc in 1 ch space, 1 ch, miss 1 st; repeat from * to end of row ending with 1 dc/sc in last st, 1 turning ch.
row 4: (with A) 1 dc/sc in first st, * 1 ch, miss 1 st, 1 dc/sc in 1 ch space; repeat from * to end of row ending with 1 dc/sc in last st, 1 turning ch.
repeat rows 1–4

multiple of 6, 3 turning ch

base row: (with A) work 1 tr/dc in fourth ch from hook and all subsequent ch to end of row, 3 turning ch.
row 1: * (with A) 1 tr/dc in each first 3 sts, (with B), 1 tr/dc in each next 3 sts; repeat from * to end of row, 3 turning ch.
repeat row 1

MULTI-COLOUR PATTERNS

any number of stitches, 1 turning ch

base row: work 1 dc/sc in second ch from hook and all subsequent ch to end of row, 1 turning ch.
row 1: 1 dc/sc in every st to end of row, 1 turning ch.
repeat row 1
using this as a base, thread a needle with contrast yarn and embroider the contrast colours on to the work

multiple of 2+1, 5 turning ch

base row: work 1 tr/dc in sixth ch from hook, * 1 ch, miss 1 ch, 1 tr/dc in next ch; repeat from * to end of row, 4 turning ch.
row 1: miss first st, * 1 tr/dc in next st, 1 ch, 1 tr/dc in next st; repeat from * to end of row ending with 1 tr/dc in turning ch, 4 turning ch.
repeat row 1
using this as a base thread a needle with contrast yarn and work it through the ch spaces

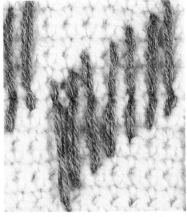

any number of stitches, 1 turning ch

base row: work 1 dc/sc in second ch from hook and all subsequent ch to end of row, 1 turning ch.
row 1: 1 dc/sc in every st to end of row, 1 turning ch.
repeat row 1
using this as a base, thread a needle with contrast yarn and embroider the contrast colours on to the work

multiple of 5+3, 3 turning ch

base row: (with A and B together) work 1 tr/dc in fourth ch from hook, 1 tr/dc in each next 2 ch, * 1 ch, miss 1 ch, 1 tr/dc in each next 4 sts; repeat from * to end of row, 3 turning ch.
row 1: miss first st, 1 tr/dc in each next 3 sts, * 1 ch, miss 1 st, 1 tr/dc in each next 4 sts; repeat from * to end of row ending with the last tr/dc in turning ch.
repeat row 1
using this as a base, thread a needle with contrast yarn and work it through the 1 ch spaces.

multiple of 4+2, 1 turning ch

base row: (with A) work 1 dc/sc in second ch from hook and all subsequent ch to end of row.
row 1: (with B) sl.st to first st, 1 ch, 1 dc/sc in next and all subsequent sts to end of row, 1 turning ch.
row 2: (with B) as row 1
row 3: (with A) sl.st to first st, 1 ch, 1 dc/sc in first st, 1 dc/sc in next st, * (1 r.f.tr/dc in next st of base row) twice, 1 dc/sc in each next 2 sts, repeat from * to end of row 1 turning ch.
row 4: (with A) 1 dc in every st to end of row.
row 5: (with B) sl.st to first st, 1 ch, 1 dc/sc in first st, 1 dc/sc in next st, * (1 r.f.tr/dc in next st of row 3) twice, 1 dc/sc in each next 2 sts; repeat from * to end of row, 1 turning ch.
row 6: (with B) as row 4
row 7: (with A) as row 5
repeat rows 4–7

multiple of 2+1, 5 turning ch

base row: work 1 tr/dc in sixth ch from hook, * 1 ch, miss 1 ch, 1 tr/dc in next ch; repeat from * to end of row, 4 turning ch.

row 1: miss first st, * 1 tr/dc in next st, 1 ch, 1 tr/dc in next st; repeat from * to end of row ending with 1 tr/dc in turning ch, 4 turning ch.
repeat row 1
using this as a base thread a needle with contrast yarn and work it through the ch spaces

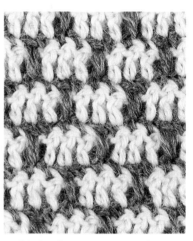

multiple of 4+3, 1 turning ch

base row: (with A) work 1 dc/sc in second ch from hook and all subsequent ch to end of row.
row 1: (with B) sl.st to first st, 3 ch, miss first st, 1 tr/dc in each next 2 sts, * 1 ch, miss 1 st, 1 tr/dc in each next 3 sts, repeat from * to end of row.
row 2: (with A) sl.st to first st, 1 ch, 1 dc/sc in each next 3 sts, * 1 tr/dc in the missed st (working over the 1 ch space), 1 dc/sc in each next 3 sts; repeat from * to end of row ending with 1 dc/sc in turning ch.
row 3: (with B) sl.st to first st, 4 ch, miss first 2 sts, * 1 tr/dc in each next 3 sts, 1 ch, miss 1 st; repeat from * to end of row ending with 1 tr/dc in last st.
row 4: (with A) sl.st to first st, 1 ch, 1 dc/sc in first st, * 1 tr/dc in the missed st (working over the 1 ch space), 1 dc/sc in each next 3 sts; repeat from * to end of row ending with 1 dc/sc in first missed st of previous row, 1 dc/sc in the third of 4 ch.
repeat rows 1–4

MULTI-COLOUR PATTERNS

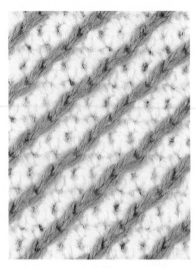

any number of stitches, 1 turning ch

base row: work 1 dc/sc in second ch from hook and all subsequent ch to end of row, 1 turning ch.
row 1: 1 dc/sc in every st to end of row, 1 turning ch.
repeat row 1
using this as a base, work the contrast colours on to the work with a crochet hook

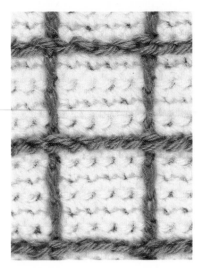

any number of stitches, 1 turning ch
base row: work 1 dc/sc in second ch from hook and all subsequent ch to end of row, 1 turning ch.
row 1: 1 dc/sc in every st to end of row, 1 turning ch.
repeat row 1
using this as a base, work the contrast colours on to the work with a crochet hook

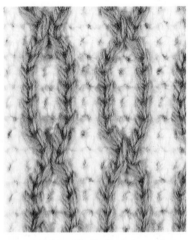

any number of stitches, 1 turning ch

base row: work 1 dc/sc in second ch from hook and all subsequent ch to end of row, 1 turning ch.
row 1: 1 dc/sc in every st to end of row, 1 turning ch.
repeat row 1
using this as a base, work the contrast colours on to the work with a crochet hook

any number of stitches, 1 turning ch

base row: work 1 dc/sc in second ch from hook and all subsequent ch to end of row, 1 turning ch.
row 1: 1 dc/sc in every st to end of row, 1 turning ch.
repeat row 1
using this as a base, work the contrast colours on to the work with a crochet hook

any number of stitches, 1 turning ch

base row: work 1 dc/sc in second ch from hook and all subsequent ch to end of row, 1 turning ch.
row 1: 1 dc/sc in every st to end of row, 1 turning ch.
repeat row 1
using this as a base, thread a needle with contrast yarn and embroider the contrast colours on to the work

any number of stitches, 1 turning ch

base row: work 1 dc/sc in second ch from hook and all subsequent ch to end of row, 1 turning ch.
row 1: 1 dc/sc in every st to end of row, 1 turning ch.
repeat row 1
using this as a base, thread a needle with contrast yarn and embroider the contrast colours on to the work

any number of stitches, 1 turning ch

base row: work 1 dc/sc in second ch from hook and all subsequent ch to end of row, 1 turning ch.
row 1: 1 dc/sc in every st to end of row, 1 turning ch.
repeat row 1
using this as a base, thread a needle with contrast yarn and embroider the contrast colours on to the work

any number of stitches, 1 turning ch

base row: work 1 dc/sc in second ch from hook and all subsequent ch to end of row, 1 turning ch.
row 1: 1 dc/sc in every st to end of row, 1 turning ch.
repeat row 1
using this as a base, thread a needle with contrast yarn and embroider the contrast colours on to the work

MULTI-COLOUR PATTERNS

multiple of 8+3, 1 turning ch

base row: (with A) work 1 dc/sc in second ch on hook and all subsequent ch to end of row, 1 turning ch.

row 1: miss first st, 1 dc/sc in every st to end of row, 1 turning ch.

rows 2–7: as row 1

row 8: (with B) sl.st to first st, 1 ch, miss first st, 1 dc/sc in next st, * hook into next dc/sc 7 rows down, yoh and draw up a loop then finish as a dc/sc, hook into next dc/sc 6 rows down, yoh and draw up a loop then finish as a dc/sc, hook into next dc/sc 5 rows down, yoh and draw up a loop then finish as a dc/sc, hook into next dc/sc 4 rows down, yoh and draw up a loop then finish as a dc/sc, hook into next st 3 rows down, yoh and draw up a loop then finish as a dc/sc, hook into next st 2 rows below, yoh and draw up a loop then finish as a dc/sc, hook into next st 1 row below, yoh and draw up a loop then finish as a dc/sc, 1 dc/sc in next st; repeat from * to end of row ending with 1 dc/sc in turning ch.

rows 9–15: (with B) as row 1

row 16: (with A) 1 ch, miss first st, 1 dc/sc in next st, * 1 dc/sc in first st, hook into next st 1 row below, yoh and draw up a loop then finish as a dc/sc, hook into next st 2 rows below, yoh and draw up a loop then finish as a dc/sc, hook into next st 3 rows below, yoh and draw up a loop then finish as a dc/sc, hook into next st 4 rows below, yoh and draw up a loop then finish as a dc/sc, hook into next st 5 rows below, yoh and draw up a loop then finish as a dc/sc, hook into next st 6 rows below yoh and draw up a loop then finish as a dc/sc, hook into next st 7 rows below, yoh and draw up a loop then finish as a dc/sc; repeat form * to end of row ending with 1 dc/sc in turning ch, 1 turning ch.

repeat rows 1–16

multiple of 3+1, 3 turning ch

base row: (with A) work 2 tr/dc in fourth ch from hook, * miss 2 ch, (1 dc/sc, 2 tr/dc) in next ch; repeat from * to end of row ending with 1 tr/dc in last st, 2 turning ch.

row 1: (with A) 1 tr/dc in every st to end of row, 2 turning ch.

row 2: (with B) 2 tr/dc in first st, * miss 2 sts, (1 dc/sc, 2 tr/dc) in next st; repeat from * to end of row ending with 1 tr/dc in last st, 2 turning ch.

row 3: (with B) as row 1

row 4: (with A) as row 2

repeat rows 1–4

any number of stitches, 2 turning ch

base row: (with A) work 1 tr/dc in fourth ch from hook and all subsequent ch to end of row, 2 turning ch.
Do not turn work
row 1: (with B) miss first st, 1 h.tr/h.dc in every st ending with 1 h.tr/h.dc in top of turning ch.
row 2: (with A) 1 tr/dc in every st to end of work working in back loop only, 1 tr/dc in turning ch.
repeat rows 1–2

multiple of 9+4, 3 turning ch.

base row: (with A) work 1 tr/dc in fourth ch from hook, 1 tr/dc in next ch, * 1 ch, miss 1 ch, 1 tr/dc in each next 8 ch; repeat from * to end of row ending with 1 tr/dc in each last 2 ch, 3 turning ch.
row 1: miss first st, 1 tr/dc in next st, * 1 ch, miss 1 ch, 1 tr/dc in each next 8 sts; repeat from * to end of row ending with 1 tr/dc in turning ch, 3 turning ch.
rows 2–4: as row 1 but omitting the turning ch on row 4
row 5: with (B) 1 dc/sc in every st to end of row. Fasten off.
row 6: (with C) sl.st to first st, 3 ch, miss first st, 1 tr/dc in next st, * 1 ch, miss 1 ch, 1 tr/dc in next st; repeat from * to end of row ending with 1 tr/dc in turning ch, 3 turning ch.
rows 7–9: as row 6
row 10: as row 5
repeat rows 1–10
on this base and using a crochet hook work a sl.st up the vertical 1 ch space

any number of stitches, 4 turning ch

base row: (with A) work 1 d.tr/tr in fifth ch from hook and all subsequent ch to end of row, 2 turning ch.
row 1: (with B) miss first st, 1 h.tr/h.dc in every st to end of row ending with 1 h.tr/h.dc in turning ch, 4 turning ch.
row 2: (with A) miss first st, 1 d.tr/tr in back loop of each st to end of row, 1 d.tr/tr in turning ch.
repeat rows 1–2

Openwork and Lace Patterns

A variety of patterns featuring simple openwork designs through to more complex lace effects

multiple of 5+1, 3 turning ch

base row: work 1 tr/dc in fourth ch from hook, * miss 4 ch, ([1 tr/dc, 1 ch] three times, 1 tr/dc) in next ch; repeat from * to end of row ending with (1 tr/dc, 1 ch, 1 tr/dc) in last ch, 4 turning ch.
row 1: 1 tr/dc in first 1 ch space, * ([1 tr/dc, 1 ch] three times, 1 tr/dc) in centre ch space of shell; repeat from * to end of row ending with (1 tr/dc, 1 ch, 1 tr/dc) in last 1 ch space, 4 turning ch.
repeat row 1

multiple of 7+4, 3 turning ch

base row: work 1 tr/dc in fourth ch from hook, miss 2 ch, * 5 tr/dc in next ch, miss 2 ch, 1 tr/dc in each next 2 ch, miss 2 ch; repeat from * to end of row ending with 3 tr/dc in last ch, 3 turning ch.
row 1: 1 tr/dc between first 2 sts, miss next 2 sts, * 5 tr/dc between the 2 tr/dc, (1 tr/dc between second and third, 1 tr/dc between third and fourth sts) of 5 tr/dc group; repeat from * to end of row ending

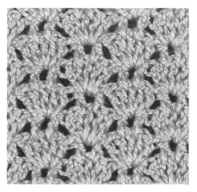

with 3 tr/dc in turning ch, 3 turning ch.
repeat row 1

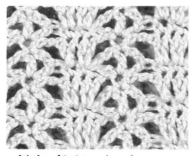

multiple of 9, 3 turning ch

base row: work 2 tr/dc in fourth ch from hook, * 2 ch, miss 3 ch, 1 dc/sc in next ch, 2 ch, miss 3 ch, (2 tr/dc in next ch) twice; repeat from * to end of row, ending with 2 tr/dc in last ch, 1 turning ch.
row 1: * 1 dc/sc in first st, * (1 tr/dc, 2 ch, 1 tr/dc, 2 ch, 1 tr/dc) in dc/sc, 1 dc/sc in 2nd and 3rd tr/dc; repeat from * to end of row, 3 turning ch.
row 2: as base row but working the dc/sc in centre st of group.
repeat rows 1–2

Published by kind permission of Pingouin, instructions: page 175.   53

OPENWORK AND LACE PATTERNS

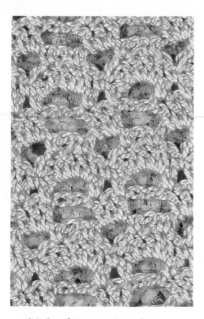

multiple of 6, 4 turning ch

row 1: work 1 tr/dc into fifth ch
from hook, * 3 ch, miss 3 ch, 1 tr/dc
in next 3 ch; repeat from * to end of
row, ending with 1 tr/dc in last 2
sts, 3 turning ch.
row 2: 1 dc/sc in 2nd tr/dc, * 5 ch,
1 dc/sc in first tr/dc, 2 ch, 1 dc/sc in
third tr/dc; repeat from * to end of
row ending with 1 dc/sc in last tr/
dc, 1 ch, 1 h.tr/h.dc in turning ch, 1
turning ch.
row 3: 1 dc/sc in h.tr/h.dc, * 5 tr
round the 5 ch, 1 dc/sc in 2 ch
space; repeat from * to end of row,
ending with 1 dc/sc in turning ch, 4
turning ch.
row 4: * 1 dc/sc in 2nd tr/dc, 2 ch, 1
dc/sc in fourth tr/dc, 3 ch; repeat
from * to end of row, 1 ch, 1 tr/dc
on last dc/sc, 3 turning ch.
repeat rows 1–4 working with 3 tr/
dc of row 1 around the 3 ch.

multiple of 6, 3 turning ch

base row: work 1 tr/dc in fourth ch
from hook, 2 ch, * 1 dc/sc in next 2
ch, 3 ch, 1 dc/sc in next ch, 2 ch, in
next 3 ch work 3 tr/dc together, 3
ch; repeat from * to end of row
ending with 2 tr/dc worked
together in last 2 ch, 5 turning ch.
row 1: 1 tr/dc in first st, * 1 ch, (1 tr/
dc, 3 ch, 1 tr/dc) in top of 3 tr/dc;
repeat from * to end of row ending
with (1 tr/dc, 1 ch, 1 tr/dc) in
turning ch, 2 turning ch.

row 2: 1 tr/dc in 1 ch space, 2 ch, * 1
dc/sc in next 2 sts, 3 ch, 1 dc/sc in
next st, 2 ch, 3 tr/dc worked
together in 3 ch space, 3 ch; repeat
from * to end of row ending with 2
tr/dc worked together in the
turning ch, 5 turning ch.
repeat rows 1–2

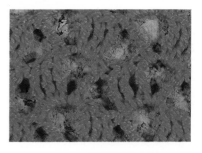

multiple of 6, 6 turning ch

base row: work 1 d.tr/tr in seventh
ch from hook, 1 d.tr/tr in next 2 ch,
3 ch, 1 d.tr/tr in next ch, * miss 2 ch,
1 d.tr/tr in next 3 ch, 3 ch, 1 d.tr/tr
in next ch; repeat from * ending
with 1 missed ch, 1 d.tr/tr in last ch,
4 turning ch.
row 1: * (3 d.tr/tr, 3 ch, 1 d.tr/tr) in 3
ch space; repeat from * to end of
row ending with 1 d.tr/tr in
turning ch, 4 turning ch.
repeat row 1

multiple of 10+1, 1 turning ch

base row: work 1 dc/sc in 2nd st
from hook, * 3 ch, miss 4 ch, (1 tr/
dc, 3 ch, 1 tr/dc, 3 ch, 1 tr/dc) in
next ch, 3 ch, miss 4 ch, 1 dc/sc in
next ch; repeat from * to end of
row, 1 turning ch.
row 1: * 1 dc/sc in first dc/sc, 3 ch,
3 tr/dc in 3 ch space, 3 ch, 1 dc/sc in
centre tr/dc, 3 ch, 3 tr/dc in 3 ch
space, 3 ch; repeat from * to end of
row, 1 dc/sc, 3 turning ch.
row 2: * 1 tr/dc in first tr/dc, 3 ch, 1
dc/sc in top of 3 ch, 3 ch, 1 dc/sc in
top of 3 ch, 3 ch, 1 tr/dc in the third
tr/dc, 1 tr/dc in the dc/sc; repeat
from * to end of row, ending with 1
tr/dc in the dc/sc, 1 turning ch.
row 3: as base row but working the
3 tr/dc group in centre 3 ch space.
repeat rows 1–3.

multiple of 11, 3 turning ch

base row: work 1 tr/dc in fourth ch
from hook, * 3 ch, 1 dc/sc in third
ch, 5 ch, 1 dc/sc in fourth ch, 3 ch, 1
tr/dc in third and fourth ch; repeat
from * to end of row ending with 1
tr/dc in last ch, 3 turning ch.
row 1: 1 tr/dc in tr/dc, 1 tr/dc in first
ch, * 1 ch, 3 tr/dc round 5 ch, 1 ch, 1

tr/dc in last ch, 2 tr/dc in tr/dc, 2 tr/
dc in next tr/dc, 1 tr/dc in first ch;
repeat from * to end of row ending
with 1 tr/dc in last ch, 2 tr/dc in last
tr/dc, 3 turning ch.
row 2: * 3 ch, 1 dc/sc in 1 ch space, 5
ch, 1 dc/sc in 1 ch space, 3 ch, miss
2 sts, 1 tr/dc in each next 2 sts;
repeat from * to end, 1 tr/dc in
turning ch, 3 turning ch.
repeat rows 1–2

multiple of 10+1, 3 turning ch

base row: work 1 tr/dc in 4th ch
from hook, * 3 ch, miss 4 ch, 1 dc/sc
in next ch, 3 ch, 3 tr/dc in same ch,
miss 4 ch, (1 tr/dc, 1 ch, 1 tr/dc) in
next ch; repeat from * to end of
row, 2 tr/dc, 3 turning ch.
row 1: 1 tr/dc in first tr/dc, * 3 ch, 1
dc/sc in top of 3 ch, 3 ch, 3 tr/dc
around 3 ch of previous row, (1 tr/
dc, 1 ch, 1 tr/dc) in 1 ch space;
repeat from * to end of row ending
with 2 tr/dc in top of turning ch, 3
turning ch.
repeat row 1.

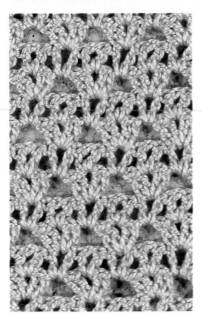

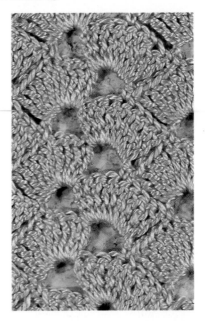

multiple of 3+2, 3 turning ch

base row: work 1 tr/dc in fourth ch from hook, miss 1 ch, (1 tr/dc, 1 ch, 1 tr/dc) in next ch, * miss 2 ch, (1 tr/dc, 1 ch, 1 tr/dc) in next ch; repeat from * to end of row ending with 1 tr/dc in last ch, 3 turning ch.
row 1: * (2 tr/dc, 1 ch, 2 tr/dc) in 1 ch space, 1 ch; repeat from * to end of row ending with 1 tr/dc in last tr/dc, 3 turning ch.
row 2: (1 tr/dc, 1 ch, 1 tr/dc) in each 1 ch space to end of row ending with 1 tr/dc in turning ch, 3 turning ch.
row 3: 1 tr/dc in first tr/dc, * 1 ch, (2 tr/dc, 1 ch, 2 tr/dc) in second 1 ch space; repeat from * to end of row ending with 1 ch, 2 tr/dc in turning ch, 3 turning ch.
row 4: as row 2.
repeat rows 1–4

multiple of 9+5, 5 turning ch

base row: work 3 d.tr/tr in sixth ch from hook, miss 3 ch, 1 dc/sc in next ch, * 2 ch, miss 3 ch, 5 d.tr/tr in next ch, 4 d.tr/tr in next ch, miss 3 ch, 1 dc/sc in next ch; repeat from * to end of row, 5 turning ch.
row 1: 3 d.tr/tr in dc/sc, * 1 dc/sc between fourth and fifth d.tr/tr of previous row, 2 ch, 9 d.tr/tr under the 2 ch space; repeat from * to end

of row ending with 1 dc/sc in top of turning ch, 5 turning ch.
repeat row 1

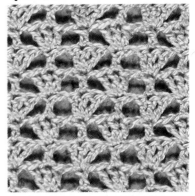

multiple of 6+1, 3 turning ch

base row: work 1 tr/dc in fourth ch from hook, 1 ch, miss 2 ch, * 3 tr/dc in next ch, 1 ch, miss 2 ch, 1 tr/dc in next ch, 1 ch, miss 2 ch; repeat from * to end of row ending with 2 tr/dc in last ch, 3 turning ch.
row 1: 2 tr/dc in first tr/dc, * 1 ch, 1 tr/dc in centre tr/dc of group, 1 ch, 3 tr/dc in single tr/dc; repeat from * to end of row ending with 2 tr/dc in last tr/dc, 3 turning ch.
row 2: 1 tr/dc in first tr/dc, * 1 ch, 3 tr/dc in next tr/dc, 1 ch, 1 tr/dc in centre tr/dc of group; repeat from * to end of row ending with 1 tr/dc in last tr/dc, 3 turning ch.
repeat rows 1–2

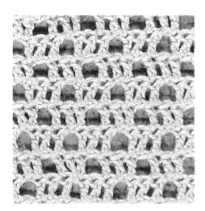

multiple of 4+2, 4 turning ch

base row: work 1 tr/dc in fifth ch from hook, * 1 tr/dc in each next 2 ch, 1 ch, miss 1 ch, 1 tr/dc in next ch; repeat from * to end of row ending with 1 tr/dc in last ch, 4 turning ch.

row 1: 1 tr/dc in third tr/dc, 1 tr/dc in 1 ch, 1 tr/dc in next tr/dc, * 1 ch, miss 1 st, 1 tr/dc in next st, 1 tr/dc in 1 ch, 1 tr/dc in next st; repeat from * to end of row ending with 1 tr/dc in turning ch, 3 turning ch.

row 2: 1 tr/dc in 1 ch, 1 tr/dc in next st, * 1 ch, miss 1 st, 1 tr/dc in next st, 1 tr/dc in 1 ch, 1 tr/dc in next st; repeat from * to end of row, 2 tr/dc in turning ch, 4 turning ch.

repeat rows 1–2

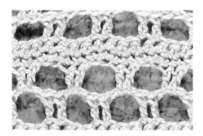

multiple of 4+2, 1 turning ch

base row: work 1 dc/sc in second ch from hook and all subsequent ch to end of row, 1 turning ch.

row 1: as base row, 3 turning ch.

row 2: 1 tr/dc in each first two dc/sc, * 2 ch, miss 2 sts, 1 tr/dc in each next two dc/sc; repeat from * to end of row, 4 turning ch.

row 3: * 2 tr/dc in 2 ch space, 2 ch; repeat from * to end of row, 1 tr/dc in turning ch, 1 turning ch.

row 4: 1 dc/sc in every st and ch to end of row, 1 turning ch.

repeat rows 1–4

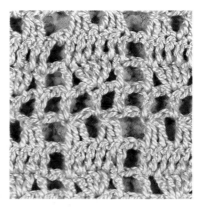

multiple of 9+3, 2 turning ch

row 1: work 1 tr/dc in third ch from hook, * 2 ch, miss 2 ch, 1 tr/dc in next st; repeat from * to end of row, 2 turning ch.

row 2: 1 tr/dc in first tr/dc, * 2 ch, 1 tr/dc in next tr/dc, 4 tr/dc in next tr/dc, 1 tr/dc in next tr/dc; repeat from * to end of row ending with 2 ch, 1 tr/dc in last tr/dc, 2 turning ch.

row 3: 1 tr/dc in first tr/dc, * 2 ch, 1 tr/dc in each next 6 tr/dc, repeat from * to end of row ending with 1 tr/dc in last tr/dc, 2 turning ch.

row 4: 1 tr/dc in first tr/dc, * 3 ch, in next three tr/dc, work 3 tr/dc together, 2 ch, in next three tr/dc work 3 tr/dc together; repeat from * to end of row ending with 1 tr/dc in last tr/dc, 2 turning ch.

repeat rows 1–4

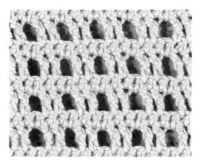

multiple of 3, 1 turning ch

row 1: work 1 dc/sc in second ch from hook and all subsequent sts to end of row, 2 turning ch.

row 2: 1 tr/dc in first dc/sc, * 1 ch, miss 1 st, 1 tr/dc in each next 2 dc/sc; repeat from * to end of row ending with 1 tr/dc in last dc/sc, 1 turning ch.

repeat rows 1–2

OPENWORK AND LACE PATTERNS

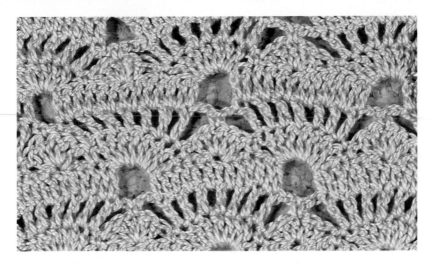

multiple of 14+1, 3 turning ch

base row: work 3 tr/dc in fourth ch from hook, * miss 3 ch, 1 dc/sc in next ch, miss 2 ch, 5 tr/dc in next ch, miss 2 ch, 1 dc/sc in next ch, miss 3 ch, 7 tr/dc in next ch; repeat from * to end of row ending with 4 tr/dc in last ch, 4 turning ch.
row 1: 1 tr/dc in second tr/dc, (1 ch, 1 tr/dc) in each next 2 sts, * 2 ch, 1 dc/sc in centre tr/dc of group, 2 ch, for next group, 1 tr/dc in first st, (1 ch, 1 tr/dc) in next 6 sts; repeat from * to end of row ending with (1 tr/dc, 1 ch) in each last 3 sts, 1 tr/dc in turning ch, 3 turning ch.
row 2: 1 tr/dc in each tr/dc and 1 ch of first group, * 2 ch, 13 tr/dc in the group of 7 tr/dc and ch; repeat from * to end of row ending with 7 tr/dc in group of 3 tr/dc and ch, 3 turning ch.
row 3: 2 tr/dc in first tr/dc, 1 dc/sc in fourth tr/dc, * 7 tr/dc in 2 ch space, 1 dc/sc in fourth tr/dc, 5 tr/dc in third tr/dc, 1 dc/sc in third tr/dc; repeat from * to end of row, 2 tr/dc in turning ch, 1 turning ch.
row 4: 1 dc/sc in first tr/dc, * 2 ch, (1 tr/dc, 1 ch) in each next six tr/dc, 1 tr/dc in last tr/dc, 2 ch, 1 dc/sc in centre tr/dc of group; repeat from * to end of row ending with 2 ch, 1 dc/sc in turning ch, 3 turning ch.
row 5: * 13 tr/dc in group of 7 tr/dc and ch, 2 ch; repeat from * to end of row, ending with 1 tr/dc in last st, 3 turning ch.
row 6: 3 tr/dc in first st, * miss 3 sts, 1 dc/sc in next st, miss 2 sts, 5 tr/dc in next st, miss 2 sts, 1 dc/sc in next st, 7 tr/dc in 2 ch space; repeat from * to end of row ending with 4 tr/dc in turning ch, 4 turning ch.
repeat rows 1–6

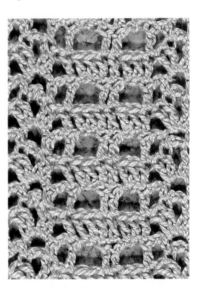

multiple of 15, 3 turning ch

row 1: work 1 tr/dc into fourth ch from hook, 1 tr/dc in next three st, * (2 tr/dc, 2 ch, 2 tr/dc) in fourth st, miss 3 ch, 1 tr/dc in next 8 sts; repeat from * to last four sts, 1 tr/dc in each of these sts, 3 turning ch.
row 2: miss first st, * 1 tr/dc in each next 3 tr/dc, * 2 ch, 1 tr/dc in second st, 2 ch, miss 2 ch, 1 tr/dc in next st, 2 ch, (1 tr/dc in first tr/dc, 2 ch, 1 tr/dc in fourth tr/dc) twice; repeat from * to end of row ending with 1 tr/dc each last 4 sts, 3 turning ch.
repeat rows 1–2 beginning row 1 by missing first tr/dc and working the 2 tr/dc, 3 ch, 2 tr/dc in 2 ch space.

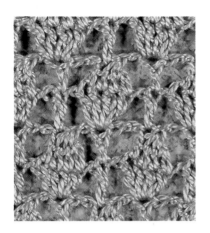

multiple of 6+1, 3 turning ch

row 1: work 1 tr/dc in fourth ch from hook, * 1 ch, miss 2 ch, 4 tr/dc in next st, 1 ch, miss 2 ch, 1 tr/dc in next st; repeat from * to end of row, 5 turning ch.

row 2: * work 4 tr/dc together in top of 4 tr/dc, 2 ch, 1 tr/dc in tr/dc, 2 ch; repeat from * to end of row, 1 tr/dc in turning ch, 3 turning ch.

row 3: 1 tr/dc in first st, * 1 ch, 1 tr/dc in top of 4 tr/dc group, 1 ch, 4 tr/dc in tr/dc; repeat from * to end of row ending with 2 tr/dc in turning ch, 3 turning ch.

row 4: 1 tr/dc in second tr/dc, * 2 ch, 1 tr/dc in next tr/dc, 2 ch, 4 tr/dc worked together; repeat from * ending with 1 tr/dc in last tr/dc and 1 tr/dc in the turning ch worked together, 3 turning ch.

repeat rows 1–4 beginning row 1 with 1 tr/dc in first tr/dc

multiple of 8+2, 3 turning ch

row 1: work 1 tr/dc in fourth ch from hook and all subsequent sts to end of row, 3 turning ch.

row 2: miss first tr/dc, * 1 tr/dc in next tr/dc, 3 ch, miss 2 sts, 1 dc/sc in next st, 3 ch, 1 dc/sc in next st, 3 ch, miss 2 sts, 1 tr/dc in next tr/dc; repeat from * to end of row ending with 1 tr/dc in turning ch, 3 turning ch.

row 3: miss first tr/dc, * 1 tr/dc in next tr/dc, 1 ch, 4 tr/dc in 3 ch space, 1 ch, 1 tr/dc in next tr/dc; repeat from * to end of row, 1 tr/dc in turning ch, 3 turning ch.

row 4: miss first tr/dc, * 1 tr/dc in next tr/dc, 2 ch, 1 tr/dc in centre 2 sts of group, 2 ch, 1 tr/dc in next tr/dc; repeat from * to end of row ending with 1 tr/dc in turning ch, 3 turning ch.

repeat rows 1–4 beginning row 1 in second tr/dc.

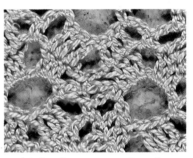

multiple of 20+9, 7 turning ch

row 1: work 1 dc/sc in eighth ch from hook, 5 ch, miss 4 ch, * 1 dc/sc in next st, 5 ch, miss 4 sts, repeat from * to end of row ending with 2 ch, 1 h.tr/h.dc in last st, 3 turning ch.

row 2: 3 tr/dc in 2 ch space, * 2 ch, 1 dc/sc round 5 ch, 2 ch, (3 tr/dc, 2 ch, 3 tr/dc) round next 5 ch; repeat from * to end of row ending with 4 tr/dc in turning ch, 1 turning ch.

row 3: 1 dc/sc in first tr/dc, 3 ch, 1 tr/dc in next three tr/dc, * 1 tr/dc in next three tr/dc, 3 ch, 1 dc/sc in 2 ch space, 3 ch, 1 tr/dc in next 3 tr/dc; repeat from * to end of row ending with 3 ch, 1 dc/sc in turning ch, 5 turning ch.

row 4: * 1 dc/sc in first tr/dc, 5 ch, 1 dc/sc in sixth tr/dc, 5 ch; repeat from * to end of row ending with 2 ch, 1 tr/dc in last st, 1 turning ch.

row 5: 1 dc/sc in first st, * 2 ch, (3 tr/dc, 2 ch, 3 tr/dc) round 5 ch, 2 ch, 1 dc/sc in 5 ch space, 2 ch; repeat from * to end of row ending with 1 dc/sc in turning ch, 3 turning ch.

row 6: * 1 tr/dc in next three tr/dc, 3 ch, 1 dc/sc in 2 ch space, 3 ch, 1 tr/dc in next three tr/dc; repeat from * to end of row ending with 1 tr/dc in last st, 5 turning ch.

repeat rows 1–6 starting row 1 with 1 dc/sc in third tr/dc.

OPENWORK AND LACE PATTERNS

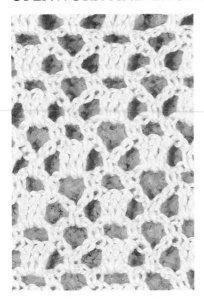

multiple of 6+2, 2 turning ch

base row: work 1 h.tr/h.dc in third ch from hook, 1 ch, miss 1 ch, * 1 dc/sc in next ch, 3 ch, miss 2 ch; repeat from * ending with 1 dc/sc, 1 ch, miss 1 ch, 1 h.tr/h/dc in last st, 3 turning ch.
row 1: 1 tr/dc in first st, * 3 ch, 1 dc/sc in 3 ch space, 3 ch, 3 tr/dc in 3 ch space; repeat from * to end of row ending with 1 tr/dc in 1 ch space, 1 tr/dc in h.tr/h.dc, 3 turning ch.
row 2: * 1 dc/sc in first ch, 3 ch, 1 dc/sc in final ch of group; repeat from * to end of row ending with 1 ch, 1 h.tr/h.dc in turning ch, 3 turning ch.
rows 3 & 5: as row 1.
rows 4 & 6: as row 2 but ending row 6 with 1 turning ch.
row 7: 1 dc/sc in first st, 3 ch, * 3 tr/dc in 3 ch space, 3 ch, 1 dc/sc in next 3 ch space; repeat from * to end of row ending with 1 dc/sc in turning ch. 3 turning ch.
row 8: as row 2.
repeat rows 1–8

multiple of 6+1, 1 turning ch

base row: work 1 dc/sc in second ch from hook, * miss 2 ch, (1 tr/dc, [1 ch, 1 tr/dc] four times) in next ch, miss 2 ch, 1 dc/sc in next ch; repeat from * to end of row, 5 turning ch.
row 1: * 1 dc/sc in second 1 ch space, 1 ch, 1 dc/sc in third 1 ch

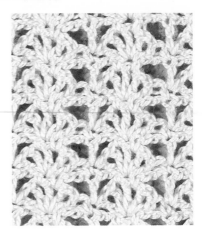

space, 2 ch, 1 tr/dc in dc/sc, 2 ch; repeat from * to end of row ending with 1 tr/dc, 1 turning ch.
row 2: 1 dc/sc in first st, (1 tr/dc [1 ch, 1 tr/dc] four times) in 1 ch space, 1 dc/sc in tr/dc; repeat from * to end of row ending with 1 dc/sc in turning ch, 5 turning ch.
repeat rows 1–2.

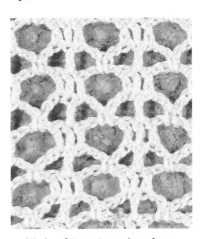

multiple of 6+1, 3 turning ch

base row: work 1 tr/dc in fourth ch from hook, * 3 ch, miss 2 ch, 1 dc/sc in next ch, 3 ch, miss 2 ch, 1 tr/dc in next ch; repeat from * to end of row, 3 turning ch.
row 1: 1 tr/dc in first st, * 3 ch, 1 tr/dc in the ch before the tr/dc, the tr/dc and the next ch; repeat from * to end of row, 1 tr/dc in last st, 1 tr/dc in turning ch, 3 turning ch.
row 2: 1 tr/dc in first tr/dc, * 3 ch, 1 dc/sc in middle of 3 ch space, 3 ch, 1 tr/dc in centre tr/dc; repeat from * to end of row ending with 1 tr/dc in turning ch, 3 turning ch.
repeat rows 1–2

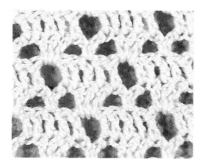

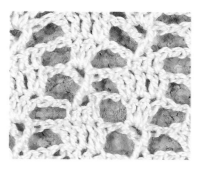

multiple of 6+1, 3 turning ch

base row: work 1 tr/dc in the fourth ch from the hook and in each of the next 5 ch, * 1 ch, miss 1 ch, 1 tr/dc in each next 5 ch; repeat from * to end of row ending with a further tr/dc in last ch, 3 turning ch.
row 1: 1 tr/dc in first st, * 2 ch, 1 dc/sc in third tr/dc, 2 ch, 3 tr/dc in 1 ch space; repeat from * to end of row ending with 2 tr/dc in turning ch, 3 turning ch.
row 2: 1 tr/dc in second tr/dc, 1 tr/dc in first ch, * 1 ch, 1 tr/dc in last ch, the 3 tr/dc, the first ch; repeat from * to end of row ending with 3 tr/dc, 1 turning ch.
row 3: 1 dc/sc in first st, * 2 ch, 3 tr/dc in 1 ch space, 2 ch, 1 dc/sc in third tr/dc; repeat from * to end of row ending with 1 dc/sc in turning ch, 3 turning ch.
row 4: * 1 tr/dc in second ch, 1 tr/dc in each next 3 sts, 1 tr/dc in first ch, 1 ch; repeat from * to end of row ending with 1 tr/dc in last st, 3 turning ch.
repeat rows 1–4

multiple of 10, 3 turning ch

base row: work 1 tr/dc in fourth ch from hook, * 3 ch, miss 2 ch, 1 dc/sc in each next 3 ch, 3 ch, miss 2 ch, 1 tr/dc in each next 3 ch; repeat from * to end of row ending with 1 tr/dc in last 2 sts, 3 turning ch.
row 1: 2 tr/dc in second tr/dc, * 1 ch, 1 d.tr/tr in third dc/sc, 1 ch, 1 d.tr/tr in first dc/sc, 1 ch, 2 tr/dc in first tr/dc, 1 tr/dc in centre tr/dc, 2 tr/dc in last tr/dc; repeat from * to end of row ending with 2 tr/dc in last st, 1 tr/dc in turning ch, 1 turning ch.
row 2: 1 dc/sc in first two tr/dc, * 3 ch, 3 tr/dc in centre 1 ch space, 3 ch, 1 dc/sc in each next 3 tr/dc; repeat from * to end of row ending with 2

dc/sc, 5 turning ch.
row 3: * 2 tr/dc in first tr/dc, 1 tr/dc in centre tr/dc, 2 tr/dc in last tr/dc, 1 ch, 1 d.tr/tr in third dc/sc, 1 ch, 1 d.tr/tr in first dc/sc, 1 ch; repeat * to end of row ending with 1 tr/dc in last two dc/sc, 3 turning ch.
row 4: 1 tr/dc in first st, * 3 ch, 1 dc/sc in each centre 3 tr/dc, 3 ch, 3 tr/dc in 1 ch space; repeat from * to end of row, 2 tr/dc in turning ch, 3 turning ch.
repeat rows 1–4.

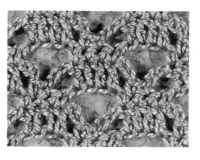

multiple of 8+3, 3 turning ch

row 1: work 1 tr/dc in fourth ch from hook, * 3 ch, miss 1 st, 1 dc/sc in next two sts, 3 ch, miss 1 st, 1 tr/dc in each next 4 sts; repeat from * to end of row ending with 1 dc/sc in last st, 4 turning ch.
row 2: * 1 dc/sc in each 4 tr/dc, 4 ch; repeat from * to end of row ending with 2 dc/sc, 1 turning ch.
row 3: 1 dc/sc in first st, 3 ch, * 4 tr/dc in 4 ch space, 3 ch, 1 dc/sc in 2 centre dc/sc, 3 ch; repeat from * to end of row ending with 2 tr/dc in turning ch, 1 turning ch.
row 4: 2 dc/sc in tr/dc, * 4 ch, 1 dc/sc in each of 4 tr/dc; repeat from * to end of row ending with 1 ch, 1 tr/dc in last st, 3 turning ch.
repeat rows 1–4 beginning row 1 with 1 tr/dc in first st.

OPENWORK AND LACE PATTERNS

multiple of 4, 3 turning ch

base row: work 1 tr/dc in fourth ch from hook and all subsequent sts to end of row, 3 turning ch.
row 1: 1 tr/dc in every st to end of row, 3 turning ch.
row 2: miss 2 sts * (1 tr/dc, 1 ch, 1 tr/dc) in next st, miss 1 st, 1 tr/dc in next st, miss 1 st; repeat from * to end of row ending with 1 tr/dc in turning ch, 3 turning ch.
row 3: 1 tr/dc in first st, * 1 tr/dc in 1 ch space, (1 tr/dc, 1 ch, 1 tr/dc) in single tr/dc; repeat from * to end of row ending with 2 tr/dc in last st, 3 turning ch.
row 4: 1 tr/dc in every st to end of row, 3 turning ch.
repeat rows 1–4

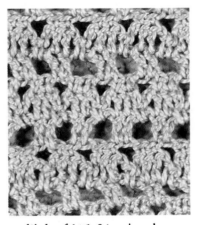

multiple of 4+1, 3 turning ch

row 1: work 1 tr/dc in fourth ch from hook, * 2 ch, miss 2 ch, 1 tr/dc in next 2 ch; repeat from * to end of row, 3 turning ch.
row 2: 1 tr/dc in second tr/dc, * 2 ch, 1 dc/sc in 2 ch space, 2 ch, 1 tr/dc in next 2 tr/dc; repeat from * to end of row, 1 turning ch.
row 3: 1 dc/sc in first two tr/dc, * 2 ch, 1 dc/sc in next two sts; repeat from * to end of row, 4 turning ch.
row 4: * 2 tr/dc in 2 ch space, 2 ch; repeat from * to end of row, 1 turning ch.
row 5: 1 dc/sc in first st, * 2 ch, 1 tr/dc in next 2 tr/dc, 2 ch, 1 dc/sc in 2 ch space; repeat from * to end of row, ending with 1 dc/sc in turning ch, 4 turning ch.
row 6: * 1 dc/sc in next 2 tr/dc, 2 ch; repeat from * to end of row, ending with 1 ch, 1 tr/dc in last st, 3 turning ch.
repeat rows 1–6 beginning row 1 with 1 tr/dc in 1 ch space and the 2 tr/dc in the 2 ch space of row 5.

multiple of 2, 1 turning ch

base row: work 1 dc/sc in second ch from hook and all subsequent ch to end of row, 1 turning ch.
row 1: 1 dc/sc in each st to end of row, 1 turning ch.
row 2: as row 1, 3 turning ch.
row 3: 1 tr/dc in second st, * 1 ch, miss 1 st, 1 tr/dc; repeat from * to end of row, 1 turning ch.
row 4: 1 dc/sc in each st and ch to end of row, 1 turning ch.
repeat rows 1–4

multiple of 16+11, 2 turning ch

base row: work 1 tr/dc in third ch from hook and all subsequent ch to end of row, 3 turning ch.
row 1: miss first st, 1 tr/dc in next 10 sts, * miss 2 sts, (1 tr/dc, 1 ch, 1 tr/dc, 1 ch, 1 tr/dc) in next st, miss 2 sts, 1 tr/dc in next 11 sts; repeat from * to end of row, 3 turning ch.
row 2: 1 tr/dc in each st to end of row, 3 turning ch.
row 3: miss first st, 1 tr/dc in next two sts, * miss 2 sts, (1 tr/dc, 1 ch, 1 tr/dc, 1 ch, 1 tr/dc) in next st, miss 2 sts, tr/dc in next 11 sts; repeat from * to end of row ending with 1 tr/dc in last 3 sts, 3 turning ch.
row 4: as row 2.
repeat rows 1–4

multiple of 6, 3 turning ch

base row: work 1 tr/dc in fourth ch from hook and all subsequent ch to end of row 3 turning ch.

row 1: 1 tr/dc in second st, * 3 ch, miss 3 sts, 1 tr/dc in each next 3 sts; repeat from * to end of row ending with 1 tr/dc in last st, 1 tr/dc in turning ch, 4 turning ch.
row 2: * 3 tr/dc in 3 ch space, 3 ch; repeat from * to end of row ending with 1 ch, 1 tr/dc in turning ch, 3 turning ch.
row 3: 1 tr/dc in 1 ch space, * 3 ch, 3 tr/dc in 3 ch space; repeat from * to end of row ending with 2 tr/dc in turning ch, 3 turning ch.
row 4: 1 tr/dc in each ch and st to end of row, 3 turning ch.
row 5 & 6: 1 tr/dc in each st to end of row, 3 turning ch.
repeat rows 1–6

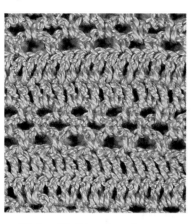

multiple of 3, 3 turning ch

base row: 1 tr/dc in fourth ch from hook and all subsequent ch to end of row, 1 turning ch.
row 1: 1 dc/sc in first st, * 3 ch, miss 2 sts, 1 dc/sc in next st; repeat from * to end of row, 3 turning ch.
row 2: * 1 dc/sc in 3 ch space, 3 ch; repeat from * to end of row ending with 1 ch, 1 h.tr/h.dc in last st, 1 turning ch.
row 3: 1 dc/sc in first st, * 3 ch, 1 dc/sc in 3 ch space; repeat from * to end of row, 3 turning ch.
row 4: * 2 tr/dc in 3 ch space, 1 tr/dc in next st; repeat from * to end of row, 3 turning ch.
row 5: miss first st, 1 tr/dc in every st to end of row, 1 tr/dc in turning ch, 3 turning ch.
repeat rows 1–5

OPENWORK AND LACE PATTERNS

multiple of 6+1, 3 turning ch

base row: work 1 tr/dc in fourth ch from hook and all subsequent ch to end of row ending with 3 turning ch.
row 1: 1 tr/dc in first st, * miss 2 sts, (2 tr/dc, 1 ch, 2 tr/dc) in next st, miss 2 ch, 1 tr/dc in next st; repeat from * to end of row, 3 turning ch.
row 2: 1 tr/dc in each st to end of row, 3 turning ch.
row 3: 2 tr/dc in first st, * miss 2 sts, 1 tr/dc in next st, miss 2 sts, (2 tr/dc 1 ch, 2 tr/dc) in next st; repeat from * to end of row ending with 3 tr/dc in last st, 3 turning ch.
row 4: as row 2.
repeat rows 1–4

multiple of 8+3, 3 turning ch

base row 1: work 1 tr/dc in fourth ch from hook, * miss 2 ch, 5 tr/dc in next ch, miss 2 ch, 1 tr/dc in next ch, miss 1 ch, 1 tr/dc in next ch; repeat from * to end of row ending with miss 1 ch, 3 tr/dc in last st, 3 turning ch.
base row 2: 2 tr/dc in second st, * 1 tr/dc in single tr/dc, 1 tr/dc in 1 ch space, 1 tr/dc in next tr/dc, 5 tr/dc in third st of 5 tr/dc group; repeat from * to end of row ending with 1 tr/dc in last st, 1 tr/dc in turning ch, 3 turning ch.
row 1: miss first st, 1 tr/dc in next st, * miss 2 sts, 5 tr/dc in next st, miss 2 sts, 1 tr/dc in next st, 1 ch, miss 1 st, 1 tr/dc in next st; repeat from * to end of row ending with

miss 1 st, 1 tr/dc in next st, 2 tr/dc in turning ch, 3 turning ch.
row 2: 2 tr/dc in second st, * 1 tr/dc in single tr/dc, 1 tr/dc in 1 ch space, 1 tr/dc in next tr/dc, 5 tr/dc in third st of 5 tr/dc group; repeat from * to end of row ending with 1 tr/dc in last st, 1 tr/dc in turning ch, 3 turning ch.
repeat rows 1–2

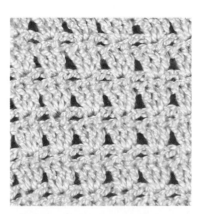

multiple of 3+1, 1 turning ch

base row: work 1 dc/sc in second ch from hook, * 2 ch, miss 2 ch, 1 dc/sc in next ch; repeat from * to end of rown, 3 turning ch.
row 1: 1 tr/dc in first st, * 3 tr/dc in each dc/sc; repeat from * to end of row ending with 2 dc/sc in last sc, 1 turning ch.
row 2: 1 dc/sc in first st, * 2 ch, 1 dc/sc in centre tr/dc of 3 tr/dc group; repeat from * to end of row, 1 dc/sc in turning ch, 3 turning ch.
repeat rows 1–2

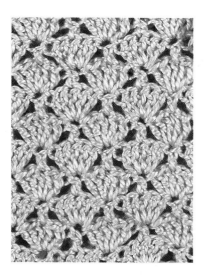

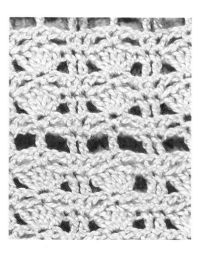

to end of row ending with 1 tr/dc in turning ch, 2 turning ch.
repeat rows 1–6

multiple of 6+5, 3 turning ch

base row: work 1 tr/dc in fourth ch from hook and all subsequent ch to end of row, 3 turning ch.
row 1: miss first st, 1 tr/dc in next st, * miss 2 sts, 5 tr/dc in next st, miss 2 sts, 1 tr/dc in next st; repeat from * to end of row ending with 3 tr/dc in turning ch, 3 turning ch.
row 2: miss first st, 1 tr/dc in next st, * 5 tr/dc in single tr/dc, 1 tr/dc in third st of 5 tr/dc group; repeat from * to end of row ending with 3 tr/dc in turning ch, 3 turning ch.
repeat rows 1–2

multiple of 7+2, 3 turning ch

base row: work 1 tr/dc in fourth ch from hook, 1 tr/dc in next ch, * 2 ch, miss 2 ch, 1 tr/dc in next ch, 2 ch, miss 2 ch, 1 tr/dc in each next 2 ch; repeat from * to end of row, 2 turning ch.
row 1: miss first st, * 1 dc/sc in next st, 2 ch, 1 dc/sc in next st, 1 dc/sc in next st; repeat from * to end of row, 1 dc/sc in last st, 3 turning ch.
row 2: miss first st, * 1 tr/dc in next st, 5 tr/dc in dc/sc, 1 tr/dc in each next 2 sts; repeat from * to end of row, 2 turning ch.
row 3: as row 1 but working a dc/sc in centre st of tr/dc group, 3 turning ch.
row 4: as row 2
row 5: as row 3
row 6: miss first st, 1 tr/dc in next st, * 2 ch, 1 tr/dc in next st, 2 ch, 1 tr/dc in each next 2 sts; repeat from *

multiple of 8+1, 3 turning ch

base row: work 2 tr/dc in fourth ch from hook, * miss 3 ch, (1 tr/dc, 3 ch, 1 tr/dc) in next ch, miss 3 ch, (1 tr/dc, 1 ch, 1 tr/dc) in next ch; repeat from * to end of row ending with 2 tr/dc in last st, 3 turning ch.
row 1: miss first st, 1 tr/dc in next st, * 6 d.tr/tr in 3 ch space, (1 tr/dc, 1 ch, 1 tr/dc) in 1 ch space; repeat from * to end of row ending with 2 tr/dc in last st, 4 turning ch.
row 2: miss first st, 1 tr/dc in next st, * (1 tr/dc, 3 ch, 1 tr/dc) between third and fourth st of d.tr/tr group, (1 tr/dc, 1 ch, 1 tr/dc) in 1 ch space; repeat from * to end of row ending with 2 tr/dc in turning ch, 3 turning ch.
repeat rows 1–2

OPENWORK AND LACE PATTERNS

multiple of 3+2, 4 turning ch

base row: work (1 tr/dc, 1 ch, 1 tr/
dc) in fifth ch from hook, * miss 2
ch, (1 tr/dc, 1 ch, 1 tr/dc) in next ch;
repeat from * to end of row ending
with 1 tr/dc in last st, 3 turning ch.
row 1: * 3 tr/dc in 1 ch space leaving
all loops on hook, yarn over hook
and draw loop through, 2 ch;
repeat from * to end of row, 1 tr/dc
in turning ch, 3 turning ch.
row 2: miss first st, 1 tr/dc in every
st to end of row, 1 tr/dc in turning
ch, 3 turning ch.
row 3: (1 tr/dc, 1 ch, 1 tr/dc) in
second st, * miss 2 sts, (1 tr/dc, 1 ch,
1 tr/dc) in next st; repeat from * to
end of row ending with 1 tr/dc in
turning ch, 3 turning ch.
repeat rows 1–3

multiple of 12+11, 4 turning ch

base row: work 1 tr/dc in fifth ch
from hook, 1 tr/dc in each of next 3
sts, * 3 ch, miss 2 ch, 1 tr/ch in each
of next 10 sts; repeat from * to end
of row ending with 5 tr/dc, 3
turning ch.
row 1: miss 1 tr/dc, 1 tr/dc in each
next 2 sts, * 3 ch, 1 dc/sc in 3 ch
space, 3 ch, miss 2 tr/dc, 1 tr/dc in
each next 6 sts, miss 2 tr/dc; repeat
from * to end of row ending with 1
tr/dc in last 2 sts, 1 tr/dc in turning
ch, 6 turning ch.
row 2: * 1 dc/sc in 3 ch space, 3 ch, 1
dc/sc in next 3 ch space, 3 ch, miss 2
tr/dc, 1 tr/dc in each next 2 sts, 3 ch;
repeat from * to end of row ending
with 1 tr/dc in turning ch, 3 turning
ch.
row 3: as row 1 but with 3 turning
ch and working new tr/dc in ch sts.
row 4: miss 1 tr/dc, 1 tr/dc in each

next 2 sts, 2 tr/dc in 3 ch space, * 3
ch, 2 tr/dc in 3 ch space, 1 tr/dc in
each next 6 sts, 2 tr/dc in 3 ch space;
repeat from * to end of row ending
with 1 tr/dc in turning ch, 3 turning
ch.
repeat rows 1–4

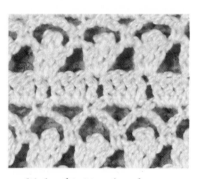

multiple of 4, 3 turning ch

base row: work 1 tr/dc in fourth ch
from hook and all subsequent sts to
end of row, 3 turning ch.
row 1: miss first 2 sts, 2 tr/dc in next
st, 3 ch picot, 1 tr/dc in same st, * 2
ch, miss 3 sts, 2 tr/dc in next st, 3 ch
picot, 1 tr/dc in same st; repeat
from * to end of row ending with
miss 1 st, 1 tr/dc in turning ch, 1
turning ch.
row 2: 1 dc/sc in first st, * 5 ch, 1 dc/
sc in 2 ch space; repeat from * to
end of row ending with 1 dc/sc in
turning ch, 3 turning ch.
row 3: * 1 dc/sc in 5 ch space, 3 ch;
repeat from * to end of row ending
with 1 ch, 1 h.tr/h.dc in last st, 3
turning ch.
row 4: miss first st, 1 tr/dc in next
and all subsequent sts and ch to
end of row ending with 2 tr/dc in
turning ch, 3 turning ch.
repeat rows 1–4

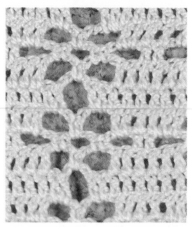

multiple of 8+1, 3 turning ch

base row: work 1 tr/dc in fourth ch
from hook, * 1 ch, miss 1 ch, 1 tr/dc
in next ch; repeat from * to end of
row, 3 turning ch.
row 1: miss 2 tr/dc, * (3 tr/dc, 2 ch, 3
tr/dc) in next tr/dc, miss 1 tr/dc, 1
tr/dc in next tr/dc, miss 1 tr/dc;
repeat from * to end of row ending
with 1 tr/dc in turning ch, 6 turning
ch.
row 2: * 1 dc/sc in 2 ch space, * 3 ch,
1 tr/dc in next single tr/dc, 3 ch;
repeat from * to end of row ending
with 1 tr/dc in turning ch, 4 turning
ch.
row 3: * 1 tr/dc in 3 ch space, 1 ch, 1
tr/dc in dc/sc, 1 ch, 1 tr/dc in 3 ch
space, 1 ch, 1 tr/dc in next tr/dc, 1
ch; repeat from * to end of row
ending with 1 tr/dc in turning ch, 3
turning ch.
row 4: 1 tr/dc in every st and ch to
end of row, 4 turning ch.
row 5: 1 tr/dc in third st, * 1 ch, miss
1 st, 1 tr/dc in next st; repeat from *
to end row ending with 1 tr/dc in
turning ch, 3 turning ch.
repeat rows 1–5

multiple of 7+6, 3 turning ch

base row: work 1 tr/dc in fourth ch
from hook and all subsequent ch to
end of row, 3 turning ch.
row 1: miss 1 tr/dc, 1 tr/dc in next
st, * 1 ch, miss 1 st, 1 tr/dc in next
st, 1 ch, miss 1 st, 1 tr/dc in each of
next 4 sts; repeat from * to end of
row ending with 1 tr/dc in last st, 1
tr/dc in turning ch, 4 turning ch.
row 2: 1 tr/dc in first st, * 1 ch, (1 tr/
dc, 1 ch, 1 tr/dc) in second st and
third sts of 4 tr/dc group; repeat
from * to end of row ending with (1
tr/dc, 1 ch, 1 tr/dc in turning ch, 3
turning ch.
row 3: 2 tr/dc in 1 ch space, * 1 ch,
miss 1 ch space, 3 tr/dc in next 1 ch
space, 3 tr/dc in next 1 ch space;
repeat from * to end of row ending
with 2 tr/dc in 1 ch space, 1 tr/dc in
turning ch, 3 turning ch.
row 4: miss first st, 1 tr/dc in next
and all subsequent sts to end of
row, 3 turning ch.
repeat rows 1–4

OPENWORK AND LACE PATTERNS

multiple of 5+1, 3 turning ch

base row: work 1 d.tr/tr in fourth ch from hook, miss 4 ch, * 5 d.tr/tr in next ch, miss 4 ch; repeat from * to end of row ending with 3 d.tr/tr in last ch, 4 turning ch.
row 1: 2 d.tr/tr in first st, * 5 d.tr/tr in centre st of shell; repeat from * to end of row ending with 2 d.tr/tr in turning ch, 4 turning ch.
row 2: 1 d.tr/tr in first st, * 5 d.tr/tr in centre st of shell; repeat from * to end of row ending with 3 d.tr/tr in turning ch, 4 turning ch.
repeat rows 1–2

multiple of 5+1, 2 turning ch

base row: work 1 tr/dc in third ch from hook, miss 4 ch, * 5 tr/dc in next ch, miss 4 ch; repeat from * to end of row ending with 3 tr/dc in last ch, 3 turning ch.
row 1: miss 1 st, 2 tr/dc in next st, * 5 tr/dc in the centre of next shell; repeat from * to end of row ending with 2 tr/dc in turning ch, 3 turning ch.
row 2: miss 1 st, 2 tr/dc in next st, * 5 tr/dc in the centre of next shell; repeat from * to end of row ending with 3 tr/dc in turning ch, 3 turning ch.
repeat rows 1–2

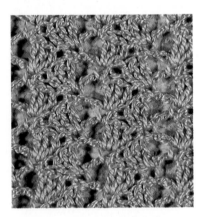

multiple of 7+4, 1 turning ch

base row: work 1 dc/sc in second ch from hook, miss 2 ch, 3 tr/dc in next ch, * 3 ch, miss 3 ch, 1 dc/sc in next ch, miss 2 ch, 3 tr/dc in next ch; repeat from * to end of work, 1 turning ch.
row 1: 1 dc/sc in first st, 3 tr/dc in dc/sc, * 3 ch, 1 dc/sc in 3 ch space, 3 tr/dc in dc/sc; repeat from * to end or row, 1 turning ch.
repeat row 1

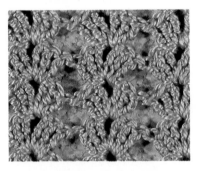

multiple of 5+1, 3 turning ch

base row: work 2 d.tr/tr in fourth ch from hook, miss 4 ch, * (3 d.tr/tr, 1 ch, 3 d.tr/tr) in next ch, miss 4 ch; repeat from * to end of row ending with 3 d.tr/tr in last ch, 4 turning ch.
row 1: 2 d.tr/tr in first st, * (3 d.tr/tr, 1 ch, 3 d.tr/tr) in 1 ch space of shell; repeat from * to end of row ending with 3 d.tr/tr in turning ch, 4 turning ch.
repeat row 1

multiple of 7+2, 3 turning ch

base row: work 1 tr/dc in fourth ch from hook, 1 tr/dc in next ch, * miss 2 ch, (3 tr/dc, 1 ch, 3 tr/dc) in next ch, miss 2 ch, 1 tr/dc in each of next 2 sts; repeat from * to end of row, 3 turning ch.
row 1: miss 1 st, 1 tr/dc in next st, * (3 tr/dc, 1 ch, 3 tr/dc) in 1 ch space; repeat from * to end of row ending with 1 tr/dc in each of last 2 sts, 3 turning ch.
repeat row 1

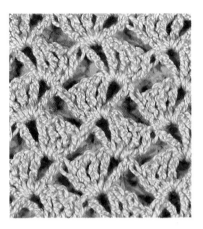

multiple of 6+1, 4 turning ch

base row: work 1 d.tr/tr in fifth ch from hook, * miss 5 ch, (1 d.tr/tr, 1 ch) 4 times, 1 d.tr/tr all in next ch; repeat from * to end of row ending with (1 d.tr/tr, 1 ch, 1 d.tr/tr) in last ch, 5 turning ch.
row 1: 1 d/tr in first 1 ch space, * (1 d.tr/tr, 1 ch) 4 times, 1 d.tr/tr all in first 1 ch space of each shell group; repeat from * to end of row ending with (1 d.tr/tr, 1 ch, 1 d.tr/tr) in last 1 ch space, 5 turning ch.
repeat row 1

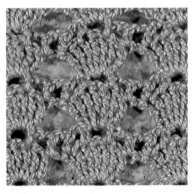

multiple of 8+1, 3 turning ch

base row: work 1 h.tr/h.dc in fourth ch from hook, * 1 ch, miss 1 ch, 1 h.tr/h.dc in next ch; repeat from * to end of row, 4 turning ch.
row 1: 3 d.tr/tr in first 1 ch space, 1 ch, miss three 1 ch spaces, * 7 d.tr/tr in next 1 ch space, 1 ch, miss three 1 ch spaces; repeat from * to end of row ending with 4 d.tr/tr in last space, 3 turning ch.
row 2: miss first st, * 1 h.tr/h.dc in next st, 1 ch, miss 1 st; repeat from * to end of row ending with 1 h.tr/h.dc in turning ch, 4 turning ch.
repeat rows 1–2

multiple of 5+1, 2 turning ch

base row 1: work 1 h.tr/h.dc in third ch from hook and all subsequent ch to end of row, 4 turning ch.
base row 2: 1 d.tr/tr in first st, * miss 4 sts, 5 d.tr/tr in next st; repeat from * to end of row ending with 3 d.tr/tr in turning ch, 2 turning ch.
row 1: miss first st, 1 h.tr/dc in next and all subsequent sts to end of row ending with 2 h.tr/h.dc in turning ch, 4 turning ch.
row 2: 1 d.tr/tr in first st, * 5 d.tr/tr in centre st of shell; repeat from * to end or row ending with 3 d.tr/tr in turning ch, 2 turning ch.
repeat rows 1–2

OPENWORK AND LACE PATTERNS

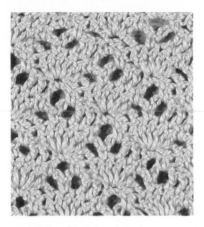

multiple of 9, 6 turning ch

base row: work 1 dc/sc in seventh ch from hook, * miss 2 ch, 5 tr/dc in next st, miss 2 sts, 1 dc/sc in next ch, 3 ch, miss 2 ch, 1 dc/sc in next ch; repeat from * to end of row ending with 5 tr/dc, miss 2 ch, 1 dc/sc in next ch, 1 ch, miss 1 ch, 1 tr/dc in last ch, 1 turning ch.
row 1: 1 dc/sc in first st, * 1 tr/dc in first tr/dc, 1 tr/dc in next st, 3 ch, 1 dc/sc in next st, 3 ch, 1 tr/dc in next st, 1 tr/dc in last st of group, 1 dc/sc in 3 ch; repeat from * to end of row ending with 1 dc/sc in turning ch, 3 turning ch.
row 2: 2 tr/dc in first st, * 1 dc/sc in 3 ch, 3 ch, 1 dc/sc in next 3 ch, 5 tr/dc in the dc/sc; repeat from * to end of row ending with 3 tr/dc in last st, 1 turning ch.
row 3: 1 dc/sc in first st, 3 ch, 1 tr/dc in each next 2 tr/dc, * 1 dc/sc in 3 ch, 1 tr/dc in first tr/dc; 1 tr/dc in next st, 3 ch, 1 dc/sc in next st, 3 ch, 1 tr/dc in next st, 1 tr/dc in last st of group; repeat from * to end of row ending with 1 dc/sc in 3 ch, 1 tr/dc in each last two sts, 3 ch, 1 dc/sc in turning ch, 4 turning ch.
row 4: * 1 dc/sc in 3 ch, 5 tr/dc in dc/sc, 1 dc/sc in 3 ch, 3 ch; repeat from * to end of row ending with 1 dc/sc in 3 ch, 1 ch, 1 tr/dc in last st, 1 turning ch.
repeat rows 1–4

multiple of 12+11, 1 turning ch

base row: work 1 dc/sc in second ch from hook, * 5 ch, miss 3 ch, 1 dc/sc in next ch; repeat from * to end of row ending with 2 ch, miss 1 ch, 1 tr/dc in last st, 1 turning ch.

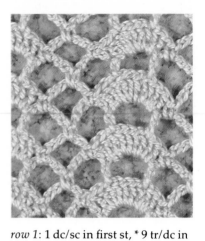

row 1: 1 dc/sc in first st, * 9 tr/dc in 5 ch loop, 1 dc/sc in 5 loop ch, 5 ch, 1 dc/sc in next 5 loop ch; repeat from * to end of row ending with 1 dc/sc in last 5 ch loop, 2 ch, 1 tr/dc in last st, 1 turning ch.
row 2: 1 dc/sc in first st, * 5 ch, 1 tr/dc in 3rd tr/dc, 5 ch, 1 tr/dc in 7th tr/dc of 9 st group, 5 ch, 1 dc/sc in 5 ch loop; repeat from * to end of row ending with 2 ch, 1 tr/dc in last st, 1 turning ch.
repeat rows 1–2

multiple of 4+1, 1 turning ch

base row: work 1 dc/sc in second ch from hook, * 2 ch, 4 tr/dc in same dc/sc, miss 3 ch, 1 dc/sc in next ch; repeat from * to end of row ending with 1 dc/sc in last ch, 3 turning ch.
row 1: 2 tr/dc in first st, * 1 dc/sc in 2 ch space, 2 ch, 4 tr/dc in same dc/sc; repeat from * to end of row ending with 2 tr/dc in last st, 3 turning ch.
row 2: 1 dc/sc in first st, * 1 dc/sc in next 2 ch space, 2 ch, 4 tr/dc in same dc/sc; repeat from * to end of row, 3 turning ch.
repeat rows 1–2

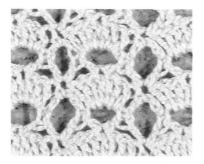

multiple of 8+1, 6 turning ch

base row: work 1 tr/dc in seventh ch
from hook, miss 3 ch, half work 1
tr/dc in next ch then finish both sts
together, * 5 ch, half work 1 tr/dc in
ch previously worked, miss 3 ch,
half work 1 tr/dc in next ch, then
finish both sts together, 5 ch, miss 3
ch, half work 1 tr/dc in next ch then
finish both sts together; repeat
from * to end of row ending with 2
ch, 1 d.tr/tr in last ch, 1 turning ch.
row 1: 1 dc/sc in first st, * 7 tr/dc in
5 ch loop, 1 dc/sc in next 5 ch loop;
repeat from * to end of row ending
with 1 dc/sc in turning ch, 6
turning ch.
row 2: half work 1 tr/dc in first st,
half work 1 tr/dc in fourth st of 7 st
group then finish both sts together
* 5 ch, half work 1 tr/dc in st
previously worked, half work 1 tr/
dc in dc/sc then finish both sts
together, 5 ch, half work 1 tr/dc in
st previously worked, half work 1
tr/dc in 4th st of 7 st group then
finish both sts together; repeat
from * to end of row ending with 2
ch, 1 d.tr/tr in last st, 1 turning ch.
repeat rows 1–2

multiple of 12+1, 3 turning ch

base row: work 1 tr/dc in fourth ch
from hook, 1 tr/dc in next 2 sts, *
miss 2 ch, 3 tr/dc in next ch, 3 ch, 3
tr/dc in next ch, 3 ch, miss 5 ch, 1 tr/
dc in each next 3 ch; repeat from *
to end of row ending with 1 tr/dc in
last ch, 3 turning ch.
row 1: 1 tr/dc in first st, 1 ch, * 3 tr/
dc in 3 ch loop, (3 tr/dc, 3 ch, 3 tr/
dc) in next 3 ch loop, 3 ch; repeat
from * to end of row ending with 2
ch, 1 tr/dc in last st, 3 turning ch.
row 2: 1 tr/dc in first st, 2 tr/dc in
loop, * (3 tr/dc, 3 ch, 3 tr/dc) in 3 ch
loop, 3 ch, 3 tr/dc in 3 ch loop, 3 ch;

repeat from * to end of row, 3 ch, 1
tr/dc in last st, 3 turning ch.
repeat rows 1–2

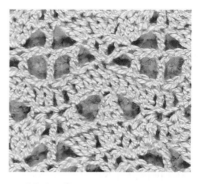

multiple of 12, 4 turning ch

base row: work 1 tr/dc in fifth ch
from hook and each subsequent ch
to end or row, 5 turning ch.
row 1: miss first 3 sts, 1 tr/dc in next
st, * miss 2 sts, (1 tr/dc, 1 ch, 1 tr/dc,
1 ch, 1 tr/dc) in next st, miss 2 sts, 1
tr/dc in next st, 2 ch, miss 2 sts, 1 tr/
dc in next st, 2 ch, miss 2 sts, 1 tr/dc
in next st; repeat from * to end of
row ending with 1 tr/dc in turning
ch, 4 turning ch.
row 2: miss first tr/dc, * 3 tr/dc in
each of next 3 tr/dc, 1 ch, 1 tr/dc in
next tr/dc, 1 ch; repeat from * to
end of row ending with 1 tr/dc in
turning ch, 3 turning ch.
row 3: * half work 1 tr/dc in each st
of first 3 tr/dc group then work
these sts tog, (4 ch, half work 1 tr/dc
in each st in next group then work
these sts tog) twice, 1 tr/dc in next
tr/dc; repeat from * to end of row
ending with 1 tr/dc in turning ch, 3
turning ch.
row 4: miss first st, 1 tr/dc in every
st to end of row, 5 turning ch.
repeat rows 1–4

OPENWORK AND LACE PATTERNS

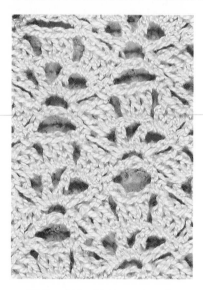 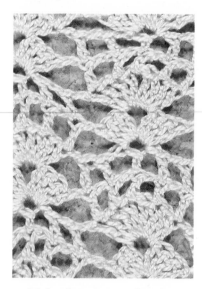

multiple of 12+11, 7 turning ch

base row: work 1 dc/sc in eighth ch
from hook, * miss 3 ch, ([1 tr/dc, 2
ch] 3 times, 1 tr/dc) in next ch, miss
3 ch, 1 dc/sc in next ch, 5 ch, miss 3
ch, 1 dc/sc in next ch; repeat from *
to end of row ending with 1 dc/sc, 2
ch, miss 1 ch, 1 tr/dc in last ch, 4
turning ch.
row 1: 1 dc/sc in 2 ch space, * 3 tr/dc
in 2 ch space, 2 ch, 3 tr/dc in next 2
ch space, 2 ch, 3 tr/dc in last 2 ch
space of 4 tr/dc group, (1 dc/sc, 3
ch, 1 dc/sc) in 5 ch space; repeat
from * to end of row ending with (1
dc/sc 1 ch, 1 h.tr/h.dc) in turning
ch, 4 turning ch.
row 2: (1 tr/dc, 2 ch, 1 tr/dc) in 1 ch
space, * 1 dc/sc in first 2 ch space, 5
ch, 1 dc/sc in last 2 ch space, ([1 tr/
dc, 2 ch] three times, 1 tr/dc) in 3 ch
space; repeat from * to end of row
ending with (1 tr/dc, 2 ch, 1 tr/dc, 1
ch, 1 tr/dc) in turning ch, 3 turning
ch.
row 3: 1 tr/dc in 1 ch space, 2 ch, 3
tr/dc in 2 ch space, * (1 dc/sc, 3 ch, 1
dc/sc) in 5 ch space, 3 tr/dc in first 2
ch space, 2 ch, 3 tr/dc in next 2 ch
space, 2 ch, 3 tr/dc in last 2 ch space
of group; repeat from * to end of
row ending with 2 tr/dc in turning
ch, 4 turning ch.
row 4: 1 dc/sc in 2 ch space, * ([1 tr/
dc, 2 ch] three times, 1 tr/dc) in 3 ch
space, 1 dc/sc in first 2 ch space, 5
ch, 1 dc/sc in last 2 ch space; repeat
from * to end of row ending with 1
dc/sc in 2 ch space, 2 ch, 1 h.tr/h.dc
in turning ch, 4 turning ch.
repeat rows 1–4

multiple of 18+2, 3 turning ch

base row: work 1 tr/dc in fourth ch
from hook, (1 ch, miss 1 ch, 1 tr/dc
in next ch) 4 times, 1 ch, * miss 4 ch,
(4 tr/dc, 1 ch, 4 tr/dc) in next ch, 1
ch, miss 4 ch, (1 tr/dc in next ch, 1
ch, miss 1 ch) five times; repeat
from * to end of row ending with 1
tr/dc in each last two ch, 3 turning
ch.
row 1: miss first st, 1 tr/dc in next
st, * 1 ch, (4 tr/dc, 1 ch, 4 tr/dc) in 1
ch space, (1 ch, 1 tr/dc in next tr/dc)
five times; repeat from * to end of
row ending with last tr/dc in
turning ch, 4 turning ch.
row 2: * (4 tr/dc, 1 ch, 4 tr/dc) in
third tr/dc of group, 1 ch, ([1 tr/dc,
1 ch] in first and third sts, the 1 ch
space, the second and fourth sts of
shell), 1 ch; repeat from * to end of
row ending with 1 tr/dc in turning
ch, 3 turning ch.
row 3: miss first st, * (1 tr/dc, 1 ch)
in each tr/dc five times, (4 tr/dc, 1
ch, 4 tr/dc) in 1 space, 1 ch;
repeat from * to end of row ending
with 1 tr/dc in turning ch, 4 turning
ch.
row 4: ([1 tr/dc, 1 ch] in first and
third sts, 1 ch space and second and
fourth sts of shell), 1 ch, (4 tr/dc, 1
ch, 4 tr/dc) in third tr/dc of next
group, 1 ch; repeat from * to end of
row ending with 1 tr/dc in turning
ch, 4 turning ch.
repeat rows 1–4

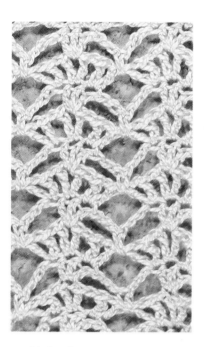

multiple of 8+1, 1 turning ch

base row: work 1 dc/sc in second ch from hook, * 3 ch, miss 3 ch, 3 tr/dc in next ch, 3 ch, miss 3 ch, 1 dc/sc in next ch; repeat from * to end of row ending with 1 dc/sc in last ch, 4 turning ch.

row 1: * (1 tr/dc, 1 ch, 1 tr/dc) in first tr/dc of group, 1 ch, (1 tr/dc, 1 ch, 1 tr/dc) in second tr/dc, 1 ch, (1 tr/dc, 1 ch, 1 tr/dc) in last tr/dc of group; repeat from * to end of row ending with 1 d.tr/tr in last st, 1 turning ch.

row 2: 1 dc/sc in first st, * 3 ch, 3 tr/dc in centre 1 ch space of group, 3 ch, 1 dc/sc between group; repeat from * to end of row ending with 1 dc/sc in turning ch, 4 turning ch.
repeat rows 1–2

multiple of 3, 5 turning ch

base row 1: work 1 tr/dc in sixth ch from hook, 2 ch, 1 tr/dc in same ch, * miss 2 ch, (1 tr/dc, 2 ch, 1 tr/dc) in next ch; repeat from * to end of row, 3 turning ch.

base row 2: 3 tr/dc in 2 ch space, * 4 tr/dc in each 2 ch space; repeat from * to end of row ending with 1 tr/dc in turning ch, 4 turning ch.

row 1: * (1 tr/dc, 2 ch, 1 tr/dc) in centre 4 ch group; repeat from * to end of row ending with 1 tr/dc in turning ch, 3 turning ch.

row 2: * 4 tr/dc in 2 ch space; repeat

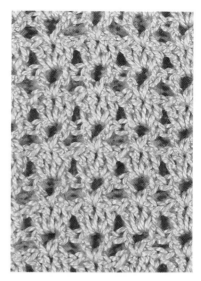

from * to end of row ending with 1 tr/dc in last st, 4 turning ch.
repeat rows 1–2

multiple of 10+8, 4 turning ch

base row: work 1 tr/dc in fifth ch from hook, * miss 1 ch, (4 tr/dc, 2 ch, 1 tr/dc) in next ch, miss 3 ch, 1 tr/dc in each next 5 ch; repeat from * to end of row ending with 1 tr/dc in each last 2 ch, 3 turning ch.

row 1: miss first st, 1 tr/dc in next st, * (4 tr/dc, 2 ch, 1 tr/dc) in 2 ch space, 1 tr/dc in each next 5 sts; repeat from * to end of row ending with 1 tr/dc in last st, 1 tr/dc in turning ch, 3 turning ch.
repeat row 1

OPENWORK AND LACE PATTERNS

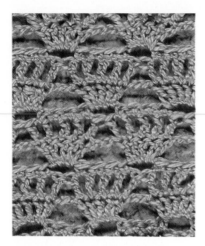

multiple of 10, 4 turning ch

multiple of 7+2, 1 turning ch

base row: work 1 dc/sc in second ch
from hook, 1 dc/sc in each next 2
ch, * 3 ch, miss 3 ch, 1 dc/sc in each
next 4 ch; repeat from * to end of
row ending with 1 dc/sc in each
last 3 ch, 4 turning ch.
row 1: * 5 tr/dc in 3 ch space, 3 ch;
repeat from * to end of row ending
with 1 ch, 1 tr/dc in last st, 3
turning ch.
row 2: (1 tr/dc, 1 ch) in each next
4 sts, 1 tr/dc in last st of group;
repeat from * to end of row, ending
with 1 tr/dc in turning ch, 1 turning
ch.
row 3: 1 dc/sc in first st, 1 ch, * 1 dc/
sc in each of the four 1 ch spaces, 3
ch; repeat from * to end of row
ending with 1 ch, 1 dc/sc in turning
ch, 3 turning ch.
row 4: 2 tr/dc in first 1 ch space, * 3
ch, 5 tr/dc in 3 ch space; repeat
from * to end of row ending with 3
tr/dc in last st, 4 turning ch.
row 5: miss first st, 1 tr/dc in next
st, 1 ch, 1 tr/dc in next st, * (1 tr/dc,
1 ch) in each of next four sts, 1 tr/dc
in last st of group; repeat from * to
end of row ending with (1 tr/dc, 1
ch) in each of last 2 sts, 1 tr/dc in
turning ch, 1 turning ch.
row 6: 1 dc/sc in first st, 1 dc/sc in
each of next two 1 ch spaces, * 3 ch,
1 dc/sc in each of the four 1 ch
spaces; repeat from * to end of row
ending with 1 dc/sc in last ch
space, 2 dc/sc in turning ch, 4
turning ch.
repeat rows 1–6

base row: work 1 tr/dc in fifth ch
from hook, 1 tr/dc in next ch, * miss
2 ch, (1 tr/dc, 3 ch, 1 tr/dc) in next
ch, miss 2 ch, 1 tr/dc in each of next
five ch; repeat from * to end of row
ending with 1 tr/dc in each of last 3
ch, 3 turning ch.
row 1: 1 tr/dc in third tr/dc. * 2 ch, 5
tr/dc in 3 ch space, 2 ch, half work 1
tr/dc in first and last tr/dc of 5 st
group then finish both together;
repeat from * to end of row ending
with 1 tr/dc in last but one st, 1 tr/
dc in turning ch worked together, 4
turning ch.
row 2: 1 tr/dc in tr/dc, * 1 tr/dc in
each of next 5 sts, (1 tr/dc, 3 ch, 1 tr/
dc) in the V; repeat from * to end of
row ending with (1 tr/dc, 1 ch, 1 tr/
dc) in last st, 3 turning ch.
row 3: 2 tr/dc in 1 ch space, * 2 ch,
half work 1 tr/dc in first and last tr/
dc of 5 st group then finish both
together, 2 ch, 5 tr/dc in 3 ch space;
repeat from * to end of row ending
with 3 tr/dc in turning ch, 3 turning
ch.
row 4: miss first st, 1 tr/dc in each of
next 2 sts, * (1 tr/dc, 3 ch, 1 tr/dc) in
the V, 1 tr/dc in each of next 5 tr/dc;
repeat from * to end of row ending
with 1 tr/dc in each of last 2 sts, 1
tr/dc in turning ch, 3 turning ch.
repeat rows 1–4

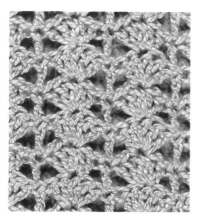

multiple of 6+1, 2 turning ch

base row: work 1 tr/dc in third ch
from the hook, * miss 2 ch, 1 tr/dc
in next ch, miss 2 ch, 5 tr/dc in next
ch; repeat from * to end of row
ending with 3 tr/dc in last ch, 3
turning ch.
row 1: 2 tr/dc in first st, * 1 tr/dc in
single next tr/dc, 5 tr/dc in centre st
of shell; repeat from * to end of
row ending with 3 tr/dc in turning
ch, 3 turning ch.
row 2: 1 tr/dc in first st, miss next
2 sts, * 1 tr/dc in next tr/dc, 5 tr/dc
in centre st of shell; repeat from * to
end of row ending with 3 tr/dc in
turning ch, 3 turning ch.
repeat rows 1–2

multiple of 6+1, 3 turning ch

base row: work 2 tr/dc in fourth ch
from hook, * miss 2 ch, 1 dc/sc in
next ch, miss 2 ch, 5 tr/dc in next
ch; repeat from * to end of row
ending with 3 tr/dc in last ch, 3
turning ch.
row 1: miss the 3 tr/dc, * 1 dc/sc in
next dc/sc, 2 ch, 1 dc/sc in centre st
of shell, 2 ch; repeat from * to end
of row ending by missing 2 tr/dc
and working 1 dc/sc in turning ch,
1 turning ch.
row 2: 1 dc/sc in first st, * 5 tr/dc in
next st, 1 dc/sc in dc/sc; repeat from
* to end of row ending with 1 dc/sc
in turning ch, 3 turning ch.
row 3: 1 dc/sc in centre st of shell, *
2 ch, 1 dc/sc in next dc/sc. 2 ch, 1
dc/sc in centre st of shell; repeat
from * to end of row ending with 2
ch, 1 dc/sc in last st, 3 turning ch.
row 4: 2 tr/dc in first dc/sc, * 1 dc/sc
in next dc/sc, 5 tr/dc in next dc/sc;

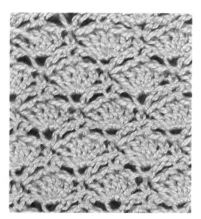

repeat from * to end of row ending
with 3 tr/dc in turning ch, 3 turning
ch.
repeat rows 1–4

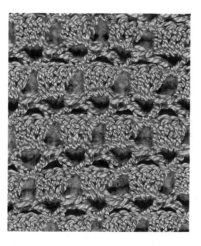

multiple of 4+3, 3 turning ch

base row: work 1 tr/dc in fourth ch
from hook, miss 2 ch, * (1 tr/dc, 3
ch, 1 tr/dc) in next ch, miss 3 ch;
repeat from * to end of row ending
with 2 missed ch, 1 tr/dc in last ch,
3 turning ch.
row 1: 1 tr/dc in first st, * 4 tr/dc in 3
ch space, 1 ch; repeat from * to end
of row ending with 1 tr/dc in last st,
4 turning ch.
row 2: 1 tr/dc in first st, (1 tr/dc, 3
ch, 1 tr/dc) in each 1 ch space and
turning ch; repeat from * to end of
row, 3 turning ch.
row 3: 2 tr/dc in 1 ch space, * 1 ch, 4
tr/dc in 3 ch space; repeat from * to
end of row, 2 tr/dc in last space, 1
tr/dc in turning ch, 4 turning ch.
row 4: * (1 tr/dc, 3 ch, 1 tr/dc) in 1 ch
space; repeat from * to end of row;
1 tr/dc in turning ch, 3 turning ch.
repeat rows 1–4

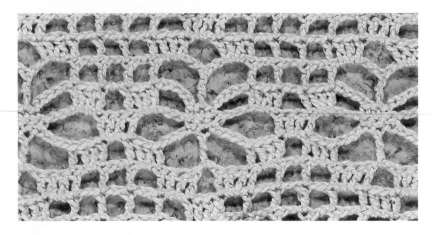

multiple of 18+1, 5 turning ch

base row: work 1 tr/dc in sixth ch from hook, * 2 ch, miss 2 ch, 1 tr/dc in next ch; repeat from * to end of row, ending with 1 tr/dc in last st, 5 turning ch.

row 1: miss first st, * (1 tr/dc in next st, 2 ch) twice, 1 tr/dc in next st, 2 tr/dc in 2 ch space, 1 tr/dc in next st, (2 ch, 1 tr/dc in next st) twice, 2 ch; repeat from * to end of row ending with 1 tr/dc in turning ch, 5 turning ch.

row 2: 1 tr/dc in second st, * (2 ch, 1 tr/dc in next st, 2 tr/dc in 2 ch space, 1 tr/dc in next st) twice, (2 ch, 1 tr/dc in next st) twice; repeat from * to end of row, ending with 1 tr/dc in turning ch, 5 turning ch.

row 3: miss first st, * 1 tr/dc in next st, 2 tr/dc in 2 ch space, 1 tr/dc in next st, 5 ch, 1 d.tr/tr in 2 ch space, 5 ch, 1 tr/dc in last tr/dc of next group, 2 tr/dc in 2 ch space, 1 tr/dc in next st, 2 ch; repeat from * to end of row ending with 1 tr/dc in turning ch, 5 turning ch.

row 4: 1 tr/dc in second st, * 5 ch, 1 dc/sc in last ch, 1 dc/sc in centre st, 1 dc/sc in first ch, 5 ch, 1 tr/dc in last st of next group, 2 tr/dc in 2 ch space, 1 tr/dc in next st; repeat from * to end of row ending with 1 tr/dc in turning ch, 5 turning ch.

row 5: 1 tr/dc in fourth st, * 1 tr/dc in each next 3 ch, 5 ch, 1 dc/sc in each next 3 sts, 5 ch, 1 tr/dc in each last 3 ch, 1 tr/dc in next st, 2 ch, 1 tr/dc in last st of group; repeat from * to end of row ending with 1 tr/dc in turning ch, 5 turning ch.

row 6: 1 tr/dc in second st, * 2 ch, miss 2 sts, 1 tr/dc in next st, 5 ch, 1 d.tr/tr in centre st, 5 ch, 1 tr/dc in first st, 2 ch, 1 tr/dc in last st of this group, 2 ch, 1 tr/dc in next st; repeat from * to end of row ending with 1 tr/dc in turning ch, 5 turning ch.

row 7: 1 tr/dc in second st, * 2 ch, 1 tr/dc in next st, 1 tr/dc in each next 3 ch, 2 ch, 1 tr/dc in each last 3 ch, 1 tr/dc in next st, 2 ch, 1 tr/dc in next st, 2ch, 1 tr/dc in next st; repeat from * to end of row ending with 1 tr/dc in turning ch, 5 turning ch.

row 8: 1 tr/dc in second st, * 2 ch, 1 tr/dc in next st, 2 ch, miss 2 sts, 1 tr/dc in next st, 2 tr/dc in 2 ch space, 1 tr/dc in next st, 2 ch, miss 2 sts, 1 tr/dc in next st, (2 ch, 1 tr/dc in next st) twice; repeat from * to end of row ending with 1 tr/dc in turning ch, 5 turning ch.

row 9: 1 tr/dc in second st, * (2 ch, 1 tr/dc in next st) twice, 2 ch, miss 2 sts, (1 tr/dc in next st, 2 ch) thrice, 1 tr/dc in next st; repeat from * to end of row ending with 1 tr/dc in turning ch, 5 turning ch.

repeat rows 1–9

multiple of 15+1, 3 turning ch

base row: work 2 tr/dc in fourth ch from hook, * 7 ch, miss 5 ch, 1 dc/sc in next ch, 3 ch, miss 2 ch, 1 dc/sc in next ch, 7 ch, miss 5 ch, (2 tr/dc, 1 ch, 2 tr/dc) in next ch; repeat from * to end of row ending with 3 tr/dc in last ch, 3 turning ch.

row 1: 2 tr/dc in first st, * 3 ch, 1 dc/sc in 7 loop ch, 5 ch, 1 dc/sc in 7 loop ch, 3 ch, (2 tr/dc, 1 ch, 2 tr/dc) in 1 ch space; repeat from * to end of row ending with 3 tr/dc in turning ch, 3 turning ch.

row 2: 2 tr/dc in first st, * 11 tr/dc in 5 ch group, (2 tr/dc, 1 ch, 2 tr/dc) in 1 ch space; repeat from * to end of

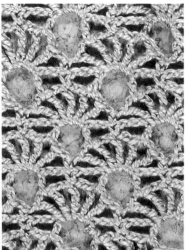

row ending with 3 tr/dc in last st, 3 turning ch.

row 3: 2 tr/dc in first st, * 2 ch, (1 dc/sc in next st, 3 ch, miss one st), 5 times, 1 dc/sc in last st, 2 ch, (2 tr/dc, 1 ch, 2 tr/dc) in 1 ch space repeat from * to end of row ending with 3 tr/dc in turning ch, 3 turning ch.

row 4: 2 tr/dc in first st, * (3 ch, 1 dc/sc in 3 ch loop) five times, 3 ch, (2 tr/dc, 1 ch, 2 tr/dc) in 1 ch space, repeat from * to end of row ending with 3 ch, 3 tr/dc in last st, 3 turning ch.

row 5: 2 tr/dc in first st, * 4 ch, 1 dc/sc in first 3 ch loop, (3 ch, 1 dc/sc) in next three 3 ch loops, 4 ch, (2 tr/dc, 1 ch, 2 tr/dc) in 1 ch space repeat from * to end of row ending with 4 ch, 3 tr/dc in last st, 3 turning ch.

row 6: 2 tr/dc in turning ch, * 5 ch, 1 dc/sc in first 3 ch loop, 3 ch, 1 dc/sc in next loop, 3 ch, 1 dc/sc in last loop, 5 ch, (2 tr/dc, 1 ch, 2 tr/dc) in 1 ch space; repeat from * to end of row ending with 5 ch, 3 tr/dc in last st, 3 turning ch.

row 7: 2 tr/dc in first st, * 7 ch, 1 dc/sc in 3 ch loop, 3 ch, 1 dc/sc in next loop, 7 ch, (2 tr/dc, 1 ch, 2 tr/dc) in 1 ch space; repeat from * to end of row ending with 3 tr/dc in turning ch, 3 turning ch.

repeat rows 1–7

multiple of 10+6, 1 turning ch

base row: 1 dc/sc in second ch from hook, * 1 ch, miss 4 ch, (1 d.tr/tr, 2 ch) in next ch four times. 1 d.tr/tr in same ch, 1 ch, miss 4 ch, 1 dc/sc in next ch; repeat from * to end of row ending with 1 ch, miss 4 ch, (1 d.tr/tr, 2 ch, 1 d.tr/tr, 2 ch, 1 d.tr/tr) in last st, 1 turning ch.

row 1: 1 dc/sc in first st, 3 ch, 1 tr/dc in second 2 ch space, * 2 ch, 1 tr/dc in first 2 ch space, 3 ch, 1 dc/sc in centre st, 3 ch, 1 tr/dc in last 2 ch space of group; repeat from * to end of row ending with 1 ch, 1 d.tr/tr in last st, 7 turning ch.

row 2: (1 d.tr/tr, 2 ch, 1 d.tr/tr) in first st, * 1 ch, 1 dc/sc in next dc/sc, 1 ch, ([1 d.tr/tr, 2 ch] four times, 1 d.tr/tr) in 2 ch space; repeat from * to end of row ending with 1 ch, 1 dc/sc in last st, 5 turning ch.

row 3: * 1 tr/dc in first 2 ch space, 3 ch, 1 dc/sc in centre st, 3 ch, 1 tr/dc in last 2 ch space, 2 ch; repeat from * to end of row ending with 1 dc/sc in turning ch, 1 turning ch.

row 4: 1 dc/sc in first st, * 1 ch, ([1 d.tr/tr, 2 ch] four times, 1 d.tr/tr) in 2 ch space. 1 ch, 1 dc/sc in next dc/sc; repeat from * to end of row ending with 1 ch, ([1 d.tr/tr, 2 ch] twice, 1 d.tr/tr) in turning ch, 1 turning ch.

repeat row 1–4

OPENWORK AND LACE PATTERNS

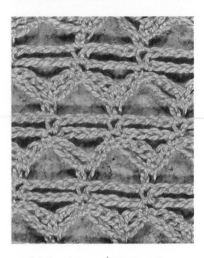

multiple of 6+1, 1 turning ch

base row: work 1 dc/sc in second ch from hook, 5 ch, miss 5 ch, 1 dc/sc in next ch; repeat from * to end of row, 1 turning ch.
row 1: 1 dc/sc in first st, * 5 ch, miss 5 ch, 1 dc/sc in next st; repeat from * to end of row, 1 turning ch.
row 2: 1 dc/sc in first st, * 7 ch, 1 dc/sc in next dc/sc; repeat from * to end of row, 1 turning ch.
row 3: as row 2 ending with 5 turning ch.
row 4: * 1 tr/dc round ch loop of previous 2 rows, 5 ch; repeat from * to end of row ending with 2 ch, 1 tr/dc in last st, 1 turning ch.
row 5: 1 dc/sc in first st, 2 ch, * 1 dc/sc in next st, 5 ch; repeat from * to end of row ending with 1 dc/sc in turning ch, 6 turning ch.
row 6: 1 dc/sc in second st, * 7 ch, 1 dc/sc in next st; repeat from * to end of row ending with 3 ch, 1 tr/dc in last st, 1 turning ch.
row 7: as row 6 beginning with 1 dc/sc in first st, 3 ch, 1 dc/sc and ending with 1 turning ch.
row 8: 1 dc/sc in first st, * 5 ch, 1 tr/dc round ch of previous 2 rows; repeat from * to end of row ending with 1 dc/sc in last st, 1 turning ch.
repeat rows 1–8

multiple of 2+1, 1 turning ch

base row: work 1 dc/sc in second ch from hook and all subsequent ch to end of row, 3 turning ch.
row 1: * miss first st, 1 tr/dc in second st, 1 tr/dc in missed st; repeat from * to end of row ending with 1 tr/dc in last st, 1 turning ch.

row 2: 1 dc/sc in every st to end of row, 3 turning ch.
repeat rows 1–2

multiple of 5+1, 1 turning ch

base row: work 1 dc/sc in second ch from hook, 4 ch, miss 4 ch, 1 dc/sc in next st; repeat from * to end of row, 3 turning ch.
row 1: * 4 tr/dc in 4 ch space, 1 ch; repeat from * to end of row ending with 1 tr/dc in last st, 1 turning ch.
row 2: 1 dc/sc in first st, * 4 ch, 1 dc/sc round 1 ch space; repeat from * to end of row ending with 1 dc/sc in turning ch, 3 turning ch.
repeat rows 1–2

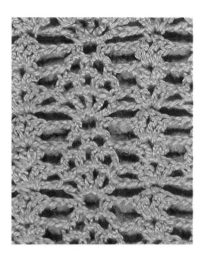
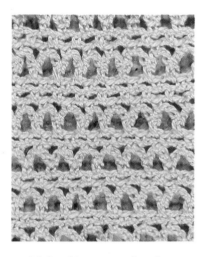

multiple of 12+7, 1 turning ch

base row: work 1 dc/sc in second ch from hook, * 3 ch, miss 5 ch, (1 tr/dc [1 ch, 1 tr/dc] four times) in next ch, 3 ch, miss 5 ch, 1 dc/sc in next ch; repeat from * to end of row ending with 3 ch, miss 5 ch, (1 tr/dc, [1 ch, 1 tr/dc] twice) in last ch, 3 turning ch.

row 1: 1 dc/sc in first 1 ch space, 3 ch, 1 dc/sc in next 1 ch space, * 1 ch, (2 tr/dc, 1 ch, 2 tr/dc) in dc/sc, 1 ch, (1 dc/sc in 1 ch space, 3 ch) three times, 1 dc/sc in next 1 ch space; repeat from * to end of row ending with 3 tr/dc in last st, 3 turning ch.

row 2: 2 tr/dc in first st, * 2 ch, 1 dc/sc in 3 ch loop, (3 ch, 1 dc/sc in 3 ch loop) twice, 2 ch, (2 tr/dc, 1 ch, 2 tr/dc) in 1 ch space; repeat from * to end of row ending with 3 ch, 1 dc/sc in turning ch, 4 turning ch.

row 3: 1 dc/sc in first 3 ch loop, * 3 ch, (2 tr/dc, 1 ch, 2 tr/dc) in 1 ch space, 1 dc/sc in 3 ch space, 3 ch, 1 dc/sc in 3 ch space; repeat from * to end of row ending with 3 tr/dc in turning ch, 1 turning ch.

row 4: 1 dc/sc in first st, * 3 ch, (1 tr/dc, [1 ch, 1 tr/dc]) four times in second 3 ch space, 3 ch, 1 dc/sc in 1 ch space; repeat from * to end of row; repeat from * to end of row ending with (1 tr/dc, [1 ch, 1 tr/dc]) twice in turning ch, 3 turning ch.

repeat rows 1–4

multiple of 3+1, 1 turning ch

base row: work 1 dc/sc in second ch from hook, * 5 ch, miss 2 ch, 1 dc/sc in next ch; repeat from * to end of row, 4 turning ch.

row 1: * 1 dc/sc in 5 ch loop, 2 ch; repeat from * to end of row ending with 1 ch, 1 tr/dc in turning ch, 1 turning ch.

row 2: 1 dc/sc in first st, 1 dc/sc in 1 ch space, * 2 ch, 1 dc/sc in 2 ch space; repeat from * to end of row ending with 1 dc/sc in turning ch, 5 turning ch.

row 3: * 1 dc/sc in 2 ch space, 5 ch; repeat from * to end of row ending with 2 ch, 1 tr/dc in last st, 1 turning ch.

row 4: 1 dc/sc in first sc, * 2 ch, 1 dc/sc in 5 ch loop; repeat from * to end of row, 1 turning ch.

row 5: 1 dc/sc in first st, 1 ch, * 1 dc/sc in 2 ch loop, 2 ch; repeat from * to end of row ending with 1 ch, 1 dc/sc in last st, 5 turning ch.

row 6: 1 dc/sc in 1 ch space, * 5 ch, 1 dc/sc in 2 ch space; repeat from * to end of row ending with 1 dc/sc in last st, 4 turning ch.

repeat rows 1–6

OPENWORK AND LACE PATTERNS

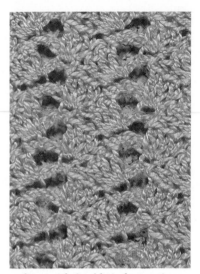

multiple of 11+3, 4 turning ch

base row: work 1 tr/dc in fifth ch from hook, 1 tr/dc in each next 2 ch, * 2 ch, miss 1 ch, 1 dc/sc in next ch, 2 ch, miss 1 ch, (1 tr/dc, 3 ch, 1 tr/dc) in next ch, 2 ch, miss 1 ch, 1 dc/sc in next ch, 2 ch, miss 1 ch, 1 tr/dc in each next 4 ch; repeat from * to end of row, 3 turning ch.

row 1: miss first st, 1 tr/dc in each next 3 sts, * 5 ch, 7 tr/dc in 3 ch loop, 5 ch, 1 tr/dc in each next 4 tr/dc sts; repeat from * to end of row, 3 turning ch.

row 2: miss first st, 1 tr/dc in each next 3 sts, * 2 ch, 1 dc/sc in 5 ch loop, 4 ch, 1 dc/sc in centre st of shell, 4 ch, 1 dc/sc in 5 ch loop, 2 ch, 1 tr/dc in each next 4 tr/dc; repeat from * to end of row, 3 turning ch.

row 3: miss first st, 1 tr/dc in each next 3 sts, * 5 ch, 1 dc/sc in 5 ch loop, 4 ch, 1 dc/sc in 5 ch loop, 5 ch, 1 tr/dc in each next 4 tr/dc; repeat from * to end of row, 3 turning ch.

row 4: miss first st, 1 tr/dc in each next 3 sts, * 2 ch, 1 dc/sc in 5 ch loop, 2 ch, (1 tr/dc, 3 ch, 1 tr/dc) in 4 ch loop, 2 ch, 1 dc/sc in 5 ch loop, 2 ch, 1 tr/dc in each next 4 tr/dc; repeat from * to end of row, 3 turning ch.

repeat rows 1–4

multiple 6+4, 9 turning ch

base row: work 1 dc/sc in tenth ch from hook, * miss 2 ch, 3 tr/dc in next ch, 3 ch, miss 2 ch, 1 dc/sc in next ch; repeat from * to end of row

ending with 3 tr/dc in last st, 1 turning ch.

row 1: * 3 tr/dc in dc/sc, 3 ch, 1 dc/sc in 3 ch loop; repeat from * to end of row ending with 1 dc/sc in turning ch, 6 turning ch.

row 2: * 1 dc/sc in 3 ch loop, 3 tr/dc in dc/sc, 3 ch; repeat from * to end of row ending with 3 tr/dc in turning ch, 1 turning ch.

repeat rows 1–2

multiple of 7+1, 2 turning ch

base row: work 1 dc/sc in third ch from hook, * miss 2 ch, 4 tr/dc in next ch, miss 2 ch, 1 dc/sc in each next 2 ch; repeat from * to end of row, 3 turning ch.

row 1: 2 tr/dc between two dc/sc, * 1 dc/sc in each two centre sts of shell, 4 tr/dc between two dc/sc; repeat from * to end of row ending with 3 tr/dc in turning ch, 1 turning ch.

row 2: 1 dc/sc in second st, * 4 tr/dc between 2 dc/sc, 1 dc/sc in each two centre sts of shell; repeat from * to end of row ending with 1 dc/sc in each last two sts, 3 turning ch.

repeat rows 1–2

WHITE

Best Before End

GREEN
&BLACK'S
ORGANIC

WHITE CHOCOLATE
WITH 30%
COCOA SOLIDS

FAIRTRADE

SOIL ASSOCIATION
ORGANIC

multiple of 8+1, 4 turning ch

base row: work 1 tr/dc in fifth ch
from hook, * miss 3 ch, (1 tr/dc, 3
ch, 1 tr/dc) in next ch; repeat from *
to end of row ending with (1 tr/dc,
1 ch, 1 tr/dc) in last ch, 4 turning ch.
row 1: 1 tr/dc in first st, * 6 tr/dc in 3
ch loop, (1 tr/dc, 3 ch, 1 tr/dc) in 3
ch loop; repeat from * to end of row
ending with (1 tr/dc, 1 ch, 1 tr/dc)
in turning ch, 4 turning ch.
row 2: 1 tr/dc in first st, * (1 tr/dc, 3
ch, 1 tr/dc) between third and
fourth st of shell, (1 tr/dc, 3 ch, 1 tr/
dc) in 3 ch loop; repeat from * to
end of row ending with (1 tr/dc, 1
ch, 1 tr/dc in turning ch, 4 turning
ch.
repeat rows 1–2

multiple of 9, 5 turning ch

base row: work 1 dc/sc in sixth ch
from hook, 1 dc/sc in each next six
ch, * 5 ch, miss 2 ch, 1 dc/sc in each
next seven ch; repeat from * to end
of row ending with 2 ch, miss 1 ch,
1 tr/dc in last ch, 1 turning ch.
row 1: 1 dc/sc in first st, * 3 ch, miss
1 dc/sc, 1 dc/sc in each next 5 dc/sc,
3 ch, 1 dc/sc in 5 ch loop; repeat
from * to end of row ending with 1
dc/sc in turning ch, 1 turning ch.
row 2: 1 dc/sc in each first two sts, *
3 ch, miss 1 dc/sc, 1 dc/sc in each
next 3 dc/sc, 3 ch, 1 dc/sc in last ch,
1 dc/sc in dc/sc, 1 dc/sc in first ch;
repeat from * to end of row ending
with 1 dc/sc in last ch, 1 dc/sc in
last dc/sc, 1 turning ch.

row 3: 1 dc/sc in each first two sts, 1
dc/sc in first ch, * 3 ch, 1 dc/sc in
centre dc/sc, 3 ch, 1 dc/sc in last ch,
1 dc/sc in each next 3 dc/sc, 1 dc/sc
in first ch; repeat from * to end of
row ending with 1 dc/sc in last ch,
1 dc/sc in last two sts, 1 turning ch.
row 4: 1 dc/sc in each first three sts,
1 dc/sc in first ch, * 5 ch, 1 dc/sc in
last ch, 1 dc/sc in each next 5 dc/sc,
1 dc/sc in first ch; repeat from *
ending with 1 dc/sc in last ch, 1 dc/
sc in last three sts, 1 turning ch.
row 5: 1 dc/sc in each first three sts,
* 3 ch, 1 dc/sc in 5 ch loop, 3 ch,
miss 1 dc/sc, 1 dc/sc in each next 3
dc/sc; repeat from * to end of row,
ending with 1 dc/sc in last three
sts, 1 turning ch.
row 6: 1 dc/sc in first two sts, * 3 ch,
1 dc/sc in last ch, 1 dc/sc in dc/sc, 1
dc/sc in first ch, 3 ch, miss 1 dc/sc, 1
dc/sc in each next 3 dc/sc; repeat
from * to end of row ending with 1
dc/sc in each last two sts, 1 turning
ch.
row 7: 1 dc/sc in first st, * 3 ch, 1 dc/
sc in last ch, 1 dc/sc in each next 3
sts, 1 dc/sc in first ch, 3 ch, 1 dc/sc
in centre dc/sc; repeat from * to end
of row ending with 1 dc/sc in last
st, 6 turning ch.
row 8: * 1 dc/sc in last ch, 1 dc/sc in
each next 5 dc/sc, 1 dc/sc in first ch,
5 ch; repeat from * to end of row,
ending with 2 ch, 1 tr/dc in last st, 1
turning ch.
repeat rows 1–8

OPENWORK AND LACE PATTERNS

multiple of 12+7, 3 turning ch

base row: work 1 tr/dc in fourth ch from hook, 4 ch, miss 5 ch, * 1 tr/dc in next ch, 4 ch, miss 5 ch, (1 tr/dc, 4 ch, 1 tr/dc) in next ch, 4 ch, miss 5 ch; repeat from * to end of row ending with 1 tr/dc in last ch, 5 turning ch.
row 1: * 1 dc/sc in 4 ch space, (4 tr/dc, 2 ch, 4 tr/dc) in 4 ch space, 1 dc/sc in next 4 ch space, 4 ch; repeat from * to end of row ending with 5 tr/dc in turning ch, 7 turning ch.
row 2: * (1 tr/dc, 4 ch, 1 tr/dc) in 4 ch space, 4 ch, 1 tr/dc in 2 ch space, 4 ch; repeat from * to end of row ending with (1 tr/dc, 1 ch, 1 tr/dc) in turning ch, 4 turning ch.
row 3: 4 tr/dc in 1 ch space, * 1 dc/sc in 4 ch space, 4 ch, 1 dc/sc in 4 ch space, (4 tr/dc, 2 ch, 4 tr/dc) in next 4 ch space; repeat from * to end of row ending with 2 ch, 1 tr/dc in turning ch, 4 turning ch.
row 4: 1 tr/dc in first st, * 4 ch, 1 tr/dc in 2 ch space, 4 ch, (1 tr/dc, 4 ch, 1 tr/dc) in 4 ch space; repeat from * to end of row ending 1 tr/dc in turning ch, 5 turning ch.
repeat rows 1–4

multiple of 10+6, 9 turning ch

base row: work 7 tr/dc in tenth ch from hook, * 1 ch, miss 4 ch, 1 tr/dc in next ch, 1 ch, miss 4 ch, 7 tr/dc in next ch; repeat from * to end of row ending with 1 tr/dc in last ch, 4 turning ch.
row 1: 1 tr/dc in first st, * 1 ch, 1 tr/dc in centre 3 sts of group, 1 ch, (1

tr/dc, 3 ch, 1 tr/dc) in single tr/dc; repeat from * to end of row ending with (1 tr/dc, 1 ch, 1 tr/dc) in turning ch, 3 turning ch.
row 2: 3 tr/dc in 1 ch space, * 1 ch, 1 tr/dc in centre st of 3 st group, 1 ch, 7 tr/dc in 3 ch space; repeat from * to end of row ending with 4 tr/dc in turning ch, 3 turning ch.
row 3: 1 tr/dc in second st, * 1 ch, (1 tr/dc, 3 ch, 1 tr/dc) in tr/dc, 1 ch, 1 tr/dc in centre 3 sts of group; repeat from * to end of row ending with 1 tr/dc in last st, 1 tr/dc in turning ch, 4 turning ch.
row 4: * 7 tr/dc in 3 ch space, 1 ch, 1 tr/dc in centre tr/dc, 1 ch; repeat from * to end of row ending with 1 tr/dc in turning ch, 4 turning ch.
repeat rows 1–4

multiple of 10+1, 1 turning ch

base row: work 1 dc/sc in first ch, 1 dc/sc in next ch, * 1 ch, miss 3 ch, (1 tr/dc, 3 ch, 1 tr/dc) in next ch, 1 ch, miss 3 ch, 1 dc/sc in each next 3 ch, repeat from * to end of row ending with 1 dc/sc in last 2 ch, 3 turning ch.

row 1: * 1 tr/dc in first tr/dc, 1 ch, 5 tr/dc in 3 ch space, 1 ch, 1 tr/dc in last tr/dc of group; repeat from * to end of row ending with 1 tr/dc in last st, 4 turning ch.

row 2: * 1 tr/dc in first tr/dc of group, 1 ch, 1 dc/sc in centre 3 sts, 1 ch, 1 tr/dc in last tr/dc of group, 3 ch; repeat from * to end of row ending with 1 ch, 1 tr/dc in turning ch, 3 turning ch.

row 3: 2 tr/dc in 1 ch space, 1 ch, 1 tr/dc in next st, * 1 tr/dc in first tr/dc of next group, 1 ch, 5 tr/dc in 3 ch space, 1 ch, 1 tr/dc in last tr/dc of group; repeat from * to end of row ending with 1 tr/dc, 1 ch, 3 tr/dc in turning ch, 1 turning ch.

row 4: 1 dc/sc in first st, 1 dc/sc in next st, 1 ch, 1 tr/dc in tr/dc, * 3 ch, 1 tr/dc in first tr/dc of group, 1 ch, 1 dc/sc in centre 3 sts, 1 ch, 1 tr/dc in last st of group; repeat from * to end of row ending with 1 dc/sc in last st, 1 dc/sc in turning ch, 3 turning ch.

repeat rows 1–4

multiple of 5+4, 6 turning ch

base row: work (4 tr/dc, 3 ch, 1 tr/dc) in seventh ch from hook, * miss 4 ch, (4 tr/dc, 3 ch, 1 tr/dc) in next ch; repeat from * to end of row ending with 2 missed ch, 1 tr/dc in last ch, 3 turning ch.

row 1: * (4 tr/dc, 3 ch, 1 tr/dc) in 3 ch space; repeat from * to end of row ending with 1 tr/dc in turning ch, 3 turning ch.

repeat row 1

multiple of 7+1, 4 turning ch

base row: work 1 tr/dc in fifth ch from hook, * 2 ch, miss 6 ch, (1 tr/dc, 3 ch, 1 tr/dc) in next ch; repeat from * to end of row ending with (1 tr/dc, 1 ch, 1 tr/dc) in last ch, 3 turning ch.

row 1: 3 tr/dc in 1 ch space, * 8 tr/dc in 3 ch space; repeat from * to end of row ending with 5 tr/dc in turning ch, 4 turning ch.

row 2: 1 tr/dc in first st, * 2 ch, (1 tr/dc, 3 ch, 1 tr/dc) in space between fourth and fifth sts of group; repeat from * to end of row, (1 tr/dc, 1 ch, 1 tr/dc in last st, 3 turning ch.

repeat rows 1–2

OPENWORK AND LACE PATTERNS

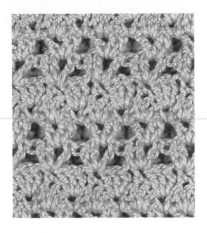

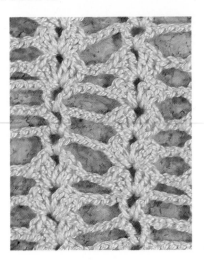

multiple of 24+5, 3 turning ch

base row: work 1 tr/dc in fourth ch from hook, miss 5 ch, * (3 tr/dc, 2 ch, 3 tr/dc) in next ch, 2 ch, miss 5 ch; repeat from * to end of row ending with 2 missed ch, 1 tr/dc in last ch, 3 turning ch.
row 1: 1 tr/dc in second st, * (3 tr/dc, 2 ch, 3 tr/dc) in 2 ch space, 2 ch (3 tr/dc, 2 ch, 3 tr/dc) in 2 ch space, (4 ch, [1 tr/dc, 2 ch, 1 tr/dc] in 2 ch space twice), repeat from * to end of row ending with 1 ch, 1 tr/dc in last st and turning ch, 3 turning ch.
row 2: 1 tr/dc in second st, * (4 ch, [1 tr/dc, 2 ch, 1 tr/dc] in 2 ch sp) twice, 4 ch, (3 tr/dc, 2 ch, 3 tr/dc) in 2 ch sp, 2 ch, (3 tr/dc, 2 ch, 3 tr/dc) in 2 ch sp; repeat from * to end, 1 tr/dc in last st and turning ch, 3 turning ch.
row 3: as row 1
row 4: 1 tr/dc in second st, * (3 tr/dc, 2 ch, 3 tr/dc) in 2 ch space, 2 ch; repeat from * to end of row, 1 tr/dc in last st and turning ch, 3 turning ch.
row 5: 1 tr/dc in second st, 2 ch, * ([1 tr/dc, 2 ch, 1 tr/dc] in 2 ch space, 4 ch) twice, ([3 tr/dc, 2 ch, 3 tr/dc] in 2 ch space, 2 ch) twice; repeat from * to end of row, 1 tr/dc in last st and turning ch, 3 turning ch.
row 6: 1 tr/dc in second st, * ([3 tr/dc, 2 ch, 2 tr/dc] in 2 ch sp, 2 ch) twice, ([1 tr/dc, 2 ch, 1 tr/dc] in 2 ch sp, 4 ch) twice, 2 ch; repeat from * to end, 1 tr/dc in last st and turning ch, 3 turning ch.
row 7: as row 5
row 8: as row 4
repeat rows 1–8

multiple of 4+3, 2 turning ch

base row: work 1 dc/sc in third ch from hook, * miss 1 ch, 3 tr/dc in next ch, miss 1 ch, 1 dc/sc in next ch; repeat from * to end of row, 2 turning ch.
row 1: * 1 dc/sc in centre tr/dc, 3 tr/dc in dc/sc; repeat from * to end of row, 2 turning ch.
row 2: 1 tr/dc in centre tr/dc, * (2 tr/dc, 1 ch, 1 tr/dc) in dc/sc; repeat from * to end of row, 2 turning ch.
row 3: (1 tr/dc, 1 ch, 1 tr/dc) in first 1 ch space, * (2 tr/dc, 1 ch, 1 tr/dc) in 1 ch space; repeat from * to end of row ending with 2 tr/dc in turning ch, 2 turning ch.
row 4: 1 dc/sc between first 2 sts, * 3 tr/dc in 1 ch space, 1 dc/sc between this and next group; repeat from * to end of row, 2 turning ch.
repeat rows 1–4

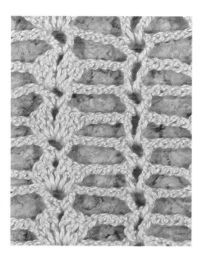

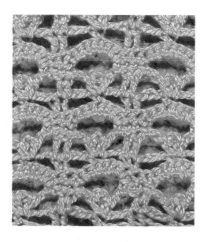

multiple of 12+3, 4 turning ch

base row: work (1 tr/dc, 2 ch, 1 tr/dc) in fifth ch from hook, * 4 ch, miss 5 ch, (1 tr/dc, 2 ch, 1 tr/dc) in next ch; repeat from * to end of row ending with 1 missed ch, 1 tr/dc in last ch, 3 turning ch.
row 1: 1 tr/dc in first st, * (1 tr/dc, 2 ch, 1 tr/dc) in 2 ch space, 4 ch, (3 tr/dc, 2 ch, 3 tr/dc) in 2 ch space, 4 ch; repeat from * to end of row ending with 1 tr/dc in turning ch, 3 turning ch.
row 2: 1 tr/dc in first st, (1 tr/dc, 2 ch, 1 tr/dc) in 2 ch space, 4 ch; repeat from * to end of row ending with 1 tr/dc in turning ch, 3 turning ch.
repeat rows 1–2

multiple of 7+2, 2 turning ch

base row: work 1 h.tr/h.dc in third ch from hook and next ch, * 3 ch, miss 2 ch, 1 dc/sc in next ch, 3 ch, miss 2 ch, 1 h.tr/h.dc in each next 2 ch; repeat from * to end of row, 2 turning ch.
row 1: 1 h.tr/h.dc in each first 2 sts, * 2 ch, (1 dc/sc, 3 ch, 1 dc/sc) in next st, 3 ch, 1 h.tr/h.dc in each next 2 sts; repeat from * to end of row, 1 turning ch.
row 2: 1 dc/sc in each first 2 sts, * 1 dc/sc in 3 ch space, 5 ch, 1 dc/sc in next 3 ch space, 1 dc/sc in each next 2 sts; repeat from * to end of row, 1 turning ch.
row 3: 1 dc/sc in each first 2 sts, * 7 dc/sc in 5 ch space, 1 dc/sc in each next 2 sts; repeat from * to end of row, 2 turning ch.

row 4: 1 h.tr/h.dc in each first 2 sts, * 3 ch, 1 dc/sc in centre dc/sc, 3 ch, 1 h.tr/h.dc in each next 2 sts; repeat from * to end of row, 2 turning ch.
repeat rows 1–4

multiple of 8+1, 1 turning ch

row 1: work 1 dc/sc in second ch from hook, * 1 h.tr/hdc in next ch, 1 tr/dc in next ch, 1 d.tr/tr in next ch, 1 t.tr/d.tr in next ch, 1 d.tr.tr/tr in next ch, 1 tr/dc in next ch, 1 h.tr/dc in next ch, 1 dc/sc in next ch; repeat from * to end of row, 3 turning ch.
row 2: 1 tr/dc in first st, * 3 ch, 1 tr/dc in t.tr/d.tr, 3 ch, 1 tr/dc in dc/sc; repeat from * to end of row, 4 turning ch.
row 3: * 1 t.tr/d.tr in first st, (1 d.tr/tr, 1 tr/dc, 1 h.tr/h.dc) in 3 ch space, 1 dc/sc in tr/dc, (1 h.tr/h.dc, 1 tr/dc, 1 d.tr/tr) in 3 ch space, 1 t.tr/d.tr in tr/dc; repeat from * to end of row ending with 1 t.tr/d.tr in last st, 3 turning ch.
row 4: as row 2.
repeat rows 1–4

OPENWORK AND LACE PATTERNS

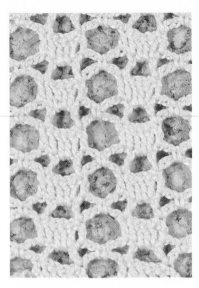

multiple of 9+8, 8 turning ch

base row: work 1 tr/dc in ninth ch
from hook, 1 tr/dc in each next 5 ch,
* 5 ch, miss 3 ch, 1 tr/dc in each next
6 ch; repeat from * to end of row
ending with 2 ch, miss 1 ch, 1 tr/dc
in last ch, 1 turning ch.
row 1: 1 dc/sc in tr/dc, * 3 ch, 1 tr/dc
in first tr/dc, 1 ch, 1 tr/dc in last tr/
dc of group, 3 ch, 1 dc/sc in 5 ch
space; repeat from * to end of row
ending with 1 dc/sc in turning ch, 5
turning ch.
row 2: 1 tr/dc in last of 3 ch, * 1 tr/dc
in tr/dc, 2 tr/dc in 1 ch space, 1 tr/dc
in tr/dc, 1 tr/dc in first ch of 3 ch
group, 5 ch, 1 tr/dc in last ch of next
3 ch group; repeat from * to end of
row ending with 2 ch, 1 tr/dc in dc/
sc, 1 turning ch.
repeat rows 1–2

multiple of 10+7, 8 turning ch

base row: work 1 tr/dc in ninth ch
from hook, 1 tr/dc in each next 3 ch,
* 2 ch, miss 2 ch, 1 tr/dc in each next
2 ch, 2 ch, miss 2 ch, 1 tr/dc in each
next 4 ch; repeat from * to end of
row ending with 1 tr/dc in last ch, 1
turning ch.
row 1: 1 dc/sc in tr/dc, * 3 tr/dc in
second tr/dc of group, 2 ch, 3 tr/dc
in third tr/dc, miss next st, 1 dc/sc
in each next 2 tr/dc; repeat from * to
end of row ending with 1 dc/sc in
turning ch, 6 turning ch.
row 2: * 2 dc/sc in 2 ch space, 3 ch, 1
tr/dc in each next 2 dc/sc, 3 ch;
repeat from * to end of row ending

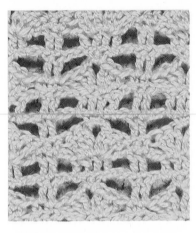

with 1 tr/dc in dc/sc, 5 turning ch.
row 3: * 1 tr/dc in last ch of 3 ch
group, 1 tr/dc in each next 2 dc/sc, 1
tr/dc in first ch of 3 ch group, 2 ch, 1
tr/dc in each next 2 tr/dc, 2 ch;
repeat from * to end of row ending
with 1 tr/dc in turning ch, 1 turning
ch.
repeat rows 1–3

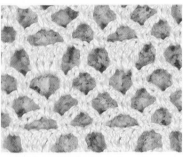

multiple of 8+1, 1 turning ch

base row: work 1 dc/sc in second ch
from hook, * 5 ch, miss 3 ch, 1 dc/sc
in next ch; repeat from * to end of
row, 5 turning ch.
row 1: * 1 dc/sc in 5 ch space, 5 ch;
repeat from * to end of row ending
with 2 ch, 1 tr/dc in last dc/sc, 3
turning ch.
row 2: 1 tr/dc in tr/dc, * 2 ch, 4 tr/dc
in 5 ch space, 2 ch, 1 tr/dc in next 5
ch space; repeat from * to end of
row ending with last tr/dc in
turning ch, 5 turning ch.
row 3: * 1 dc/sc in 2 ch space, 5 ch;
repeat from * to end or row ending
with 2 ch, 1 tr/dc in turning ch, 1
turning ch.
row 4: 1 dc/sc in tr/dc, * 5 ch, 1 dc/sc
in 5 ch space; repeat from * to end
of row ending with 1 dc/sc in
turning ch, 5 turning ch.
repeat rows 1–4

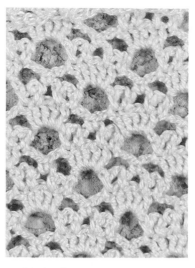

multiple of 15+1, 7 turning ch

base row: work 1 tr/dc in eighth ch from hook, * 2 ch, miss 2 ch, 1 tr/dc in next ch; repeat from * to end of row, 5 turning ch.

row 1: miss first st, * (1 tr/dc in next st, 2 tr/dc in 2 ch space) four times, 1 tr/dc in next st, 2 ch; repeat from * to end of row ending with 1 tr/dc in turning ch, 5 turning ch.

row 2: miss first st, * 1 tr/dc in each next 4 sts, 2 ch, miss 2 sts, 1 d.tr/tr in next st, 2 ch, 1 tr/dc in each next 4 sts, 2 ch; repeat from * to end of row ending with 1 tr/dc in turning ch, 5 turning ch.

row 3: miss first st, * 1 tr/dc in each next 2 sts, 5 ch, 1 dc/sc in d.tr/tr, 5 ch, miss 2 ch and 2 tr/dc, 1 tr/dc in next 2 sts, 2 ch; repeat from * to end of row ending with 1 tr/dc in turning ch, 5 turning ch.

row 4: miss first st, * 1 tr/dc in each next 2 sts and first 2 ch, 2 ch, 1 d.tr/tr in dc/sc, 2 ch, 1 tr/dc in each last 2 ch, 1 tr/dc in each next 2 sts, 2 ch; repeat from * to end of row ending with 1 tr/dc in turning ch, 5 turning ch.

row 5: miss first st, * 1 tr/dc in each next 4 sts, 2 tr/dc in 2 ch space, 1 tr/dc in next st, 2 tr/dc in 2 ch space, 1 tr/dc in each next 4 sts, 2 ch; repeat from * to end of row ending with 1 tr/dc in turning ch, 5 turning ch.

row 6: miss first st, * 1 tr/dc in next st, 2 ch, miss 2 sts; repeat from * to end of row ending with 1 tr/dc in turning ch, 5 turning ch.

repeat rows 1–6

multiple of 8+1, 1 turning ch

base row: work 1 dc/sc in second ch from hook, * 2 ch, miss 3 ch, 5 tr/dc in next ch, 2 ch, miss 3 ch, 1 dc/sc in next ch; repeat from * to end of row, 5 turning ch.

row 1: * 1 dc/sc in first tr/dc, 3 ch, 1 dc/sc in next tr/dc, 3 ch, miss 1 tr/dc, 1 dc/sc in next tr/dc, 3 ch, 1 dc/sc in last tr/dc, 5 ch; repeat from * to end of row ending with 2 ch, 1 tr/dc in dc/sc, 3 turning ch.

row 2: 2 tr/dc in first st, * 2 ch, 1 dc/sc in centre 3 ch space, 2 ch, 5 tr/dc in 5 ch space; repeat from * to end of row ending with 3 tr/dc in turning ch, 5 turning ch.

row 3: 1 dc/sc in second tr/dc, 3 ch, 1 dc/sc in next tr/dc, * 5 ch, 1 dc/sc in first tr/dc, 3 ch, 1 dc/sc in next dc/sc, 3 ch, miss 1 tr/dc, 1 dc/sc in next tr/dc, 3 ch, 1 dc/sc in last tr/dc; repeat from * to end of row ending with 1 dc/sc in first tr/dc, 3 ch, 1 dc/sc in last tr/dc, 2 ch, 1 tr/dc in turning ch, 1 turning ch.

row 4: 1 dc/sc in first st, * 2 ch, 5 tr/dc in 5 ch space, 2 ch, 1 dc/sc in centre 3 ch space; repeat from * to end of row ending with 1 dc/sc in turning ch, 5 turning ch.

repeat rows 1–4

OPENWORK AND LACE PATTERNS

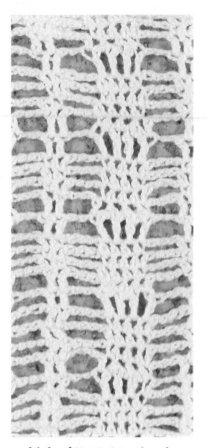

multiple of 11 +1, 2 turning ch

base row: work 1 tr/dc in third ch from hook, * (2 ch, miss 1 ch, 1 tr/dc in next ch) five times, 1 tr/dc in next ch; repeat from * to end of row, 3 turning ch.

row 1: miss first st, * 1 tr/dc in next st, 4 ch, 1 dc/sc in each next 4 tr/dc, 4 ch, 1 tr/dc in next tr/dc; repeat from * to end of row ending with 1 tr/dc in turning ch, 1 turning ch.

row 2: miss first st, * 1 dc/sc in next tr/dc, 4 ch, 1 dc/sc in each next 4 dc/sc, 4 ch, 1 dc/sc in next tr/dc; repeat from * to end of row ending with 1 dc/sc in turning ch, 1 turning ch.

row 3: as row 2

row 4: as row 2 but ending with 3 turning ch.

row 5: miss first st, * 1 tr/dc in next tr/dc, (2 ch, 1 tr/dc) in each next 4 sts, 2 ch, 1 tr/dc in next tr/dc; repeat from * to end of row ending with 1 tr/dc in turning ch, 3 turning ch.

repeat rows 1–5

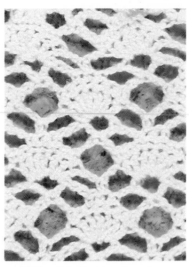

multiple of 8+2, 1 turning ch

base row: work 1 dc/sc in second ch from hook, 1 dc/sc in next ch, * 2 ch, miss 2 ch, (1 tr/dc, 3 ch, 1 tr/dc) in next ch, 2 ch, miss 2 ch, 1 dc/sc in each next 3 ch; repeat from * to end of row ending with 1 dc/sc in each last 3 ch, 1 turning ch.

row 1: 1 dc/sc in first st, * 2 ch, 7 tr/dc in 3 ch space, 2 ch, 1 dc/sc in second dc/sc; repeat from * to end of row ending with 2 ch, 1 dc/sc in last st, 1 turning ch.

row 2: 1 dc/sc in first st, 2 ch, * 1 dc/sc in each st of the 7 tr/dc group, 5 ch; repeat from * to end of row ending with 2 ch, 1 dc/sc in last st, 5 turning ch.

row 3: 1 tr/dc in first st, * 2 ch, 1 dc/sc in the third, fourth and fifth dc/sc, 2 ch, (1 tr/dc, 3 ch, 1 tr/dc) in third ch of 5 ch loop; repeat from * to end of row, 3 turning ch.

row 4: 3 tr/dc in 3 ch space, * 2 ch, 1 dc/sc in centre dc/sc, 2 ch, 7 tr/dc in 3 ch space; repeat from * to end of row ending with 4 tr/dc in turning ch, 1 turning ch.

row 5: 1 dc/sc in each first 4 sts, * 5 ch, 1 dc/sc in each st of the 7 tr/dc group; repeat from * to end of row ending with 5 ch, 1 dc/sc in each last 3 sts, 1 turning ch.

row 6: 1 dc/sc in each first 2 sts, * 2 ch, (1 tr/dc, 3 ch, 1 tr/dc) in third ch of 5 ch loop, 2 ch, 1 dc/sc in the third, fourth and fifth dc/sc; repeat from * to end of row ending with 2 ch, 1 dc/sc in each last 2 sts, 1 turning ch.

repeat rows 1–6

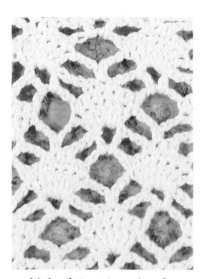

multiple of 10+1, 3 turning ch

base row: work (1 tr/dc, 3 ch, 1 tr/
dc) in fourth ch from hook, * 3 ch,
miss 3 ch, 1 dc/sc in each next 3 ch,
3 ch, miss 3 ch, (1 tr/dc, 3 ch, 1 tr/
dc) in next ch; repeat from * to end
of row, 3 turning ch.
row 1: * 7 tr/dc in 3 ch space, 3 ch, 1
dc/sc in second dc/sc, 3 ch; repeat
from * to end of row ending with 7
tr/dc in last 3 ch space, 1 turning
ch.
row 2: * 1 dc/sc in each st of 7 tr/dc
group, 5 ch; repeat from * to end of
row, 5 turning ch.
row 3: * 1 dc/sc in third, fourth and
fifth sts of 7 tr/dc group, 3 ch, (1 tr/
dc, 3 ch, 1 tr/dc) in third st of 5 ch
loop, 3 ch; repeat from * to end of
row ending with 1 dc/sc in third,
fourth and fifth sts of last group, 3
ch, 1 tr/dc in last st, 5 turning ch.
row 4: * 1 dc/sc in second dc/sc, 3
ch, 7 tr/dc in 3 ch space, 3 ch; repeat
from * to end of row ending with 1
dc/sc in second st, 3 ch, 1 dc/sc in
turning ch, 5 turning ch.
row 5: * 1 dc/sc in each st of 7 tr/dc
group, 5 ch; repeat from * to end of
row ending with 1 dc/sc in turning
ch, 3 turning ch.
row 6: * (1 tr/dc, 3 ch, 1 tr/dc) in
third st of 5 ch loop, 3 ch, 1 dc/sc in
third, fourth and fifth sts of 7 tr/dc
group, 3 ch; repeat from * to end of
row ending with 1 dc/sc in turning
ch, 3 turning ch.
repeat rows 1–6

multiple of 8+1, 1 turning ch

base row: work 1 dc/sc in second ch
from hook, 1 dc/sc in each next 2
ch, * 5 ch, miss 3 ch, 1 dc/sc in each
next 5 ch; repeat from * to end of
row ending with 1 dc/sc in each
last 3 ch, 2 turning ch.
row 1: miss 2 sts, 1 dc/sc in next st, *
9 d.tr/tr in 5 ch space, 1 dc/sc in
first dc/sc, 2 ch, miss 3 sts, 1 dc/sc
in last dc/sc of group; repeat from *
to end of row ending with 1 dc/sc
in first of 3 last sts, 1 ch, 1 dc/sc in
last st, 6 turning ch.
row 2: * 1 dc/sc in each of the 3
centre d.tr/tr sts, 3 ch, 1 d.tr/tr in 2
ch space, 3 ch; repeat from * to end
of row ending with 3 ch, 1 d.tr/tr in
turning ch, 3 turning ch.
row 3: * 1 dc/sc in 3 ch space, 1 dc/
sc in each next 3 dc/sc, 1 dc/sc in 3
ch space, 5 ch, miss the next d.tr/tr;
repeat from * to end of row ending
with 3 ch, 1 dc/sc in turning ch, 3
turning ch.
row 4: 4 d.tr/tr in first 3 ch space, * 1
dc/sc in first dc/sc, 2 ch, 1 dc/sc in
last dc/sc of group, 9 tr/dc in 5 ch
space; repeat from * to end of row
ending with 1 dc/sc, 2 ch, 5 d.tr/dc
in turning ch, 2 turning ch.
row 5: 1 dc/sc in first 2 sts, * 3 ch, 1
d.tr/tr in 2 ch space, 3 ch, 1 dc/sc in
each of the 3 centre d.tr/tr sts;
repeat from * to end of row ending
with 3 ch, 1 dc/sc in each last 2 sts,
1 turning ch.
row 6: as row 4
repeat rows 1–6

Puffs, Picots, Clusters and Popcorns

A selection of designs using four different methods of creating close groups of stitches to be worked as part of the overall pattern

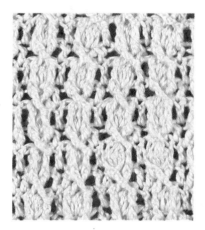

multiple of 4+2, 3 turning ch

base row 1: work 1 tr/dc in fourth ch from hook and all subsequent ch to end of row, 3 turning ch.
base row 2: miss first st, 1 tr/dc in next st, * r.b.d.tr/dc in next st, 1 five loop puff in next st, 1 r.b.d.tr/tr in next st, 1 tr/dc in next st; repeat from * to end of row ending with 1 tr/dc in last st, 1 tr/dc in turning ch, 3 turning ch.
row 1: miss first st, 1 tr/dc in next st, * keeping loop of each st on hook, 1 tr/dc in next st, miss puff stitch, 1 r.f.d.tr/tr in next st, yoh, draw through all 3 loops on hook, 1 tr/dc in top of puff stitch, keeping loop of each st on hook, 1 r.f.d.tr/tr in st before puff stitch, 1 tr/dc in st after puff st, yoh, draw through all 3 loops on hook, 1 tr/dc in next st; repeat from * to end of row ending with 1 tr/dc in last st, 1 tr/dc in turning ch, 3 turning ch.
row 2: as base row 2 but working the relief sts into the stem only of the previous raised stitches.
repeat rows 1–2

multiple of 8, 6 turning ch

base row: work a 3 loop puff in seventh ch from hook, * 3 ch, miss 3 ch, 1 dc/sc in next ch, 3 ch, miss 3 ch, 3 loop puff in next ch, 5 ch, 3 loop puff in same ch; repeat from * to end of row ending with a puff in last st, 1 d.tr/tr in same st, 1 turning ch.
row 1: 1 dc/sc in first st, * 2 ch, 3 tr/dc in dc/sc, 2 ch, 1 dc/sc in 5 ch loop; repeat from * to end of row ending with 1 dc/sc in turning ch, 1 turning ch.
row 2: 1 dc/sc in first st, * 3 ch, (3 loop puff, 5 ch, 3 loop puff) in centre tr/dc, 3 ch, 1 dc/sc in dc/sc; repeat from * to end of row ending with 1 dc/sc in last st, 3 turning ch.
row 3: 1 tr/dc in first st, * 2 ch, 1 dc/sc in 5 ch loop, 2 ch, 3 tr/dc in dc/sc; repeat from * to end of row ending with 2 tr/dc in last st, 6 turning ch.
row 4: 3 loop puff in first st, * 3 ch, 1 dc/sc in dc/sc, 3 ch, (3 loop puff, 5 ch, 3 loop puff) in centre tr/dc; repeat from * to end of row ending with (3 loop puff, 2 ch, 1 d.tr/tr) in last st, 1 turning ch.
repeat rows 1–4

PUFFS, CLUSTERS AND PICOTS

multiple of 11+7, 4 turning ch

base row: work 1 tr/dc in fifth ch from hook, * 3 ch, miss 3 ch, 1 dc/sc in next ch, (3 ch, 1 dc/sc in next ch) 3 times, 3 ch, miss 3 ch, (1 tr/dc, 2 ch, 1 tr/dc) in next ch; repeat from * to end of row ending with 3 ch, miss 3 ch, 1 dc/sc in next ch, 3 ch, 1 dc/sc in next ch, 1 ch, 1 h.tr/h.dc in last ch, 4 turning ch.

row 1: 1 tr/dc in 1 ch space, * 3 ch, ([1 dc/sc, 3 ch] 3 times, 1 dc/sc) in 2 ch space, 3 ch, (1 tr/dc, 2 ch, 1 tr/dc) in centre 3 ch space; repeat from * to end of row ending with 3 ch, (1 dc/sc in tr/dc, 3 ch, (1 dc/sc, 1 ch, 1 h.tr/h.dc) in turning ch, 4 turning ch.

repeat row 1

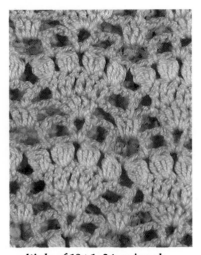

multiple of 10+1, 3 turning ch

base row: work 1 tr/dc in fourth ch from hook, 1 tr/dc in next ch, * 2 ch, miss 3 ch, 5 tr/dc in next ch, 2 ch, miss 3 ch, 1 tr/dc in each next 3 ch;

repeat from * to end of row ending with 1 tr/dc in each last 2 ch, 5 turning ch.

row 1: * (1 tr/dc in first tr/dc, 2 tr/dc in next st, 1 tr/dc in next st, 2 tr/dc in next st, 1 tr/dc) in last st of 5 tr/dc group, 2 ch, 1 tr/dc in centre st of 3 tr/dc group, 2 ch; repeat from * to end of row ending with 1 tr/dc in last st, 3 turning ch.

row 2: 1 tr/dc in first st, * (1 four loop cluster, 2 ch) in first, third and fifth sts of tr/dc group, 1 tr/dc in seventh st of group; repeat from * to end of row ending with 1 tr/dc in turning ch, 3 turning ch.

row 3: 1 tr/dc in first st, 2 ch, * 1 tr/dc in first 2 ch space, 2 ch, (1 tr/dc, 2 ch, 1 tr/dc) in next space, 2 ch, 1 tr/dc in next space, 3 ch; repeat from * to end of row ending with 1 tr/dc in turning ch, 3 turning ch.

row 4: 1 tr/dc in first st, 1 tr/dc in 2 ch space, * 2 ch, miss next 2 ch space, 5 tr/dc in 2 ch space, 2 ch, miss 2 ch space, 3 tr/dc in 3 ch space; repeat from * to end of row ending with 1 tr/dc in last 2 ch space, 1 tr/dc in last st, 5 turning ch.

repeat rows 1–4

multiple of 6+5, 3 turning ch

base row: work 1 cluster in fourth ch from hook thus ([yarn over hook, draw through a loop, yarn over hook and draw through first 2 loops on hook, yarn over hook and draw through all four loops on hook] four times, 1 ch to secure), * miss 2 ch, (1 tr/dc, 2 ch, 1 tr/dc) in next ch, miss 2 ch, 1 cluster in next ch; repeat from * to end of row ending with 1 tr/dc in last ch, 3 turning ch.
row 1: * 1 cluster in 2 ch space, (1 tr/dc, 2 ch, 1 tr/dc) under the two threads securing the cluster of previous row; repeat from * to end of row ending with 1 tr/dc in turning ch, 3 turning ch.
repeat row 1

multiple of 8+1, 3 turning ch

base row: work 1 tr/dc in fourth ch from hook, 2ch, (1 three loop cluster, 1 ch, 1 three loop cluster) in fourth ch, (three tr/dc keeping all loops on hook, yarn over hook, pull yarn through to secure cluster), * 2 ch, miss 3 ch, 1 tr/dc in next ch, 2 ch, miss 3 ch, (1 cluster, 1ch, 1 cluster) in next ch; repeat from * ending with 1 tr/dc in last ch, 5 turning ch.
row 1: * (1 cluster, 1 ch, 1 cluster) in 1 ch space, 2 ch, 1 tr/dc in tr/dc, 2 ch; repeat from * to end of row ending with 1 tr/dc in turning ch, 3 turning ch.
row 2: 1 cluster in first st, * 2 ch, 1 tr/dc in 1 ch space, 2 ch, (1 cluster, 1 ch, 1 cluster) in tr/dc; repeat from * to end of row ending with (1 cluster, 1 tr/dc) in turning ch, 5 turning ch.
row 3: * (1 cluster, 1 ch, 1 cluster) in tr/dc, 2 ch, 1 tr/dc in 1 ch space, 2

ch; repeat from * to end of row, 1 tr/dc in turning ch, 5 turning ch.
repeat rows 1–3

multiple of 5, 3 turning ch

base row: work 1 three loop cluster in fourth ch from hook, * 1 ch, 1 three ch picot, 1 ch, miss 4 ch, (1 three loop cluster, 1 ch, 1 three loop cluster) in next ch; repeat from * to end of row ending with (1 three loop cluster, 1 tr/dc) in last ch, 3 turning ch.
row 1: 2 tr/dc in first st, * 5 tr/dc in 1 ch space between clusters; repeat from * to end of row ending with 3 tr/dc in turning ch, 3 turning ch.
row 2: * (1 three loop cluster, 1 ch, 1 three loop cluster) between 5 tr/dc groups, 1 ch, 1 three ch picot, 1 ch; repeat from * to end of row ending with 1 tr/dc in last st, 3 turning ch.
row 3: * 5 tr/dc in 1 ch space between clusters; repeat from * to end of row ending with 1 tr/dc in turning ch, 3 turning ch.
row 4: 1 three loop cluster in first st, * 1 ch, 1 three ch picot, 1 ch, (1 three loop cluster, 1 ch, 1 three loop cluster) between tr/dc groups; repeat from * to end of row ending with (1 three loop cluster, 1 tr/dc) in turning ch, 3 turning ch.
repeat rows 1–4

PUFFS, CLUSTERS AND PICOTS

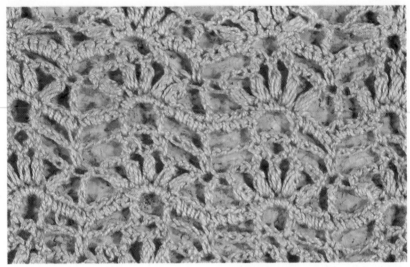

multiple of 8+1, 1 turning ch

base row: work 1 dc/sc in second ch from hook, * 3 ch, miss 3 ch, (1 tr/dc, 3 ch, 1 tr/dc) in next ch, 3 ch, miss 3 ch, 1 dc/sc in next ch; repeat from * to end of row, 1 turning ch.
row 1: 1 dc/sc in first st, * 3 dc/sc in ch loop, 1 dc/sc in tr/dc, 5 dc/sc in next loop, 1 dc/sc in tr/dc, 3 dc/sc in next loop, 1 dc/sc in dc/sc; repeat from * to end of row, 3 turning ch.
row 2: miss first 5 dc/sc, * 1 three loop puff (yarn over hook, hook in st, pull up a loop three times, yarn over hook, draw through 6 loops, yarn over hook and pull yarn through the 2 loops), (3 ch, 1 puff) four times, miss 4 sts, 1 d.tr/tr in dc/sc, miss 4 sts; repeat from * to end of row ending with 1 d.tr/tr in last st, 1 turning ch.
row 3: 1 dc/sc in d.tr/tr, * ch 4, miss next ch loop, 1 dc/sc in next ch loop, 3 ch, 1 dc/sc in next ch loop, miss next ch loop, 4 ch, 1 dc/sc in d.tr/tr; repeat from * to end of row ending with 1 dc/sc in turning ch, 1 turning ch.
row 4: 1 dc/sc in first st, * 3 ch, miss 4 ch loop, (1 tr/dc, 3 ch, 1 tr/dc) in 3 ch loop, 3 ch, miss 4 ch loop, 1 dc/sc in next dc/sc; repeat from * to end of row, 1 turning ch.
repeat rows 1–4

multiple of 3+2, 1 turning ch

base row: work 1 dc/sc in second ch from hook and all subsequent ch to end of row, 4 turning ch.
row 1: miss one st, 1 seven loop puff, ([hook into next st, draw through a loop, yarn over hook] three times, 7 loops on hook, yarn over hook and draw loop through), * 2 ch, miss 2 sts, 1 seven loop puff in next st; repeat from * to end of row ending with 1 tr/dc in last st, 1 turning ch.
row 2: 1 dc/sc in each st and puff to end of row ending with 1 dc/sc in turning ch, 4 turning ch.
repeat rows 1–2

multiple of 4+1, 5 turning ch

base row: work 1 five loop popcorn in sixth ch from hook, (5 tr/dc keeping all loops on hook, take loop off hook, hook into first st and into dropped loop and draw loop through, 1 ch to secure stitch), * 1 ch, miss 1 ch, 1 tr/dc in next ch, 2 ch, miss 1 ch, 1 popcorn in next ch; repeat from * to end of row, 3 turning ch.

row 1: * 1 tr/dc in popcorn, 1 tr/dc in 2 ch space, 1 tr/dc in next tr/dc, 1 tr/dc in 2 ch space; repeat from * to end or row ending with 1 tr/dc in popcorn, 1 tr/dc in turning ch, 4 turning ch.

row 2: 1 popcorn in first st, * 1 ch, miss 1 st, 1 tr/dc in next st, 2 ch, miss 1 st, 1 popcorn in next st; repeat from * to end of row, 3 turning ch.

repeat rows 1–2

multiple of 6, 3 turning ch

base row: work (1 tr/dc, 1 ch, 1 tr/dc, 3 ch, 1 tr/dc, 1 ch, 1 tr/dc) in sixth ch from hook, * miss 5 ch, (1 tr/dc, 1 ch, 1 tr/dc, 3 ch, 1 tr/dc, 1 ch, 1 tr/dc) in next ch; repeat from * to end

of row ending with miss 2 ch, 1 tr/dc in last ch, 3 turning ch.

row 1: * (a 3 loop cluster, 3 ch, a 3 loop cluster) in 3 ch sp, 1 ch; repeat from * to end or row ending with 1 tr/dc in turning ch, 5 turning ch.

row 2: * 1 tr/dc in 3 ch sp, 2 ch, 1 tr/dc in 1 ch sp, 2 ch; repeat from * to end of row ending with 1 tr/dc in turning ch, 2 turning ch.

row 3: miss first st, * (1 tr/dc, 1 ch, 1 tr/dc, 3 ch, 1 tr/dc, 1 ch, 1 tr/dc) in next tr/dc, miss next tr/dc; repeat from * to end of row ending with 1 tr/dc in turning ch, 3 turning ch.

repeat rows 1–3

multiple of 2, 4 turning ch

base row: work a 3 loop puff in fifth ch from hook, * 1 ch, miss 1 ch, a 3 loop puff in next ch; repeat from * to end of row ending with 1 tr/dc in last ch, 4 turning ch.

row 1: * a 3 loop puff in 1 ch sp, 1 ch; repeat from * to end of row ending with 1 tr/dc in turning ch, 3 turning ch.

row 2: * a 3 loop puff in 1 ch sp, 1 ch; repeat from * to end of row ending with 1 tr/dc in turning ch, 4 turning ch.

repeat rows 1–2

PUFFS, CLUSTERS AND PICOTS

multiple of 12, 5 turning ch.

base row: work 1 tr/dc in seventh ch
from hook, * (1 ch, miss 1 ch, 1 tr/
dc) in next st twice, miss 2 ch, (a 3
loop puff st, 3 ch, a 3 loop puff st) in
next ch, miss 2 ch, 1 tr/dc in next
ch, 1 ch, miss 1 ch, 1 tr/dc in next
ch; repeat from * to end of row
ending with miss 2 ch, 1 tr/dc in
last ch, 4 turning ch.

row 1: * (a 3 loop puff st, 3 ch, a 3
loop puff st) in 3 ch sp, (1 tr/dc in
next st, 1 ch) three times, 1 tr/dc in
next st; repeat from * to end of row,
1 tr/dc in turning ch, 4 turning ch.

row 2: miss first st, 1 tr/dc in next
st, (1 ch, 1 tr/dc in next st) twice, *
(a 3 loop puff st, 3 ch, a 3 loop puff
st) in 3 ch sp, (1 tr/dc, 1 ch in next
st) three times 1 tr/dc in next st;
repeat from * to end of row, 1 tr/dc
in turning ch, 3 turning ch.

row 3: * (a 3 loop puff st, 3 ch, a 3
loop puff st, 1 ch) in 3 ch space, (a 3
loop puff st, 3 ch, a 3 loop puff st, 1
ch) in first and third 1 ch spaces;
repeat from * to end of row ending
with 1 tr/dc in turning ch, 4 turning
ch.

row 4: 1 tr/dc in second puff st, 1
ch, 1 tr/dc in next puff st, 1 ch, 1 tr/
dc in next puff st, * (a 3 loop puff st,
3 ch, a 3 loop puff st) in 3 ch sp, (1
tr/dc, 1 ch in puff st) three times, 1
tr/dc in next puff st; repeat from *
to end of row ending with 1 tr/dc in
turning ch.
repeat rows 1–4

multiple of 3, 3 turning ch

base row: work 1 tr/dc in fourth ch
from hook and all subsequent ch to
end of row, 1 turning ch.
row 1: 1 dc/sc in first st, * 4 ch, 3

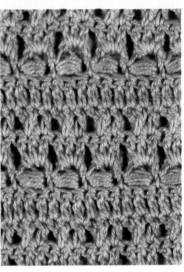

loop puff in next dc/sc, miss 1 st, 1
dc/sc in next st; repeat from * to
end of row ending with 1 dc/sc in
turning ch, 4 turning ch.

row 2: * 3 tr/dc in 4 ch sp; repeat
from * to end of row ending with 1
d.tr/tr in last st, 2 turning ch.

row 3: * miss first tr/dc, 1 tr/dc in
each next 2 sts, 1 tr/dc in missed st;
repeat from * to end of row, 1 tr/dc
in turning ch, 3 turning ch.

row 4: miss first st, 1 tr/dc in every
st to end of row ending with 1 tr/dc
in turning ch, 1 turning ch.
repeat rows 1–4

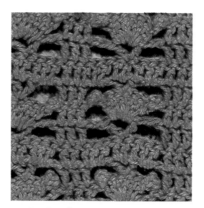

multiple of 10, 4 turning ch

base row: 1 tr/dc in fifth ch from
hook, * 2 ch, miss 3 ch, (1 tr/dc, 2
ch, 1 tr/dc) in next ch, 2 ch, miss 3
ch, 1 tr/dc in each next 3 ch; repeat
from * to end of row ending with 1
tr/dc in each last 2 ch, 3 turning ch.
row 1: miss first st, 1 tr/dc in next
st, * (1 tr/dc, 3 ch picot, 5 tr/dc, 3 ch
picot, 1 tr/dc) in 2 ch space, 1 tr/dc
in each next 3 sts; repeat from * to
end of row ending with 1 tr/dc in
last st, 1 tr/dc in turning ch, 3
turning ch.
row 2: miss first st, 1 tr/dc in next
st, * 2 ch, (1 tr/dc, 1 ch, 1 tr/dc) in
centre st of 7 tr/dc group, 2 ch, 1 tr/
dc in each next 3 sts; repeat from *
to end of row ending with 1 tr/dc in
last st, 1 tr/dc in turning ch, 3
turning ch.
row 3: miss first st, 1 tr/dc in each st
and ch space to end of row, 3
turning ch.
row 4: miss first st, 1 tr/dc in next
st, * 2 ch, miss 3 sts, (1 tr/dc, 2 ch, 1
tr/dc) in next st, 2 ch, miss 3 sts, 1
tr/dc in each next 3 sts; repeat from
* to end of row ending with 1 tr/dc
in last st, 1 tr/dc in turning ch, 3
turning ch.
repeat rows 1–4

multiple of 6+1, 1 turning ch

base row: work 1 dc/sc in second ch
from hook, 3 ch, miss 2 ch, a 4 loop
popcorn in next ch, 3 ch, miss 2 ch,
1 dc/sc in next ch; repeat from * to
end of row, 1 turning ch.
row 1: 1 dc/sc in first st, * 3 dc/sc in
each 3 ch sp; repeat from * to end of
row ending with 1 dc/sc in last st, 2
turning ch.
row 2: a 2 loop popcorn in first st, *
3 ch, 1 dc/sc between the dc/sc

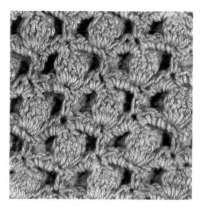

either side of popcorn, 3 ch, a 4
loop popcorn between sts either
side of dc/sc; repeat from * to end
of row ending with 3 ch, a 2 loop
popcorn in last st, 1 turning ch.
row 3: as row 1
row 4: 1 dc/sc in first st, * 3 ch, a
four loop popcorn between sts
either side of dc/sc, 3 ch, 1 dc/sc
between sts either side of popcorn;
repeat from * to end of row, 1
turning ch.
repeat rows 1–4

multiple of 9+1, 1 turning ch

base row: work 1 dc/sc in second ch
from hook, * 3 ch, miss 2 ch, 1 dc/sc
in next ch; repeat from * to end of
row, 3 turning ch.
row 1: * a 3 loop cluster in 3 ch sp, 5
ch, 1 dc/sc in next 3 ch sp, 5 ch, a 3
loop cluster in next 3 ch space;
repeat from * to end of row ending
with a 3 loop cluster in last 3 ch sp,
1 tr/dc in last st, 1 turning ch.
row 2: 1 dc/sc in first st, * 3 ch, 1 dc/
sc in 5 ch sp, 3 ch, 1 dc/sc in next 5
ch sp, 3 ch, 1 dc/sc between the two
3 loop clusters; repeat from * to end
of row ending with last dc/sc in
turning ch, 3 turning ch.
repeat rows 1–2

PUFFS, CLUSTERS AND PICOTS

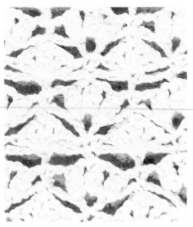

multiple of 10+1, 4 turning ch

base row: work (1 tr/dc, 1 ch, 1 tr/
dc) in fifth ch from hook, 1 ch, *
miss 4 ch, 1 dc/sc in next ch, 1 ch,
miss 4 ch, (1 tr/dc, [1 ch, 1 tr/dc]
five times) in next ch, 1 ch; repeat
from * to end of row ending with (1
tr/dc, [1 ch, 1 tr/dc] twice) in last ch,
1 turning ch.
row 1: 1 dc/sc in first st, * 3 ch, (1 tr/
dc, 3 ch, 1 tr/dc) in next dc/sc, 3 ch,
1 dc/sc in centre space of 6 tr/dc
group; repeat from * to end of row
ending with 1 dc/sc in turning ch, 1
turning ch.
row 2: 1 dc/sc in first st, * 2 ch, (1
three loop cluster, 2 ch, 1 three loop
cluster, 2 ch, 1 three loop cluster) in
3 ch space, each cluster worked
thus, (half work 1 tr/dc three times,
yarn over hook and draw through
all loops), 2 ch, 1 dc/sc in next dc/
sc; repeat from * to end of row, 7
turning ch.
row 3: * 1 dc/sc in centre cluster, 4
ch, 1 tr/dc in dc/sc, 4 ch; repeat
from * to end of row ending with 1
tr/dc in last st, 4 turning ch.
row 4: (1 tr/dc, 1 ch, 1 tr/dc) in first
st, 1 ch, * 1 dc/sc in dc/sc, 1 ch, (1 tr/
dc, [1 ch, 1 tr/dc] five times) in tr/
dc, 1 ch; repeat from * to end of row
ending with (1 tr/dc, [1 ch, 1 tr/dc]
twice) in last st, 1 turning ch.
repeat rows 1–4

multiple of 4+1, 5 turning ch

base row: work (1 dc/sc, 3 ch, 1 dc/
sc) in sixth ch from hook, * 5 ch,
miss 3 ch, (1 dc/sc, 3 ch, 1 dc/sc) in
next ch; repeat from * to end of row
ending with 1 dc/sc in last ch, 5
turning ch.
row 1: * (1 dc/sc, 3 ch, 1 dc/sc) in

third ch of 5 ch loop, 5 ch; repeat
from * to end of row ending with 5
ch, 1 dc/sc in turning ch, 5 turning
ch.
repeat row 1

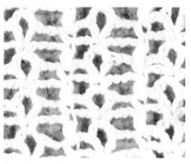

multiple of 8+1, 1 turning ch

base row: work 1 dc/sc in second ch
from hook, * 2 ch, miss 3 ch, (1 tr/
dc, 3 ch, 1 tr/dc) in next ch, 2 ch,
miss 3 ch, 1 dc/sc in next ch; repeat
from * to end of row, 6 turning ch.
row 1: * 1 dc/sc in 3 ch loop, 3 ch, 1
puff in dc/sc worked thus (yarn
over hook, draw through a loop 3
times, yarn over hook and draw
through all 7 loops on hook, 1 ch to
secure), 3 ch; repeat from * to end
of row ending with 1 tr/dc in last
dc/sc, 1 turning ch.
row 2: 1 dc/sc in first st, * 2 ch, (1 tr/
dc, 3 ch, 1 tr/dc) in dc/sc, 2 ch, 1 dc/
sc in top of puff; repeat from * to
end of row ending with 1 dc/sc in
turning ch, 6 turning ch.
repeat rows 1–2

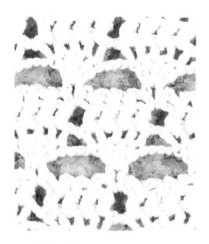

multiple of 9, 3 turning ch

base row: work 1 tr/dc in fourth ch from hook, 1 ch, miss 3 ch, 5 tr/dc in next ch, * 4 ch, miss 8 ch, 5 tr/dc in next ch; repeat from * to end of row ending with 1 ch, miss 3 ch, 1 tr/dc in last ch, 3 turning ch.

row 1: * (1 tr/dc, 1 ch) in each next 5 tr/dc; repeat from * to end of row, 1 tr/dc in last st, 3 turning ch.

row 2: (1 three loop cluster, 1 ch) worked thus, (half work 3 tr/dc, yarn over hook and draw through all loops), in each first three 1 ch spaces, 1 cluster in next space, * 2 ch, (1 cluster, 1 ch) in first three 1 ch space of 5 tr/dc group, 1 cluster in last space; repeat from * to end of row, 1 tr/dc in turning ch, 1 turning ch.

row 3: 1 dc/sc in first st, * (3 ch, 1 dc/sc) in next three 1 ch spaces, 3 ch, (1 dc/sc, 4 ch, 1 dc/sc) in 2 ch space; repeat from * to end of row ending with last dc/sc in turning ch, 4 turning ch.

row 4: 2 tr/dc in first 3 ch loop, * 4 ch, 5 tr/dc in 4 ch loop; repeat from * to end of row, 2 tr/dc in last 3 ch loop, 1 d.tr/tr in last st, 4 turning ch.

row 5: (1 tr/dc, 1 ch) in next 2 tr/dc, * (1 tr/dc, 1 ch) in each next 5 sts; repeat from * to end of row ending with (1 tr/dc, 1 ch) in each last 2 sts, 1 tr/dc in turning ch, 4 turning ch.

row 6: (1 cluster, 1 ch) in first space, 1 cluster in next space, * 2 ch, (1 cluster in 1 ch space, 1 ch) three times, 1 cluster; repeat from * to end of row ending with 2 ch, 1 cluster in first space, (1 ch, 1 cluster, 1 tr/dc in turning ch, 1 turning ch.

row 7: 1 dc/sc in first st, 3 ch, 1 dc/sc in 1 ch space, * 3 ch, (1 dc/sc, 4 ch, 1

dc/sc) in 2 ch space, (3 ch, 1 dc/sc) in next three 1 ch spaces; repeat from * to end of row ending with 3 ch, 1 dc/sc in last 1 ch space, 3 ch, 1 dc/sc in turning ch, 5 turning ch.

row 8: * 5 tr/dc in four ch loop, 4 ch; repeat from * to end of row 1 ch, 1 tr/dc in last st, 3 turning ch.

repeat rows 1–8

multiple of 8+6, 3 turning ch

base row: work 1 tr/dc in fourth ch from hook, 1 tr/dc in each next 5 ch, * 1 ch, miss 1 ch, 1 tr/dc in each next 7 ch; repeat from * to end of row, 3 turning ch.

row 1: miss first st, 1 tr/dc in each next 2 sts, * 4 loop popcorn in next st, 1 tr/dc in each next 3 sts, 1 ch, 1 tr/dc in each next 3 sts; repeat from * to end of row, 1 tr/dc in turning ch, 3 turning ch.

row 2: miss first st, 1 tr/dc in each next 2 sts, * 1 tr/dc in popcorn, 1 tr/dc in each next 3 sts, 1 ch, 1 tr/dc in each next 3 sts; repeat from * to end of row, 1 tr/dc in turning ch, 4 turning ch.

row 3: miss 2 sts, (1 tr/dc in next st, 1 ch, miss next st) twice, 1 tr/dc in next st, * 1 ch, (1 tr/dc in next st, 1 ch, miss next st) three times, 1 tr/dc; repeat from * to end of row, 1 tr/dc in turning ch, 3 turning ch.

row 4: miss first st, (1 tr/dc in 1 ch sp, 1 tr/dc in next st) three times, * 1 ch, (1 tr/dc in next st, 1 tr/dc in 1 ch sp) three times, 1 tr/dc in next st; repeat from * ending with 2 tr/dc in turning ch, 3 turning ch.

repeat rows 1–4

PUFFS, CLUSTERS AND PICOTS

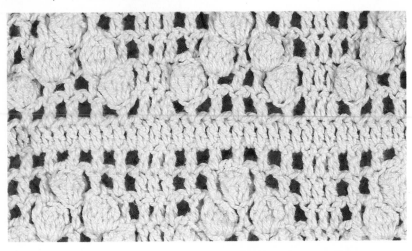

multiple of 14+2, 3 turning ch

base row: work 1 tr/dc in fourth ch from hook and all subsequent ch to end of row, 3 turning ch.
row 1: miss first st, 1 tr/dc in each next 2 sts, * (1 ch, miss 1 st, 1 tr/dc in next st) six times, 1 tr/dc in each next 2 sts; repeat from * to end of row ending with 1 tr/dc in turning ch, 3 turning ch.
row 2: miss first st, 1 tr/dc in each next 2 sts, * 1 ch, a 5 loop popcorn in next st, (1 ch, 1 tr/dc in next st) three times, 1 ch, a 5 loop popcorn in next st, 1 ch, 1 tr/dc in each next 3 sts; repeat from * to end of row, 1 tr/dc in turning ch, 3 turning ch.
row 3: miss first st, 1 tr/dc in each next 2 sts, * 1 ch, 1 tr/dc in popcorn, 1 ch, a 5 loop popcorn in next st, 1 ch, 1 tr/dc in next st, 1 ch, a 5 loop popcorn in next st, 1 ch, 1 tr/dc in popcorn, 1 ch, 1 tr/dc in each next 3 sts; repeat from * to end of row, 1 tr/dc in turning ch, 3 turning ch.
row 4: miss first st, 1 tr/dc in each next 2 sts, * 1 ch, 1 tr/dc in next st, 1 ch, 1 tr/dc in popcorn, 1 ch, a 5 loop popcorn in next st, 1 ch, 1 tr/dc in popcorn, 1 ch, 1 tr/dc in next st, 1 ch, 1 tr/dc in each next 3 sts; repeat from * to end of row, 3 turning ch.
row 5: miss first st, 1 tr/dc in each next 2 sts, * (1 ch, 1 tr/dc in next st) twice, 1 ch, 1 tr/dc in popcorn, 1 ch, (1 tr/dc in next st, 1 ch) twice, 1 tr/dc in each next 3 sts; repeat from * to end of row, 3 turning ch.
row 6: miss first st, 1 tr/dc in each next 2 sts, * 1 tr/dc in each 1 ch sp, 1 tr/dc in each st; repeat from * to end of row, 3 turning ch.
repeat rows 1–6

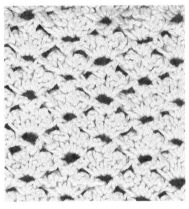

multiple of 8+1, 1 turning ch

base row 1: work 1 dc/sc in second ch from hook, 1 dc/sc in each next 3 ch, * 1 ch, miss 1 ch, 1 dc/sc in each next 7 ch; repeat from * to end of row ending with 1 dc/sc in each last 4 ch, 3 turning ch.
base row 2: (1 tr/dc, 2 ch, 1 tr/dc) in first st, * 3 picots (work [1 dc/sc, 3 ch] three times, 1 dc/sc) in next 1 ch space, (1 dc/sc, 2 ch, 1 dc/sc) in fourth dc/sc; repeat from * to end of row, 1 turning ch.
row 1: 2 picots in first 2 ch loop, * (1 tr/dc, 2 ch, 1 tr/dc) in centre picot of 3 picot group, 3 picot in 2 ch loop; repeat from * to end of row ending with 2 picots in last 1 ch space, 3 turning ch.
row 2: (1 tr/dc, 2 ch, 1 tr/dc) in first picot, miss next picot, * 3 picot in next 2 ch space, (1 tr/dc, 2 ch, 1 tr/dc) in centre picot of 3 picot group; repeat from * to end of row ending with (1 tr/dc, 2 ch, 1 tr/dc) in last 1 picot, 1 turning ch.
repeat rows 1–2

multiple of 3 +1, 5 turning ch.

base row: work 1 tr/dc in sixth ch from hook, * 2 ch, half work 1 tr/dc in same ch, miss 2 ch, half work 1 tr/dc in next ch and finish off tog; repeat from * to end of row ending with (1 tr/dc, 1 ch, 1 tr/dc) in last ch, 4 turning ch.
row 1: * a four loop puff in top of 2 tr/dc, 3 ch; repeat from * to end of row ending with 1 tr/dc in turning ch, 3 turning ch.
row 2: 1 tr/dc in 3 ch loop, * 2 ch, half work 1 tr/dc in same loop, half work 1 tr/dc in next loop and finish off tog; repeat from * to end of row ending with second tr/dc half worked in turning ch then finished tog, (1 ch, 1 tr/dc in turning ch), 4 turning ch.
repeat rows 1–2

multiple of 14+1, 3 turning ch

base row: work 1 tr/dc in fourth ch from hook, * 2 ch, miss 2 ch, 1 dc/sc in next ch, miss 3 ch, (1 tr/dc [1 ch, 1 tr/dc] four times) in next ch, miss 3 ch, 1 dc/sc in next ch, 2 ch, miss 2 ch, (1 tr/dc, 1 ch, 1 tr/dc) in next ch; repeat from * to end of row, 4 turning ch.
row 1: 1 dc/sc in second st, * 3 ch, (1 dc/sc, 3 ch, 1 dc/sc) in each next four 1 ch spaces, 3 ch, (1 tr/dc, 3 ch, 1 tr/dc) in next 1 ch space; repeat from * to end of row ending with 1 dc/sc in last st, 1 ch, 1 h.tr/h.dc in turning ch, 3 turning ch.
row 2: 1 tr/dc in first st, * 3 ch, 1 dc/sc in second 3 ch loop, 3 ch, 1 dc/sc in third 3 ch loop, 3 ch, (1 tr/dc, 1 ch, 1 tr/dc) in single 3 ch loop;

repeat from * to end of row ending with 2 tr/dc in turning ch, 4 turning ch.
row 3: 1 tr/dc in second st, * 2 ch, (1 tr/dc [1ch, 1 tr/dc] four times) in 3 ch loop, 2 ch, (1 dc/sc, 1 ch, 1 dc/sc) in 1 ch space; repeat from * to end of row ending with 1 tr/dc in last st, 1 ch, 1 tr/dc in turning ch, 4 turning ch.
repeat rows 1–3

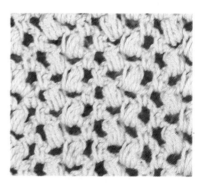

multiple of 6+1, 1 turning ch

base row: work 1 dc/sc in second ch from hook, * miss 2 ch, 3 ch, a 3 loop puff st in next ch, miss 2 sts, 3 ch, 1 dc/sc in next ch; repeat from * to end of row, 7 turning ch.
row 1: 1 dc/sc in 3 ch sp, * 3 ch, a 3 loop puff st in next 3 ch sp, 3 ch, 1 dc/sc in 3 ch sp; repeat from * to end of row ending with a 3 loop puff in last 3 ch sp, 1 tr/dc in last st, 1 turning ch.
row 2: 1 dc/sc in first st, 3 ch, * a 3 loop puff in next 3 ch sp, 3 ch, 1 dc/sc in next 3 ch sp, 3 ch; repeat from * to end of row ending with 1 dc/sc in turning ch, 7 turning ch.
repeat rows 1–2

Filet Patterns

Designs based on a simple mesh construction and worked from charts. The patterns are made from filling in the designated squares with stitches

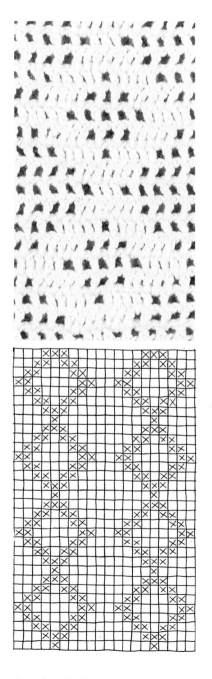

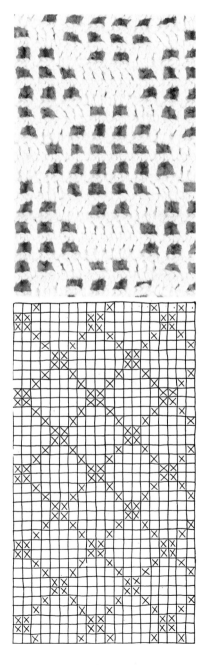

Reproduced by kind permission of Pingouin, instructions: page 177.

FILET PATTERNS

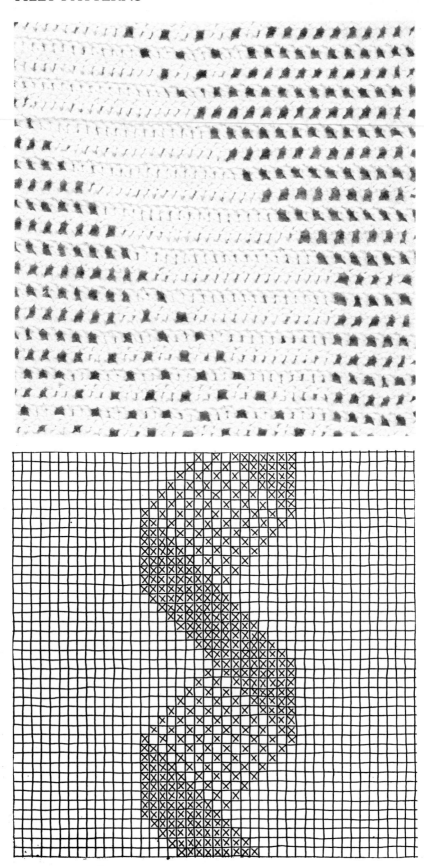

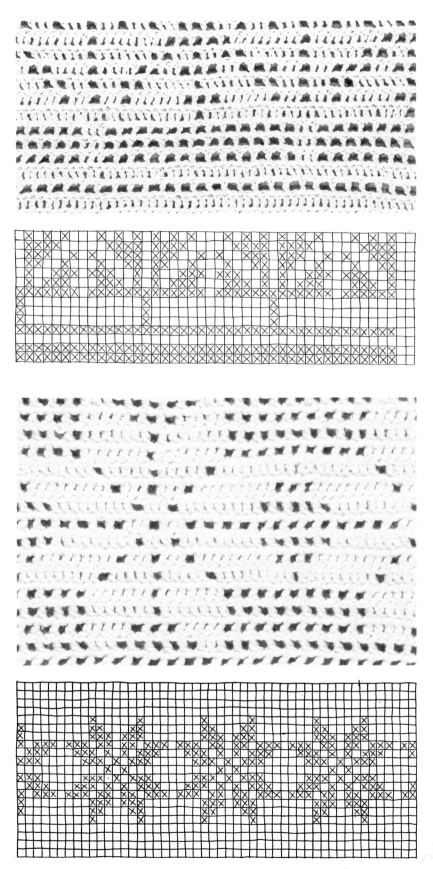

FILET PATTERNS

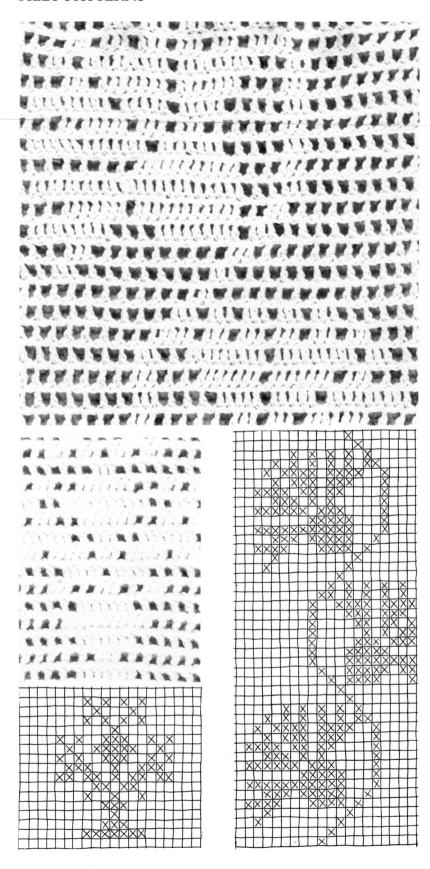

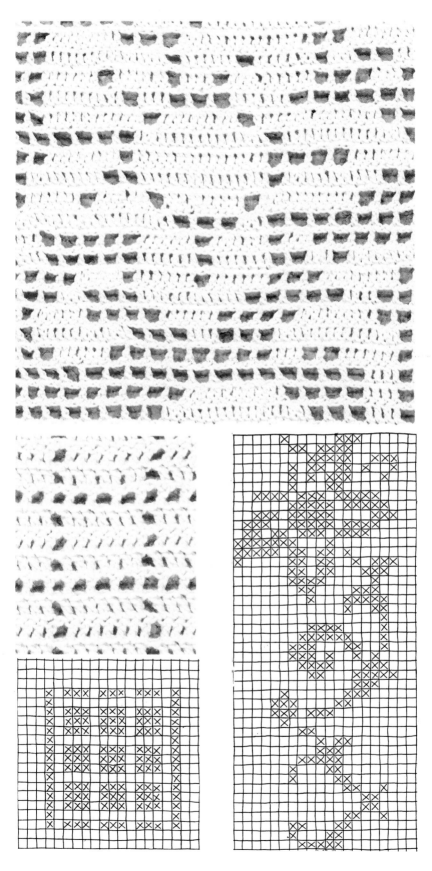

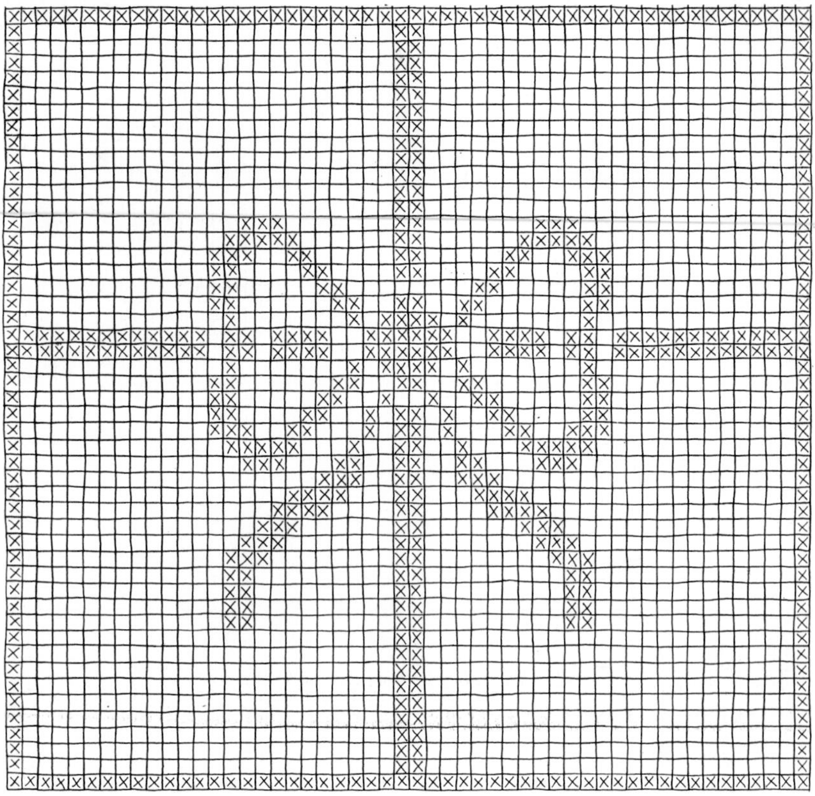

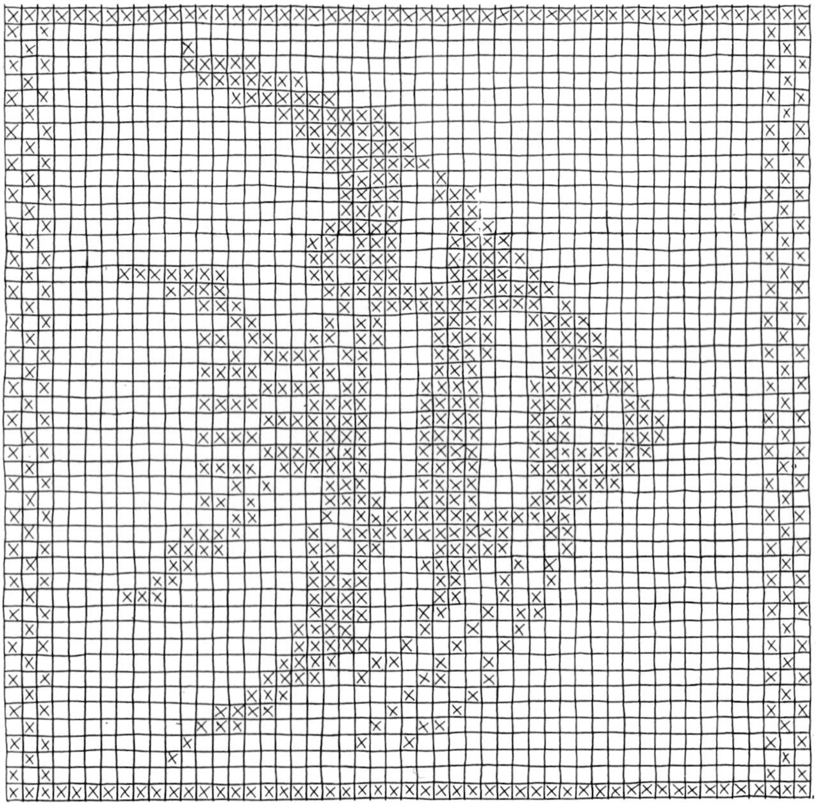

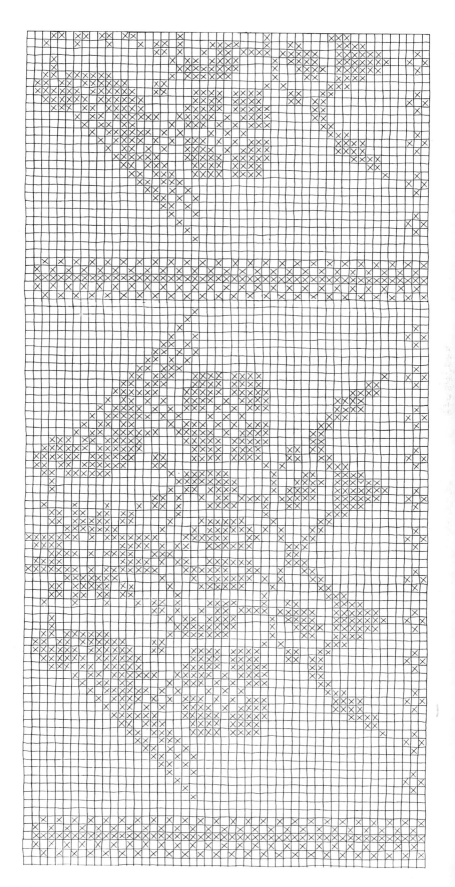

FILET PATTERNS

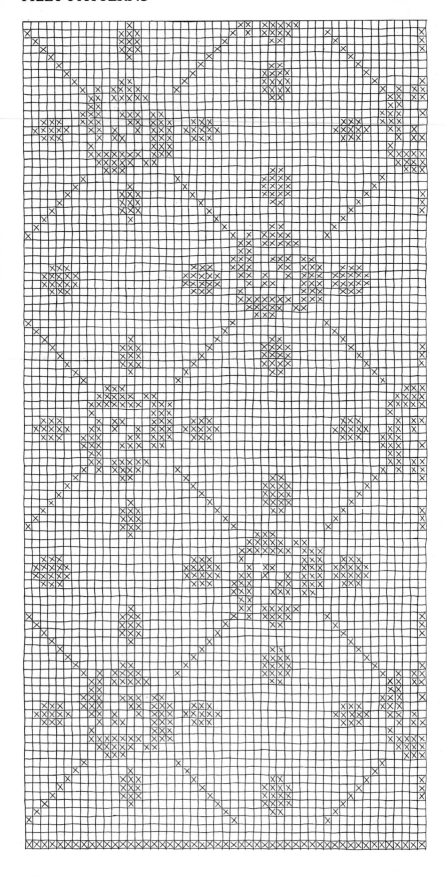

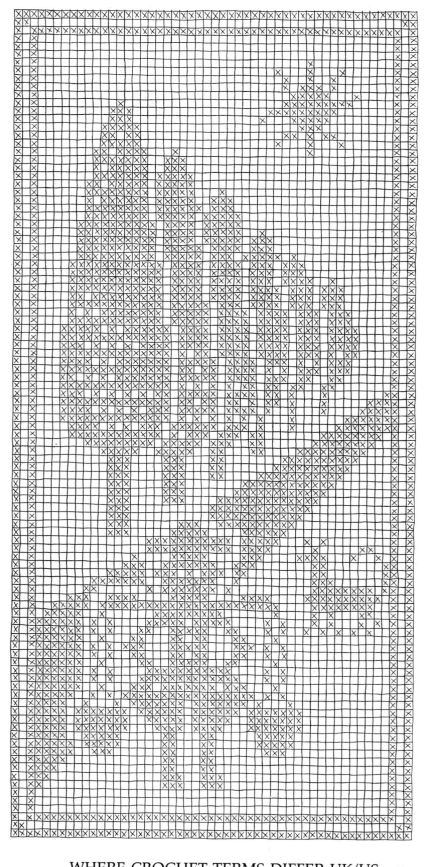

Tunisian Crochet

Worked with a special hook half way between a knitting needle and a crochet hook. How to work it is given in more detail on page 152

Basic Tunisian Crochet 1
any number of sts

row 1 (outward): put hook into second ch from hook, yoh, draw loop through and leave on hook, * put hook into next ch, yoh, draw loop through and leave on hook; repeat from * to end of row.
row 2 (return): yoh, draw loop through first st on hook, * yoh, draw through next 2 loops; repeat from * until only 1 loop remains on hook, 1 ch.
repeat rows 1–2

'Knitted' Tunisian Stitch
any number of stitches

rows 1 & 2: worked as for Basic Tunisian Stitch 1.
row 3 (outward): miss first st, * put hook through next loop and under the bar, yoh and draw loop through; repeat from * to end of row.

row 4 (return): as row 2.
repeat rows 3–4

'Purl' Tunisian Stitch
any number of stitches

rows 1 & 2: worked as for Basic Tunisian Stitch 1.
row 3 (outward): miss first st, * yarn forward, put hook through next loop, yarn back, yoh and draw loop through; repeat from * to end of row.
row 4 (return): as row 2.
repeat rows 3–4

Published originally in Vogue Knitting, Butterick Company, instructions: page 179.

Alternating Tunisian Stitch 1
any number of sts

row 1 (outward): put hook into second ch from hook, yoh, draw loop through and leave on hook, * put hook into next ch, yoh, draw loop through and leave on hook; repeat from * to end of row.

row 2 (return): yoh, draw loop through first st on hook, * yoh, draw through next 2 loops; repeat from * until only 1 loop remains on hook.

row 3 (outward): 1 ch, * put between 2 vertical sts and under the ch edge of previous row, yoh, draw loop through; repeat from * to end of row.

row 4 (return): yoh, draw loop through first st on hook, * yoh, draw through next 2 loops; repeat from * until only 1 loop remains on hook.

repeat rows 3–4

but on subsequent odd numbered rows, move 1 st over to the left; to keep total number of sts correct, pick up 1 st in last st of previous row, yoh and draw loop through.

even numbered rows: as row 4

Alternating Tunisian Stitch 2
any number of sts

row 1 (outward): put hook into second ch from hook, yoh, draw loop through and leave on hook, * put hook into next ch, yoh, draw loop through and leave on hook; repeat from * to end of row.

row 2 (return): yoh, draw loop through first st on hook, * yoh, draw through next 2 loops; repeat from * until only 1 loop remains on hook.

row 3 (outward): 1 ch, * put hook

from bottom to top between the vertical st of previous row, yoh, draw loop through; repeat from * to end of row.

row 4 (return): yoh, draw loop through first st on hook, * yoh, draw through next 2 loops; repeat from * until only 1 loop remains on hook.

repeat rows 3–4

Rib Effect Tunisian Stitch
any number of sts

row 1 (outward): put hook into second ch from hook, yoh, draw loop through and leave on hook, * put hook into next ch, yoh, draw loop through and leave on hook; repeat from * to end of row.

row 2 (return): yoh, draw loop through first st on hook, * yoh, draw through next 2 loops; repeat from * until only 1 loop remains on hook.

row 3 (outward): 1 ch, * put hook from right to left under vertical st of previous row, yoh, draw, loop through then draw next loop under the chain edge after these 2 sts; repeat from * to the last st and at end of row, draw through another loop under last vertical st.

row 4 (return): yoh, draw loop through first st on hook, * yoh, draw through next 2 loops; repeat from * until only 1 loop remains on hook.

repeat rows 3–4

Tunisian Rib Stitch 1
multiple of 2, 1 turning ch

row 1 (outward): put hook into second ch from hook, yoh, draw loop through and leave on hook, * put hook into next ch, yoh, draw loop through and leave on hook; repeat from * to end of row.
row 2 (return): yoh, draw loop through first st on loop, * yoh, draw through next 2 loops; repeat from * until only 1 loop remains on hook.
row 3 (outward): 1 ch, * yoh, put hook from front to back into second st, yoh, pull loop through, miss next vertical st; repeat from * to end of row.
row 4 (return): yoh, draw loop through first st on loop, * yoh, draw through next 2 loops; repeat from * until only 1 loop remains on hook.
repeat rows 3–4

Tunisian Rib Stitch 2
multiple of 4, 1 turning ch

row 1 (outward): put hook into second ch from hook, yoh, draw loop through and leave on hook, * put hook into next ch, yoh, draw loop through and leave on hook; repeat from * to end of row.
row 2 (return): yoh, draw loop through first st on loop, * yoh, draw through next 2 loops; repeat from * until only 1 loop remains on hook.
row 3 (outward): 1 ch, * (put hook under vertical st from right to left, yoh, draw through loop) twice, (yarn in front of work, put hook from right to left through vertical st of previous row) twice; repeat from * to end of row.
row 4 (return): yoh, draw loop through first st on hook, * yoh, draw through next 2 loops; repeat from * until only 1 loop remains on hook.
repeat rows 3–4

Fancy Tunisian Stitch

any even number of sts

row 1 (outward): put hook into second ch from hook, yoh, draw loop through and leave on hook, * put hook into next ch, yoh, draw loop through and leave on hook; repeat from * to end of row.
row 2 (return): yoh, draw loop through first st on hook, * yoh, draw through next 2 loops; repeat from * until only 1 loop remains on hook.
row 3 (outward): 1 ch, miss first, * work next st as for 'Knit' Tunisian Stitch, work next st as for 'Purl' Tunisian Stitch; repeat from * to end of row ending with hook in last st and loop at back of st, yoh, draw a loop through to make an edge st.
row 4 (return): yoh, draw loop through first st on hook, * yoh, draw through next 2 loops; repeat from * until only 1 loop remains on hook.
row 5 (outward): miss first vertical st, * work next st as for 'Purl' Tunisian Stitch, work next st as for 'Knit' Tunisian Stitch; repeat from * to end of row ending with hook in last st and loop at back of st, yoh, draw through a 1 loop.
row 6: as row 4
repeat rows 3–6

Basic Tunisian Crochet 2

any number of sts

row 1 (outward): put hook into second ch from hook, yoh, draw loop through and leave on hook, * put hook into next ch, yoh, draw loop through and leave on hook; repeat from * to end of row.
row 2 (return): yoh, draw loop through first st on hook, * yoh, draw through next 2 loops; repeat from * until only 1 loop remains on hook.
row 3 (outward): 2 ch, miss first st, * put hook from right to left under next vertical st, yoh, draw loop through, yoh and draw through loop; repeat from * to end of row.
row 4 (return): yoh, draw loop through first st on hook, * yoh, draw through next 2 loops; repeat from * until only 1 loop remains on hook.
repeat rows 3–4

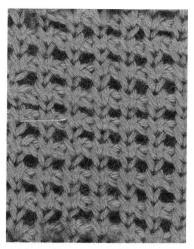

Tunisian Mesh Stitch

multiple of 2+1, 1 turning ch

row 1: (outward): put hook into second ch from hook, yoh, draw loop through and leave on hook, * put hook into next ch, yoh, draw loop through and leave on hook; repeat from * to end of row.

row 2 (return): yoh, draw loop through first st on loop, * yoh, draw through next 2 loops; repeat from * until only 1 loop remains on hook.

row 3 (outward): 1 ch, * put hook through vertical st of previous row, yoh and pull through loop, 1 ch, miss 1 st; repeat from * to end of row.

row 4 (return): yoh, draw loop through first st on hook, * yoh, draw through next 2 loops; repeat from * until only 1 loop remains on hook.

repeat rows 3–4

Tunisian Basket Stitch

multiple of 8+4, 1 turning ch

row 1 (outward): put hook into second ch from hook, yoh, draw loop through and leave on hook, * put hook into next ch, yoh, draw loop through and leave on hook; repeat from * to end of row.

row 2 (return): yoh, draw loop through first st on loop, * yoh, draw through next 2 loops; repeat from * until only 1 loop remains on

hook.

row 3 (outward): 1 ch, miss first st, 1 Tunisian knit st (hook from front to back through ch formed in previous row, yoh, draw loop through) in each next 3 sts, * 1 Tunisian purl st (yarn to front, hook from right to left behind single vertical thread, yoh, draw loop through) in each next 4 sts, 1 Tunisian knit st in each next 4 sts; repeat from * to end of row.

row 4 (return): yoh, draw loop through first st on hook, * yoh, draw through next 2 loops; repeat from * until only 1 loop remains on hook.

rows 3, 5 and 7: as row 1.
rows 4, 6, and 8: as row 2.
row 9: 1 ch, miss first st, Tunisian purl st in each next 3 sts, * Tunisian knit st in each next 4 sts, Tunisian purl st in each next 4 sts; repeat from * to end of row.

rows 10, 12, 14 and 16: as row 2.
rows 11, 13 and 15: as row 9.

repeat rows 1–16

Crossed Tunisian Stitch

multiple of 4, 1 turning ch

row 1 (outward): put hook into second ch from hook, yoh, draw loop through and leave on hook, * put hook into next ch, yoh, draw loop through and leave on hook; repeat from * to end of row.

row 2 (return): yoh, draw loop through first st on hook, * yoh draw through next 2 loops; repeat from * until only 1 loop remains on hook.

row 3 (outward): 1 ch, put hook from right to left under second vertical st, yoh, draw through loop, * put hook from right to left under the fourth vertical st, yoh, draw through loop, put hook from right to left under third vertical st, yoh and draw loop through; repeat from * to end of row.

row 4 (return): yoh, draw loop through first st on hook, * yoh, draw through next 2 loops; repeat from * until only 1 loop remains on hook.

row 5: 1 ch, work as for row 1 but working 1 st further to left for each crossed st row.

repeat rows 4–5

Tunisian Pebble Stitch 1

multiple of 2, 1 turning ch

row 1: (outward): put hook into second ch from hook, yoh, draw loop through and leave on hook, * put hook into next ch, yoh, draw loop through and leave on hook; repeat from * to end of row.

row 2 (return): yoh, draw loop through first st on hook, * yoh, draw through 2 loops; repeat from * until only 1 loop remains on hook, 1 ch.

row 3 (outward): miss first st, * hook in top of next st, yoh and draw loop through; repeat from * to end of row.

row 4 (return): yoh, draw through a loop, yoh, draw through 2 loops, * 3 ch, (yoh, draw through 2 loops) twice; repeat from * to end or row, 1 ch.

row 5 (outward): as row 3 watching that the 3 ch loops are through at front of work.

row 6: yoh, draw through a loop, * (yoh, draw through 2 loops) twice, 3 ch; repeat from * to end of row ending with yoh, draw through last 2 loops, 1 ch.

repeat rows 3–6

Tunisian Bobble Stitch 1

multiple of 4+3, 1 turning ch

row 1 (outward): put hook into second ch from hook, yoh, draw loop through and leave on hook, * put hook into next ch, yoh, draw loop through and leave on hook; repeat from * to end of row.

row 2 (return): yoh, draw loop through first ch on hook, * yoh, draw through next 2 loops; repeat from * until only 1 loop remains on hook.

row 3: miss first st, (hook into next st, yoh and draw through loop) twice, * tr/dc3tog in next st to make a bobble (yoh, hook into st, yoh and draw loop through three times, yoh and draw through all loops), (hook in next st, yoh and draw loop through) three times; repeat from * to end of row.

row 4: as row 2

row 5: as row 1.

row 6: as row 2.

row 7: miss first st, tr/dc3tog in next st, (hook in next st, yoh and draw through loop) three times; repeat from * to end of row ending with tr/dc3tog in last but one st, hook in last st, yoh and draw through loop.

row 8: as row 2.

row 9: as row 3.

row 10: as row 4.

repeat rows 3–8

Tunisian Bobble Stitch 2

multiple of 6+4, 1 turning ch

row 1 (outward): put hook into second ch from hook, yoh, draw loop through and leave on hook, * put hook into next ch, yoh, draw loop through and leave on hook; repeat from * to end of row.

row 2 (return): yoh, draw loop through first st on hook, * yoh, draw through 2 loops; repeat from * until only 1 loop remains on hook, 1 ch.

row 3: hook into first st, yoh and draw loop through, * tr/dc3tog in next st to make a bobble (yoh, hook into st, yoh and draw loop through three times, yoh and draw through all loops), hook in next st, yoh and draw loop through five times; repeat from * to end of row ending with tr/dc3tog in last but one st, hook in next st, yoh and draw loop through.

rows 4, 6 and 8: as row 2.

rows 5 and 7: as row 1.

row 9: hook in first st, yoh and draw loop four times, tr/dc3tog in next st, hook in next st, yoh and draw through loop five times; repeat from * to end of row ending with hook into last st, yoh and draw through loop.

rows 10, 12 and 14: as row 2.

rows 11 and 13: as row 1.

repeat rows 3–14.

Eyelet Tunisian Stitch

multiple of 2

row 1 (outward): * yoh twice, put hook into third ch from hook, yoh and draw through a loop, yoh, draw through 2 loops, * miss 1 ch, yoh twice, hook into next ch, yoh and draw through 1 loop, yoh and draw through 2 loops; repeat from * to end of row.
row 2 (return): yoh, draw loop through first st on hook, * yoh, draw through 2 loops; repeat from * until only 1 loop remains on hook, 2 turning ch.
row 3 (outward): * yoh twice, hook into vertical loop and slightly sloping vertical loop made in previous row, yoh and draw through 1 loop, yoh, and draw through 2 loops; repeat from * to end of row.
row 4 (return): as row 2
repeat rows 3–4

Tunisian Cluster Stitch

multiple of 4 + 1

row 1 (outward): put hook into second ch from hook, yoh, draw loop through and leave on hook, * put hook into next ch, yoh, draw loop through and leave on hook; repeat from * to end of row.
row 2 (return): yoh, draw through 2 loops, * 3 ch, yoh, draw through 5 loops; repeat from * until 4 loops remain, 3 ch, yoh, draw through last 4 loops.

row 3 (outward): 1 ch, miss first cluster * (hook into next ch, yoh, draw loop through) 3 times, hook under thread which closed next cluster, yoh, draw loop through; repeat from * to end of row.
row 4 (return): yoh, draw through 2 loops, * 3 ch, yoh draw through 5 loops; repeat from * until 4 loops remain, 3 ch, yoh, draw through last 4 loops.
repeat rows 3–4

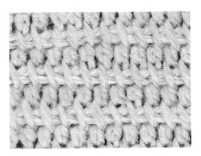

Treble Tunisian Stitch

multiple of 2

row 1 (outward): put hook into second ch from hook, yoh, draw loop through and leave on hook, * put hook into next ch, yoh, draw loop through and leave on hook; repeat from * to end of row.
row 2 (return): yoh, draw loop through first st on hook, * yoh, draw through 2 loops; repeat from * until only 1 loop remains on hook, 2 turning ch.
row 3 (outward): * yoh and put hook from right to left into vertical loop of previous row, yoh and draw through one loop, yoh and draw through 2 loops; repeat from * to end of row.
row 4 (return): as row 2
repeat rows 3–4

Tunisian Pebble Stitch 2

multiple of 2

row 1 (outward): put hook into second ch from hook, yoh, draw loop through and leave on hook, * put hook into next ch, yoh, draw loop through and leave on hook; repeat from * to end of row.
row 2 (return): yoh, draw loop through first st on hook, * yoh, draw through 2 loops; repeat from * until only 1 loop remains on hook, 1 turning ch.
row 3 (outward): * hook into third vertical loop of previous row, yoh and draw through a loop, hook into second vertical loop, yoh and draw through a loop; repeat from * working in groups of 2, crossing the threads by working the second st before the first, ending with 1 st in last loop.
row 4 (return): as row 2
row 5 (outward): hook into next vertical loop, yoh and draw through a loop, * yoh and hook into second st, draw through a loop, hook into first st, yoh and draw through a loop.
row 6 (return): as row 2
repeat rows 3–6

Tunisian Cable Stitch

multiple of 7+3

row 1 (outward): put hook into second ch from hook, yoh, draw loop through and leave on hook, * put hook into next ch, yoh, draw loop through and leave on hook; repeat from * to end of row.
row 2 (return): yoh, draw loop through first st on hook, * yoh, draw through next 2 loops; repeat from * until only 1 loop remains on hook.
row 3 (outward): 1 ch, * ** (hook under next vertical st holding yarn with thumb in front and below hook) three times, ** (holding yarn at back, hook from front to back through centre of next loop and strand behind it, yoh and pull loop through) three times; repeat from * to end of row ending with ** to **.
row 4 (return): yoh, draw through loop, (yoh, draw through 2 loops) twice, * slip next 2 sts on to a cable needle and hold at front of work, yoh and pull loop through working off the next two loops twice, slip loops from cable needle back to hook and work off making a cable, (yoh, draw through 2 loops) three times; repeat from * to end of row, 1 ch.
row 5 (outward): * (yoh, hook under vertical bar of next st holding yarn with thumb in front and below hook and pull loop through) three times, (pick up 1 vertical loop of cable, yoh, pull loop through) twice, (pick up one loop in bar at back of cable) twice; repeat from * to end of row.
row 6 (return): yoh, draw loop through first st on hook, * yoh, draw through next 2 loops; repeat from * until only 1 loop remains on hook.
row 7: as row 1.
row 8: as row 2.
repeat rows 3–8

Collars and Edgings

*Using forms of filet, lace and openwork
to make an effective finishing touch to clothes*

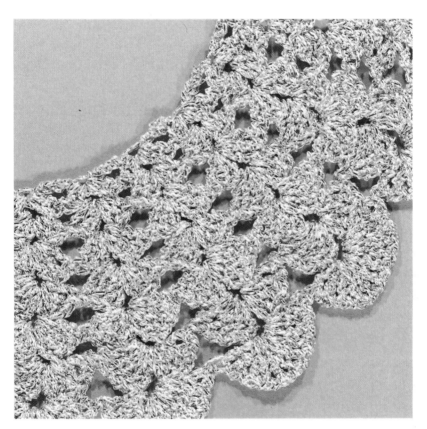

multiple of 5+1, 3 turning ch

row 1: work 1 tr/dc in fourth ch
from hook, miss 4 ch, * (2 tr/dc, 1
ch, 2 tr/dc) in next ch, miss 4 ch;
repeat from * to end of row ending
with 2 tr/dc in last ch, 3 turning ch.
row 2: 2 tr/dc in first st, (3 tr/dc, 1
ch, 3 tr/dc) in each 1 ch space
ending with 3 tr/dc in turning ch, 4
turning ch.
row 3: 2 d.tr/tr in first st, (3 d.tr/tr, 1
ch, 3 d.tr/tr) in each 1 ch space
ending with 3 d.tr/tr in turning ch,
4 turning ch.
row 4: 3 d.tr/tr in first st, (4 d.tr/tr, 2
ch, 4 d.tr/tr) in each 1 ch space
ending with 4 d.tr/tr in turning ch,
4 turning ch.
row 5: 4 d.tr/tr in first st, (5 d.tr/tr, 2
ch, 5 d.tr/tr) in each 2 ch space

ending with 5 d.tr/tr in turning ch,
4 turning ch.
row 6: (1 d.tr/tr, 1 ch) in first st
three times, 1 d.tr/tr in same st, ([1
d.tr/tr, 1 ch] five times, [1 ch, 1 d.tr/
tr] five times) in each 2 ch space
ending with (1 d.tr/tr, [1 ch, 1 d.tr/
tr] four times) in turning ch, 4
turning ch.
row 7: (1 d.tr/tr, [1 ch, 1 d.tr/tr] four
times) in first st, ([1 d.tr/tr, 1 ch] six
times, [1 ch, 1 d.tr/tr] six times) in
each 2 ch space ending with (1 d.tr/
tr, [1 ch, 1 d.tr/tr] five times) in
turning ch.

NOTE: this design is only suitable
for collars, cuffs as the pattern
curve develops with every row
worked

Published originally in Vogue Knitting, Butterick Company, instructions: page 181.

COLLARS, BRAIDS AND EDGINGS

9 chain

base row: work 5 tr/dc in ninth ch from hook, 5 turning ch.
row 1: 1 tr/dc in second st, 2 ch, 1 tr/dc in next st, 2 ch, miss 1 st, 1 tr/dc in next st, 2 ch, 5 tr/dc in 5 ch loop, 5 turning ch.
row 2: 1 tr/dc in second st, 2 ch, 1 tr/dc in next st, 2 ch, miss 1 st, 1 tr/dc in next st, 2 ch, 5 tr/dc in 5 ch loop, 5 turning ch.
repeat row 2

finish top and bottom edges by working a heading and a frill
heading
row 1: 2 tr/dc in each 5 ch loop, 5 ch to end of work, 2 tr/dc at end.
row 2: 5 ch, 1 tr/dc between the 2 tr/dc, * 2 ch, 1 tr/dc in 5 ch loop, 2 ch, 1 tr/dc between the 2 tr/dc; repeat from * to end or work, 1 tr/dc in last st.
frill
row 1: * 1 dc/sc in first 5 ch loop, 4 ch, (5 tr/dc, 2 ch, 5 tr/dc) in next 5 ch loop; repeat from * to end of work.
row 2: * 2 ch, 1 tr/dc on second tr/dc, 2 ch, 1 tr/dc in next st, 2 ch, miss 1 st, 1 tr/dc in next st, 2 ch, (1 tr/dc, 3 ch, 1 tr/dc) in 2 ch loop, 2 ch, 1 tr/dc in first st, 2 ch, miss 1 st, 1 tr/dc in next st, 2 ch, 1 tr/dc in next st, 2 ch, 1 dc/sc in 4 ch loop; repeat from * to end of work, 4 turning ch.
row 3: 1 dc/sc in space to left of first tr/dc, 4 ch, * 1 dc/sc in next tr/dc, 4 ch, 1 dc/sc in next tr/dc, 4 ch, (1 dc/sc, 4 ch, 1 dc/sc) in loop at point of frill, 4 ch, 1 dc/sc in next space, 4 ch, 1 dc/sc in next space, 4 ch, 1 dc/sc in space to right of dc/sc, 2 ch, 1 dc/sc in space to left of same dc/sc, 4 ch; repeat from * to end of work.

26 chain

base row: work 1 tr/dc in eighth ch from hook, 2 ch, miss 2 ch, 2 tr/dc in next ch, 3 ch, 2 tr/dc in next ch, 9 ch, miss 10 ch, 2 tr/dc in next ch, 3 ch, 2 tr/dc in next ch, leave last 2 ch unworked, 6 turning ch.
row 1: (1 tr/dc, 3 ch, 1 tr/dc) in 3 ch loop, 9 ch, (2 tr/dc, 3 ch, 2 tr/dc) in 3 ch loop, 1 tr/dc in last st, 2 ch, 1 tr/dc in turning ch, 5 turning ch.
row 2: 1 tr/dc in second tr/dc, 2 ch, (2 tr/dc, 3 ch, 2 tr/dc) in 3 ch loop, 9 ch, (2 tr/dc, 3 ch, 2 tr/dc) in 3 ch loop, (1 ch, 1 tr/dc) seven times in 6 ch loop, 1 ch, 1 dc/sc in last ch of foundation ch, 3 turning ch.
row 3: (1 dc/sc in 1 ch space, 1 ch) six times, 1 dc/sc in last space, (1 tr/dc, 3 ch, 1 tr/dc) in 3 ch loop, 9 ch, (2 tr/dc, 3 ch, 2 tr/dc) in 3 ch loop, 2 ch, 1 tr/dc in last st, 2 ch, 1 tr/dc in turning ch, 5 turning ch.
row 4: 1 tr/dc in second tr/dc, 2 ch, (2 tr/dc, 3 ch, 2 tr/dc) in 3 ch loop, 4 ch, 1 dc/sc round the 3 chains, 4 ch, (2 tr/dc, 3 ch, 2 tr/dc) in 3 ch loop, 6 turning ch.
repeat rows 1–4

5 chain

base row: work 3 tr/dc in fourth ch from hook, 3 ch, 3 tr/dc in last st, 3 turning ch.

row 1: (3 tr/dc, 3 ch, 3 tr/dc) in 3 ch loop, 2 ch, 1 tr/dc in last st, 5 turning ch.

row 2: 1 tr/dc in first st, 2 ch, (3 tr/dc, 3 ch, 3 tr/dc) in 3 ch loop, 3 turning ch.

row 3: (3 tr/dc, 3 ch, 3 tr/dc) in 3 ch loop, 2 ch, 1 tr/dc in last tr/dc, 2 ch, 1 tr/dc in centre st of turning ch, 5 turning ch.

row 4: 1 tr/dc on first st, 2 ch, 1 tr/dc in next st, 2 ch, 1 tr/dc in first tr/dc, 2 ch, (3 tr/dc, 3 ch, 3 tr/dc) in 3 ch loop, 3 turning ch.

row 5: (3 tr/dc, 3 ch, 3 tr/dc) in 3 ch loop, 2 ch, 1 tr/dc in last of 3 tr/dc, 5 turning ch.

repeat rows 2–5

finish the top of the edging by working * 3 tr/dc in each 3 ch turning ch, 3 ch; and work dc/sc round bottom edge.

13 chain

base row: work 1 dc/sc in sixth ch from hook, 2 ch, miss 3 ch, (2 tr/dc, 3 ch, 2 tr/dc) in next ch, 2 ch, miss 2 ch, 1 tr/dc in last ch, 5 turning ch.

row 1: (2 tr/dc, 3 ch, 2 tr/dc) in 3 ch loop, 10 ch, 1 dc/sc in turning ch.

row 2: 18 dc/sc in loop, (2 tr/dc, 3 ch, 3 tr/dc) in 3 ch loop, 2 ch, 1 tr/dc at end.

row 3: 2 ch, (2 tr/dc, 3 ch, 2 tr/dc) in 3 ch loop, 1 ch, 1 tr/dc in second tr/dc of group, (1 ch, miss next st, 1 tr/dc in next tr/dc) eight times.

row 4: (3 ch, 1 dc/sc) in 1 ch space of group eight times, 2 ch, (2 tr/dc, 3 ch, 2 tr/dc) in 3 ch loop, 2 ch, 1 tr/dc at end, 5 turning ch.

repeat rows 1–4 linking the scallop by working the 10 ch loop into the second 3 ch loop.

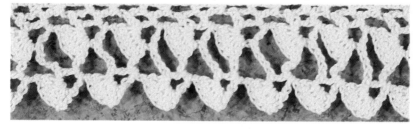

11 chain

row 1: 1 tr/dc in seventh ch from hook. 2 ch, (1 tr/dc, 3 ch, 1 tr/dc) in next ch, 4 ch, (1 tr/dc, 3 ch, 1 tr/dc) in last ch, 3 turning ch.

row 2: 5 tr/dc in first 3 ch loop, 4 ch, 6 tr/dc in next 3 ch loop, 2 ch, (1 tr/dc, 2 ch, 1 tr/dc) in turning ch, 5 turning ch.

row 3: 1 tr/dc in first 2 ch loop, 2 ch, (1 tr/dc, 3 ch, 1 tr/dc) in next loop, 4 ch, (1 tr/dc, 3 ch, 1 tr/dc) in 4 loop ch.

row 4: as row 2

repeat rows 3–4

COLLARS, BRAIDS AND EDGINGS

9 chain

row 1: join 9 ch with 1 dc/sc in first ch, 4 turning ch.
row 2: 12 d.tr/tr in 9 ch loop, 4 turning ch.
row 3: (1 tr/dc worked between the d.tr/tr, 1 ch) twelve times.
row 4: (4 ch, 1 dc/sc worked under the 1 ch of previous row) twelve times.
row 5: (6 ch, 1 dc/sc in second loop, of 4 ch of previous row, 4 turning ch.

row 6: 12 d.tr/tr in 6 ch loop, 4 turning ch.
row 7: (1 tr/dc worked between the d.tr/tr, 1 ch) twelve times, ending by joining to first scallop with a sc in fifth 4 ch loop.
row 8: (4 ch, 1 dc/sc worked under the ch of previous row) twelve times.
repeat from row 5

finish the top of the edging with * 1 tr/dc, 1 ch; repeat from * to end of work ending with 1 tr/dc.

14 chain

row 1: 1 tr/dc in eighth ch from hook, 1 tr/dc in each next 6 ch, 2 turning ch.
row 2: 1 tr/dc in third tr/dc, 1 ch, 1 tr/dc in fifth tr/dc, 1 ch, 1 tr/dc in seventh tr/dc, 4 ch, 7 tr/dc in loop, 4 turning ch.
row 3: 1 tr/dc in third tr/dc, 1 ch, 1 tr/dc in fifth tr/dc, 1 ch, 1 tr/dc in seventh tr/dc, 5 ch, 7 tr/dc in 4 ch loop, 1 d.tr/tr in first ch st at end of row, 2 turning ch.
row 4: as row 2
row 5: as row 3
row 6: 1 tr/dc in third tr/dc, 1 ch, 1 tr/dc in fifth tr/dc, 1 ch, 1 tr/dc in seventh tr/dc, 4 ch, 7 tr/dc in 5 ch loop, 9 ch, 1 sc in 4 ch of previous row.
7th row: 11 dc/sc in 9 ch loop, 1 ch, 1 tr/dc in third tr/dc, 1 ch, 1 tr/dc in fifth tr/dc, 1 ch, 1 tr/dc in seventh

tr/dc, 5 ch, 7 tr/dc in 4 loop ch, 1 d.tr/tr in first ch st at end of row, 2 turning ch.
row 8: 1 tr/dc in third tr/dc, 1 ch, 1 tr/dc in fifth tr/dc, 1 ch, 1 tr/dc in seventh tr/dc, 4 ch, 7 tr/dc in 5 ch loop, 1 d.tr/tr in first dc/sc, (2 ch, 1 d.tr/tr in next dc/sc) ten times, 1 d.tr/tr in sc of row 6, catch with a sc into 4 ch, 3 turning ch.
row 9: 1 dc/sc in second d.tr/tr, 5 ch, 1 sc in top thread of dc/sc just done, 1 dc/sc in 2 ch loop, (4 ch, 1 dc) in each next eight 2 ch loops, 2 ch, 1 dc/sc in last 2 ch loop, 1 dc/sc in d.tr/tr, 2 ch, 1 tr/dc in third tr/dc, 1 ch, 1 tr/dc in fifth tr/dc, 1 tr/dc in seventh tr/dc, 5 ch, 7 tr/dc in 4 ch loop, 1 d.tr/tr in first ch st at end of row.
NOTE on subsequent scallops, the 5 ch should be sl.st to preceding scallop then another 5 ch worked.
repeat rows 4–9

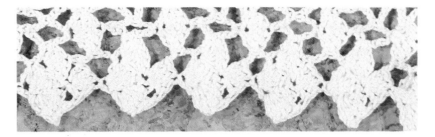

20 chain

base row: work 1 dc/sc in the eleventh ch from hook, miss 2 ch, 5 tr/dc in next ch, miss 2 ch, 1 dc/sc in next ch, 5 ch, miss 2 ch, 1 dc/sc in next ch, 3 turning ch.

row 1: 5 tr/dc in first st, 1 dc/sc in centre st of 5 ch, 5 ch, 1 dc/sc in centre st of 5 tr/dc, 5 ch, 1 dc/sc in third st of turning ch, 7 turning ch.

row 2: 1 dc/sc in centre st of 5 ch, 5 ch, 1 dc/sc in centre st of next 5 ch, 5 tr/dc in dc/sc, 1 dc/sc in centre st of 5 tr/dc, 5 tr/dc in corner st.

row 3: sl.st over first 2 tr/dc sts, 1 tr/dc in centre st of 5 tr/dc, 5 tr/dc in the dc/sc, 1 dc/sc in centre st of next 5 tr/dc, 5 ch, 1 dc/sc in centre st of next 5 ch, 5 ch, 1 dc/sc in third st of turning ch, 7 turning ch.

row 4: 1 dc/sc in centre st of 5 ch, 5 tr/dc in dc/sc, 1 dc/sc in centre st of 5 ch, 5 ch, 1 dc/sc in centre st of 5 tr/dc, 3 turning ch.

repeat rows 1–4

finish the open edge with * 1 tr/dc in end tr/dc st of fourth row, 3 ch, (1 tr/dc, 5 ch, 1 tr/dc) at point of scallop, 3 ch, 1 tr/dc in end tr/dc st of second row;

repeat from * until all scallops have been worked.

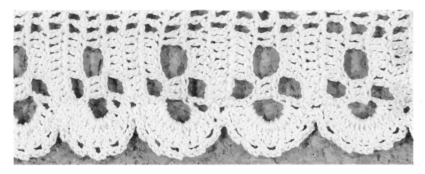

16 chain

row 1: work 1 tr/dc in fourth ch from hook, 1 tr/dc in each next 8 ch, 1 ch, miss 1 ch, 1 tr/dc in next ch, 1 ch, miss 1 ch, 1 tr/dc in last ch, 4 turning ch.

row 2: 1 tr/dc in second st, 1 ch, miss 1 ch, 1 tr/dc in each next 6 sts, 3 ch, miss 3 ch, 1 tr/dc in turning ch, 9 turning ch.

row 3: 3 tr/dc in 3 ch loop, 4 ch, miss 4 ch, 1 tr/dc in each next 2 sts, 1 ch, miss 1 ch, 1 tr/dc in next st, 1 ch, 1 tr/dc in second st of turning ch, 4 turning ch.

row 4: 1 tr/dc in second st, 1 ch, miss 1 ch, 1 tr/dc in each next 6 sts, 3 ch, miss 3 ch, 1 tr/dc in last st, 3 turning ch

row 5: 1 tr/dc in each next 9 sts, 1 ch, miss 1 ch, 1 tr/dc in next st, 1 ch, 1 tr/dc in second st of turning ch, 4 turning ch.

repeat rows 2–5

finish edging with

row 1: 1 dc/sc in corner of commencing ch, 2 ch, 1 dc/sc at corner of first row, * 13 tr/dc in 9 ch loop, 1 dc/sc at corner of fourth row, 2 ch, 1 dc/sc at corner of fifth row;

repeat from * to end of work.

row 2: * 1 dc/sc in 2 ch loop, 1 dc/sc in second st of 13 tr/dc, (3 ch, miss 1 st, 1 dc/sc in next st) five times, 3 ch; repeat from * to end of work.

COLLARS, BRAIDS AND EDGINGS

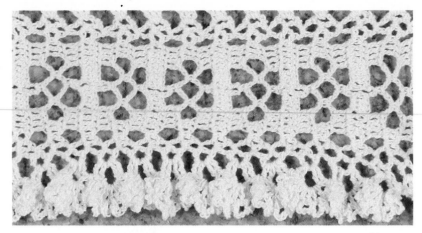

30 chain

base row: work 1 tr/dc on sixth ch from hook, 2 ch, 1 tr/dc in same ch, 1 ch, miss 1 ch, 1 dc/sc in next st, 1 ch, miss 1 ch, 1 tr/dc in each next 8 ch, 5 ch, miss 1 ch, 1 tr/dc in each next 8 ch, 1 ch, miss 1 ch, 1 dc/sc in next ch, 1 ch, miss 1 ch, (1 tr/dc, 2 ch, 1 tr/dc) in last ch, 5 turning ch.
row 1: (1 tr/dc, 2 ch, 1 tr/dc) in 2 ch loop, 2 ch, 1 tr/dc in next 4 sts, 5 ch, 1 dc/sc in 5 ch loop, 5 ch, 1 tr/dc in each last 4 tr/dc, 2 ch, (1 tr/dc, 2 ch, 1 tr/dc) in 2 ch, 5 turning ch.
row 2: (1 tr/dc, 2 ch, 1 tr/dc) in 2 ch loop, 1 ch, 1 dc/sc in next 2 ch loop, 1 ch, 1 tr/dc in each next 2 sts, 4 ch, 1 dc/sc in first 5 ch loop, 5 ch, 1 dc/sc in next 5 ch loop, 4 ch, 1 tr/dc in each last 2 tr/dc, 1 ch, 1 dc/sc in 2 ch loop, 1 ch, (1 tr/dc, 2 ch, 1 tr/dc) in last 2 ch loop, 5 turning ch.
row 3: (1 tr/dc, 2 ch, 1 tr/dc) in 2 ch loop, 2 ch, 1 tr/dc in each next 2 sts, 1 tr/dc in each next 2 ch, 5 ch, 1 dc/sc in 5 ch loop, 5 ch, 1 tr/dc in each

last 2 ch, 1 tr/dc in each 2 tr/dc, 2 ch, (1 tr/dc, 2 ch, 1 tr/dc) in 2 ch loop, 5 turning ch.
row 4: (1 tr/dc, 2 ch, 1 tr/dc) in 2 ch loop, 1 ch, 1 dc/sc in next 2 ch loop, 1 ch, 1 tr/dc in each next 4 sts, 1 tr/dc in each next 4 ch, 5 ch, 1 tr/dc in each last 4 ch, 1 tr/dc in each next 4 sts, 1 ch, 1 dc/sc in next 2 ch loop, 1 ch, (1 tr/dc, 2 ch, 1 tr/dc) in last 2 ch loop, 5 turning ch.
repeat rows 1–4

finish top and bottom edges by working a heading and a frill
heading
3 tr/dc in each 5 ch loop, 2 ch to end of work
frill.
row 1: (2 d.tr/tr, 3 ch, 2 d.tr/tr) in each 5 ch loop to end of work.
row 2: (1 tr/dc, [1 ch, 1 tr/dc] six times) in each 3 ch loop, 1 ch, to end of work.
row 3: (1 dc/sc, 5 ch) in each 1 ch space to end of work, 1 dc/sc at end.

8 chain

row 1: work 1 tr/dc in seventh ch from hook, 2 ch, 1 tr/dc in same ch, 2 ch, (1 tr/dc, 2 ch, 1 tr/dc) in last ch, 6 turning ch.
row 2: 1 tr/dc in second 2 ch space, (2 ch, 1 tr/dc in same space) three times, 7 ch, 1 dc/sc in loop at end, 4 turning ch.

row 3: 2 dc/sc in 7 ch loop, (4 ch, 2 dc/sc in same loop) twice, 4 ch, miss the first loop of 2 ch, 1 tr/dc in next, (2 ch, 1 tr/dc in same loop) three times, 6 turning ch.
repeat rows 2–3
finish top of edging with
* 5 ch, 1 dc/sc in loop; repeat from * to end of work.

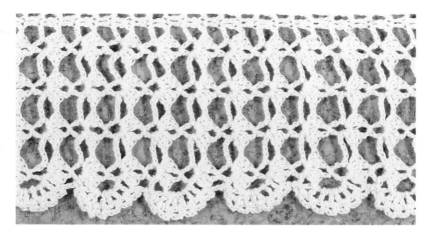

35 chain

base row: 1 tr/dc in third ch from hook, 1 ch, miss 1 ch, 1 tr/dc in each next 2 ch, 1 ch, miss 3 ch, 3 tr/dc in next ch, 3 ch, 3 tr/dc in next ch, (1 ch, miss 5 ch, 3 tr/dc in next ch, 3 ch, 3 tr/dc in next ch) three times, leave last 3 ch unworked, 3 turning ch.

row 1: (1 tr/dc, 3 ch, 1 tr/dc) in 3 ch loop, (5 ch, [1 tr/dc, 3 ch, 1 tr/dc in next 3 ch loop]) three times, 3 ch, 1 tr/dc in each two tr/dc, 1 ch, 1 tr/dc in last tr/dc, 1 tr/dc in turning ch, 3 turning ch.

row 2: 1 tr/dc in second tr/dc, 1 ch, 1 tr/dc in each next two tr/dc, (1 ch, [3 tr/dc, 3 ch, 3 tr/dc in 3 ch loop]) four times, (1 ch, 1 tr/dc) seven times in 6 ch loop, 1 sc in last ch of base row.

NOTE in future repeats, the sc is worked into the 3 ch loop of preceding pattern

row 3: (3 ch, 1 dc/sc in 1 ch loop) seven times, 3 ch, (1 tr/dc, 3 ch, 1 tr/dc) in 3 ch loop, (5 ch, [1 tr/dc, 3 ch, 1 tr/dc in 3 loop ch]) three times 3 ch, 1 tr/dc in each of 2 tr/dc, 1 ch, 1 tr/dc in tr/dc, 1 tr/dc in turning ch, 3 turning ch.

row 4: 1 tr/dc in second tr/dc, 1 ch, 1 tr/dc in each of 2 tr/dc, (1 ch, [3 tr/dc, 3 ch, 3 tr/dc in 3 ch loop]) four times, 3 turning ch.

repeat rows 1–4

multiple of 7+1, 3 turning ch

row 1: work 1 tr/dc in fourth ch from hook, * 1 ch, miss 1 ch, 1 tr/dc in next ch; repeat from * to end of row, 3 turning ch.

row 2: 1 dc/sc in first 1 ch space, * (9 ch, 1 sc in fifth ch to make a picot, 7 ch, 1 sc in fifth ch) twice, 1 ch, 1 sc in third ch from dc/sc, 3 ch, miss two 1 ch spaces, 1 dc/sc in next; repeat from * to end of row, 9 turning ch.

row 3: * 1 dc/sc in loop, 6 ch; repeat from * to end of row, 4 turning ch.

row 4: * 4 d.tr/tr in 6 ch loop, 3 ch; repeat from * to end of row, 3 turning ch.

row 5: 1 tr/dc on first d.tr/tr, 6 ch, 1 sc in fifth ch, (1 d.tr/tr, 6 ch, 1 sc in fifth ch) twice, 1 tr/dc on last d.tr/tr; repeat from * to end of row

COLLARS, BRAIDS AND EDGINGS

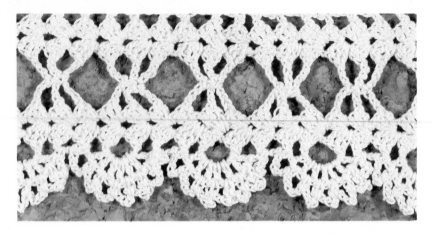

20 chain

base row: work 1 tr/dc in seventh ch from hook, 2 tr/dc in same ch, 2 ch, 3 tr/dc in next ch, 3 ch, miss 3 ch, 1 dc/sc in next ch, 3 ch, miss 3 ch, 3 tr/dc in next ch, 2 ch, 3 tr/dc in next ch, leave last 3 ch unworked, 6 turning ch.
row 1: (3 tr/dc, 2 ch, 3 tr/dc) in 2 ch loop, 3 ch, 1 dc/sc in dc/sc, 3 ch, (3 tr/dc, 2 ch, 3 tr/dc) in 2 ch loop, 1 ch, 1 tr/dc in second st of turning ch, 4 turning ch.
row 2: (3 tr/dc, 2 ch, 3 tr/dc) in 2 ch loop, 7 ch, (3 tr/dc, 2 ch, 3 tr/dc) in 2 ch loop, (1 ch, 1 tr/dc) seven times in 6 ch loop, 1 sc in last ch of base row.
row 3: (5 ch, 1 tr/dc) in each seven 1 ch spaces, 3 ch, (3 tr/dc, 2 ch, 3 tr/dc) in 2 ch loop, 3 ch, 1 dc/sc in centre st of 7 ch, 3 ch, (3 tr/dc, 2 ch, 3 tr/dc) in 2 ch loop, 1 ch, 1 tr/dc in

2nd st of turning ch, 4 turning ch.
row 4: (3 tr/dc, 2 ch, 3 tr/dc) in 2 ch loop, 3 ch, 1 dc/sc in dc/sc, 3 ch, (3 tr/dc, 2 ch, 3 tr/dc) in 2 ch loop, 6 turning ch.
row 5: (3 tr/dc, 2 ch, 3 tr/dc) in 2 ch loop, 7 ch, (3 tr/dc, 2 ch, 3 tr/dc) in 2 ch loop, 1 ch, 1 tr/dc in second st of turning ch, 4 turning ch.
row 6: (3 tr/dc, 2 ch, 3 tr/dc) in 2 ch loop, 3 ch, 1 dc/sc in centre st of 7 ch, 3 ch, (3 tr/dc, 2 ch, 3 tr/dc) in 2 ch loop, (1 ch, 1 tr/dc) seven times in 6 ch loop, 1 sc in 3 ch loop of row 3.
row 7: (5 ch, 1 tr/dc) in each seven 1 ch spaces, 3 ch, (3 tr/dc, 2 ch, 3 tr/dc) in 2 ch loop, 3 ch, 1 dc/sc in dc/sc, 3 ch, (3 tr/dc, 2 ch, 3 tr/dc) in 2 ch loop, 1 ch, 1 tr/dc in second st of turning ch, 4 turning ch.
Each scallop takes four rows but the 7 ch centre is worked every three rows.

multiple of 17+6, 2 turning ch

base row 1: 1 tr/dc in third ch from hook, * 1 ch, miss 1 ch, 1 tr/dc in next ch; repeat from * to end of row, 3 turning ch.
base row 2: as base row 1 but omitting turning ch.
row 1: sl.st along 7 sts, 8 ch, 1 sl.st in fourth st.
row 2: 16 tr/dc in 8 ch loop, sl.st last tr/dc to foundation strip.

row 3: (1 tr/dc, 1 ch) 15 times, 1 tr/dc, sl.st last st to foundation strip.
row 4: * 5 ch, 1 dc/sc in ch space; repeat to end, sl.st to foundation strip.
row 5: * 6 ch, 1 dc/sc in ch space; repeat to end, sl.st to foundation strip.

repeat from row 1 linking sections on row 5 by working 3 of first 6 ch, sl.st into previous scallop, 3 ch.

31 chain

base row: work 1 tr/dc in ninth ch
from hook, 3 ch, 1 tr/dc in next ch, 2
ch, miss 4 ch, 1 tr/dc in next ch, 1
ch, (1 tr/dc, 1 ch, 1 tr/dc) in next ch,
1 ch, 1 tr/dc in next ch, 1 ch, (1 tr/
dc, 1 ch, 1 tr/dc) in next ch, 1 ch, 1
tr/dc in next ch, 2 ch, miss 4 ch, 1 tr/
dc in next ch, 3 ch, 1 tr/dc in next
ch, 2 ch, miss 4 ch, 1 tr/dc in next
and last ch, 3 turning ch.
row 1: 1 tr/dc in first st, 2 ch, 7 tr/dc
in 3 ch loop, 2 ch, (1 dc/sc, 4 ch) in
second, third and fourth 1 ch space,
1 dc/sc in fifth 1 ch space, 2 ch, 7 tr/
dc in 3 ch loop, 2 ch, 12 tr/dc in loop
at end, 6 turning ch.
row 2: 1 dc/sc in fourth ch from
hook, 1 tr/dc in second tr/dc, (4 ch,
1 dc/sc in fourth ch from hook,
miss 1 tr/dc, 1 tr/dc in next) four

times, 2 ch, (1 tr/dc, 1 ch) in each
next 6 tr/dc, 1 tr/dc in seventh tr/
dc, 2 ch, (1 tr/dc, 3 ch, 1 tr/dc) in
centre 4 ch loop, 2 ch, (1 tr/dc, 1 ch)
in each next 6 tr/dc, 1 tr/dc in
seventh tr/dc, 2 ch, 1 tr/dc in last st,
1 tr/dc in turning ch, 3 turning ch.
row 3: 1 tr/dc in first st, 2 ch, (1 dc/
sc, 4 ch) in second, third and fourth
1 ch space, 1 dc/sc in next 1 ch
space, 2 ch, 7 tr/dc in 3 ch loop, 2
ch, (1 dc/sc, 4 ch) in second, third
and fourth 2 ch space, 1 dc/sc in
next 2 ch space, 9 turning ch.
row 4: (1 tr/dc, 3 ch, 1 tr/dc) in
centre 4 ch loop, 2 ch, 1 tr/dc in first
tr/dc, (1 ch, 1 tr/dc) in each next 6
tr/dc, 2 ch, (1 tr/dc, 3 ch, 1 tr/dc) in
centre 4 ch loop, 2 ch, 1 tr/dc in last
st, 1 tr/dc in turning ch.
repeat from row 1 but after the 12
tr/dc, work 1 sc in first picot.

multiple of 13, 3 turning ch

base row: work 1 tr/dc in third ch
from hook, * 1 tr/dc in each next 2
ch, 2 ch, 1 tr/dc in fourth and fifth
ch, (3 tr/dc, 3 ch, 3 tr/dc) in next ch,
3 ch, miss 5 ch; repeat from * to end
of row, 1 tr/dc in last ch, 3 turning
ch.
rows 1 and 2: * 3 tr/dc in 3 ch loop,

(3 tr/dc, 3 ch, 3 tr/dc) in 3 ch loop,
miss next 3 ch loop; repeat from * to
end of row ending with 1 tr/dc in
turning ch, 3 turning ch.
row 3: * 1 tr/dc in 3 ch loop, 1 ch, (2
d.tr/tr, [5 ch, 1 dc/sc in fifth ch, 2
d.tr/tr] four times) in 3 ch loop, 1
ch, miss 3 ch loop; repeat from * to
end of row, 1 tr/dc in turning ch.

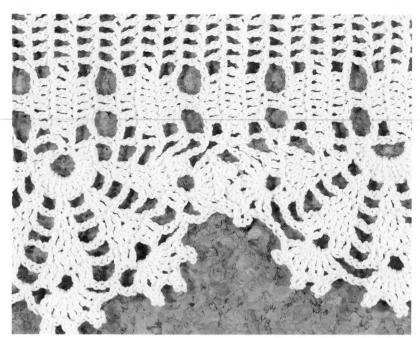

23 chain

base row: work 1 tr/dc in sixth ch
from hook, (1 ch, miss 1 ch, 1 tr/dc
in next ch) three times, 1 ch, miss 1
ch, 1 tr/dc in next 8 ch, 1 ch, miss 1
ch, 1 tr/dc in last ch, 5 turning ch.
row 1: miss first 3 tr/dc, 1 tr/dc in
each next 6 sts, miss next tr/dc, 2 ch
(1 tr/dc on tr/dc, 1 ch) four times,
miss 1 ch, 1 tr/dc in last ch, 4
turning ch.
row 2: 1 tr/dc on tr/dc, (1 ch, 1 tr/dc
on tr/dc) three times, 4 ch, 2 tr/dc in
each of centre 2 sts of 6 tr/dc group,
4 ch, 1 tr/dc in third ch of turning
ch, 5 turning ch.
row 3: miss 2 ch, 1 tr/dc in each
next 2 ch, 1 tr/dc in each 2 tr/dc, 1
tr/dc in each first 2 ch, 2 ch, 1 tr/dc
in tr/dc, (1 ch, 1 tr/dc in tr/dc) three
times, 1 ch, miss 1 ch, 1 tr/dc in
next ch, 4 turning ch.
row 4: 1 tr/dc in tr/dc, (1 ch, 1 tr/dc
in tr/dc) three times, 1 ch, miss 1
ch, 1 tr/dc in next ch, 1 tr/dc in each
next 6 tr/dc, 1 tr/dc in next ch, 1 ch,
1 tr/dc in 3rd ch of turning ch, 4
turning ch.
row 5: as row 1
row 6: as row 2
row 7: as row 3
row 8: as row 4 and for the scallop,
8 ch, 1 sc to join to end of 7th row, 2
ch, 1 sc to join to end of 6th row.
row 9: 15 tr/dc in 8 ch loop, 1 tr/dc
in tr/dc, 2 ch, 1 tr/dc in each next 6
centre sts of 8 tr/dc group, 2 ch, 1 tr/
dc on tr/dc, (1 ch, 1 tr/dc on tr/dc) 3
times, 1 ch, miss 1 ch, 1 tr/dc in last
ch, 5 turning ch.
row 10: as row 2 except that the last
tr/dc is worked on a tr/dc and for
the scallop, 2 ch, miss 2 tr/dc, 2 tr/
dc in next st, 2 ch, miss 2 sts, 2 tr/dc
in next st, 2 ch, miss 1 st, 2 tr/dc in
next st, 2 ch, miss 1 st, 2 tr/dc in
next st, 2 ch, miss 2 sts, 2 tr/dc in
next st, 2 ch, and join with 1 sc to
end of fifth row, sl.st along 2 ch to
end of fourth row, 3 turning ch.
row 11: 3 tr/dc in 2 tr/dc, (3 ch, 3 tr/
dc in 2 tr/dc) four times, 3 ch, 1 tr/
dc in tr/dc, 2 ch, 6 tr/dc, the centre 2
sts are worked in the 2 tr/dc of
previous row, 2 ch, 1 tr/dc in tr/dc,
(1 ch, 1 tr/dc on tr/dc) three times, 1
ch, miss 1 ch, 1 tr/dc in next ch, 4
turning ch.
row 12: as 4th row except that the
last tr/dc is worked on a tr/dc and
for the scallop, (4 ch, 4 tr/dc in 3 tr/
dc) five times, 4 ch, 1 sc at end of
third row, sl.st. along 2 ch to get to
end of second row, 4 turning ch.
row 13: 6 tr/dc in the 4 tr/dc, (4 ch, 4
tr/dc in 4 tr/dc) four times, 4 ch, 1
tr/dc in tr/dc, 2 ch, 6 tr/dc in centre
6 tr/dc, 2 ch, (1 ch, 1 tr/dc in tr/dc)
three times, 1 ch, miss 1 ch, 1 tr/dc
in next ch, 4 turning ch.
row 14: as row 2 except that the tr/
dc is worked in a tr/dc and for the
scallop, (4 ch, 1 tr/dc in each next 3
tr/dc of group, 3 ch, 1 tr/dc in each
last 3 tr/dc of group) five times, 4

ch, 1 sc in end of 1st row, sl.st along 2 ch st to end of base row, 3 turning ch.

row 15: * 2 d.tr/tr in 3 ch loop, (5 ch, 1 dc in fifth ch from hook, 2 d.tr/tr in same 3 ch loop) three times, 3 ch, 1 dc/sc in 4 ch loop, 3 ch, * repeat from *–* four times, 3 ch, 1 tr/dc in 1 tr/dc, 2 ch, 6 tr/dc the centre 2 sts worked in the 2 tr/dc of previous row, 2 ch, 1 tr/dc on tr/dc, (1 ch, 1 tr/dc on tr/dc) three times, 1 ch, miss 1 ch, 1 tr/dc in last ch, 4

turning ch.

this practically finishes one scallop

row 16: 1 tr/dc in tr/dc, (1 ch, 1 tr/dc in tr/dc) three times, 1 ch, miss 1 ch, 1 tr/dc in each next 8 sts. 1 ch, miss 1 ch, 1 tr/dc in tr/dc, 5 turning ch.

repeat rows 1–16

the scallops are joined by linking the first 2 picots to the 2 corresponding picots of the preceding scallop.

9 chain

row 1: work 1 tr/dc in eighth ch from hook, 2 ch, 1 tr/dc in same ch, 2 ch, (1 tr/dc, 2 ch, 1 tr/dc) in last ch, 5 turning ch.

row 2: 1 tr/dc in centre 2 ch space, (2 ch, 1 tr/dc) three times in same

space, 5 turning ch.

repeat row 2

finish the bottom edge with 9 tr/dc in each 5 loop ch.

finish the top edge with * 2 dc/sc in each 5 loop ch, 4 ch; repeat from * to end of work.

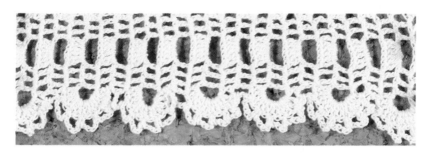

20 chain

row 1: work 1 tr/dc in the seventh ch from hook, (1 ch, miss 1 ch, 1 tr/dc in next ch) twice, 2 tr/dc in each next 2 ch, (1 tr/dc in next st, 1 ch, miss 1 ch) three times, 1 tr/dc in last st, 7 turning ch.

row 2: 1 tr/dc in first 1 ch space, (1 ch, 1 tr/dc in next 1 ch space) twice, 4 ch, (1 tr/dc in next 1 ch space, 1 ch) twice, 1 tr/dc in second st of turning ch, 1 tr/dc in next st, 4 turning ch.

row 3: (1 tr/dc in next 1 ch space, 1 ch) twice, 6 tr/dc in 4 ch loop, (1 ch, 1 tr/dc in next 1 ch space) twice, 1 ch, 12 tr/dc in 7 ch loop at end and catch with a sc in last st of commencing ch, 5 turning ch.

row 4: 1 dc/sc in second st, (5 ch, miss 1 st, 1 dc/sc on next st) five times, 1 ch, (1 tr/dc in next 1 ch space, 1 ch) twice, 1 tr/dc in next 1 ch space, 4 ch, (1 tr/dc in next 1 ch space, 1 ch) twice, 1 tr/dc in first st of turning ch, 1 tr/dc in next st, 4 turning ch.

row 5: (1 tr/dc in next 1 ch space, 1 ch) twice, 6 tr/dc in 4 ch loop, 1 ch, (1 tr/dc in next 1 ch space, 1 ch) twice, 1 tr/dc in first loop of 5 ch, 7 turning ch.

row 6: as row 2

row 7: as row 3

but after working the 12 tr/dc, work a sc into the st of 5 ch close to the tr/dc st.

row 8: as row 4

repeat rows 5–8

Medallions and Quilt Squares

Simple through to complex squares and rounds, completed separately and then linked together

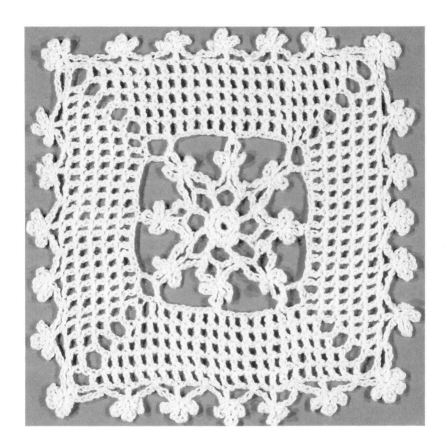

base ring: 16 ch and join with sl.st.
1st round: 1 ch, 24 dc/sc in ring, sl.st to first st.
2nd round: 1 ch, 1 dc/sc in same place, * 4 ch, half work 1 tr.tr/d.tr in each next 2 sts and finish together, in top of st just made work a set of 3 leaves thus: ([8ch, 1 qt.tr/q.tr, 7 ch, 1 dc/sc, 8 ch, 1 s.tr/qt.tr, 8 ch, 1 dc/sc, 7 ch, 1 qt.tr/q.tr, 7 ch, sl.st], 4 ch, 1 dc/sc in next st of first round, 7 ch, miss 2 sts, 1 dc/sc in next st) repeat from * three more times

omitting final dc at end of last repeat, sl.st to first dc/sc. Fasten off.
3rd round: rejoin yarn at tip of second leaf then in top of the 8 ch before the s.tr/qt.tr, 1 ch, 1 dc/sc in same place, * 2 ch, miss s.tr/qt.tr, 1 dc/sc in next ch, 5 ch, then in tip of third leaf of same set in the same way work 1 dc/sc before and after the qt.tr/q.tr, 7 ch, in tip of first leaf of next group, 1 dc/sc before and after the qt.tr/q.tr, 5 ch, in tip of second leaf of same group, 1 dc/sc

MEDALLIONS AND QUILT SQUARES

before s.tr/qt.tr; repeat from * 3 more times omitting final dc at end of last repeat, sl.st to first dc/sc.

4th round: 1 ch, 1 dc/sc in same place, * 3 dc/sc in next 2 ch space, 1 dc/sc in next st, 1 dc/sc in each next 5 ch, 1 dc/sc in each next 2 sts, 1 dc/sc in each next 7 ch, 1 dc/sc in each next 2 dc/sc, 1 dc/sc in each next 5 ch, 1 dc/sc in next dc/sc; repeat from * three more times omitting final dc/sc at end of last repeat, sl.st to first dc/sc.

5th round: sl.st along each first 2 dc/sc to corner, 4 ch, 1 tr/dc in corner place, * ([1 ch, miss 1 st, 1 tr/dc in next st] 13 times to next corner, [1 ch, 1 tr/dc, 1 ch, 3 tr/dc, 1 ch, 1 tr/dc] in corner st); repeat from * twice, (1 ch, miss 1 st, 1 tr/dc in next st) 13 times to corner, 1 ch, sl.st to third ch of 4 ch.

6th round: 4 ch, 1 tr/dc in same place, * ([1 ch, 1 tr/dc in next ch space] 15 times, 1 ch, [1 tr/dc, 1 ch, 1 tr/dc, 1 ch, 1 tr/dc] in next corner); repeat from * twice, (1 ch, 1 tr/dc in next ch space) fifteen times, 1 ch, 1 tr/dc in corner st, 1 ch, sl.st to third ch of 4 ch.

7th round: 3 ch, 1 tr/dc in same place, * 1 ch, (1 tr/dc in next ch space, 1 tr/dc in next tr/dc, 1 ch, miss 1 ch, 1 tr/dc in next tr/dc, 1 tr/dc in next ch space, 1 ch, miss 1 tr/dc) 5 times, 1 tr/dc in next ch space, 1 tr/dc in next tr/dc, 1 ch, miss 1 ch, 1 tr/dc in next tr/dc, 1 tr/dc in next ch space, 1 ch, 3 tr/dc in corner st; repeat from * twice, 1 ch, (1 tr/dc in next ch space, 1 tr/dc in next tr/dc, 1 ch, miss 1 ch, 1 tr/dc in next tr/dc, 1 tr/dc in next ch space, 1 ch, miss 1 tr/dc) five times, 1 tr/dc in next ch space, 1 tr/dc in next tr/dc, 1 ch, miss 1 ch, 1 tr/dc in next tr/dc, 1 tr/dc in next 1 ch space, 1 ch, 1 tr/dc in corner st, sl.st to top of 3 ch.

8th round: 4 ch, 1 tr/dc in same place, * (1 tr/dc in next tr/dc, [1 ch, miss 1 ch, 1 tr/dc in each next 2 sts] 13 times to next corner st, 1 ch, [1 tr/dc, 1 ch, 1 tr/dc] in same place as last tr/dc); repeat from * twice, 1 tr/dc in next tr/dc, (1 ch, miss 1 ch, 1 tr/dc in each next 2 sts) 13 times, 1 ch, sl.st to third ch of 4 ch.

9th round: 1 ch, 2 dc/sc in same place, 1 dc/sc in each ch space and each tr/dc but working 3 dc/sc in each first 3 corners and 1 dc/sc in last corner, sl.st to first dc/sc.

10th round: 5 ch, (half work 2 tr.tr/d.tr and finish together, 2 ch, half work 3 tr.tr/d.tr and finish tog) in same place, * 5 ch, miss 4 sts, half work 3 tr.tr/d.tr in next st and finish together, ([5 ch, miss 4 sts, half work 3 tr.tr/d.tr in next st and finish together] six times, 5 ch, miss 4 sts, [half work 3 tr.tr/d.tr and finish together, 2 ch, half work 3 tr.tr/d.tr and finish together] in next corner); repeat from * twice, (5 ch, miss four sts, half work 3 tr.tr/d.tr in next st and finish together) seven times, 5 ch, miss four sts, sl.st to top of cluster.

11th round: sl.st to next ch, 8 ch, 1 dc/sc in fifth ch from hook, 1 tr/dc in same 2 ch space, (5 ch, 1 picot [1 dc/sc in fifth ch from hook]), * 1 tr/dc in next cluster, (picot, miss 2 ch, 1 tr/dc in next ch, picot, miss 2 ch, 1 tr/dc in next cluster) eight times, (1 picot; [1 tr/dc, 1 picot] twice in two ch space at corner); repeat from * twice, 1 tr/dc in next cluster, [picot, miss 2 ch, 1 tr/dc in next ch, picot, 2 ch, 1 tr/dc in next cluster] eight times, 1 picot, sl.st to third of 8 ch.

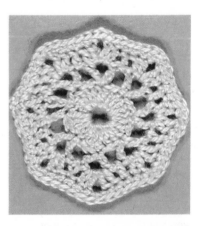

base ring: work 6 ch, join with sl.st.

1st round: 2 ch, 23 tr/dc in ring, sl.st to top of 2 ch.

2nd round: 4 ch, 1 tr/dc in same st, 1 ch, (miss 2 sts, [1 tr/dc, 2 ch, 1 tr/dc] in same st, 1 ch) seven times, sl.st to second st of 4 ch.

3rd round: 2 ch, (1 tr/dc, 2 ch, 1 tr/dc) in first 2 ch sp, (1 tr/dc in 1 ch sp, [2 tr/dc, 2 ch, 2 tr/dc] in 2 ch sp) seven times, 1 tr/dc in last 1 ch sp, sl.st to top of 2 ch.

4th round: 1 dc/sc in each st and 2 dc/sc in each 2 ch sp to end of round, sl.st to first single dc/sc.

base ring: 12 ch, join with sl.st.
1st round: 4 ch, 23 d.tr/tr in ring, sl.st'to first ch.
2nd round: 6 ch, (1 tr/dc in each next 3 sts, 3 ch) seven times, 1 tr/dc in last 2 sts, sl.st to third ch.
3rd round: 3 ch, (2 tr/dc, 3 ch, 3 tr/dc) in first 3 ch space, (1 ch, [3 tr/dc, 3 ch, 3 tr/dc] in next 3 ch space) seven times, 1 ch, sl.st to top of ch.
4th round: 3 ch, (2 tr/dc, 3 ch, 3 tr/dc) in first 3 ch space, (3 ch, [3 tr/dc, 3 ch, 3 tr/dc] in next 3 ch space) seven times, 3 ch, sl.st to top of ch.
5th round: 3 ch, (2 tr/dc, 1 ch, 3 tr/dc) in first 3 ch space, ([2 ch, 1 dc/sc, 2 ch] in next 3 ch space, [3 tr/dc, 1 ch, 3 tr/dc] in next 3 ch space) seven times, (2 ch, 1 dc/sc, 2 ch) in last 3 ch space, sl.st to top of ch and next 2 tr/dc.
6th round: (1 dc/sc in each 1 ch space, 5 ch, a five loop puff st in dc/sc, 5 ch) 8 times, sl.st to dc/sc.
7th round: 3 ch, 8 tr/dc in each 5 ch space, sl.st to top of ch.
8th round: 1 ch, 1 dc/sc in same place, (5 ch, 2 tr/dc between 8 tr/dc group, 5 ch, 1 dc/sc between next group, 5 ch, [2 d.tr/tr, 3 ch, 2 d.tr/tr]

in space above the puff st, 5 ch, 1 dc/sc between next group) four times ending last group with the 5 ch, sl.st to dc/sc.
9th round: 1 ch, 1 dc/sc in same place, (1 dc/sc in each next 15 ch and sts, 1 tr/dc in each next 4 ch, 1 tr/dc in d/tr/tr, (3 tr/dc, 3 ch, 3 tr/dc) in 3 ch space, 1 d.tr/tr in tr/dc, 1 tr/dc in each next 4 ch, 1 dc/sc in each next 2 ch and st) four times ending last group with 2 dc/sc, sl.st to last st.
10th round: 3 ch, 1 tr/dc in each st of previous row and (2 tr/dc, 3 ch, 2 tr/dc) in each 3 ch corner loop, sl.st to top of ch.
11th round: 5 ch, miss 1 st, (1 tr/dc in each next 2 sts, 2 ch, miss 2 sts) 6 times, (3 tr/dc, 3 ch, 3 tr/dc) in corner loop, ([2 ch, miss 2 sts, 1 tr/dc in each next 2 sts] nine times, 2 ch, (3 tr/dc, 3 ch, 3 tr/dc) in corner loop) three times, (2 ch, miss 2 sts, 1 tr/dc in each next 2 sts) twice, 2 ch, miss 2 sts, 1 tr/dc in next st, sl.st to third ch.
12th round: 3 ch, 1 tr/dc in every st and ch with (2 tr/dc, 3 ch, 1 tr/dc) in each corner loop, sl.st to top of ch.

MEDALLIONS AND QUILT SQUARES

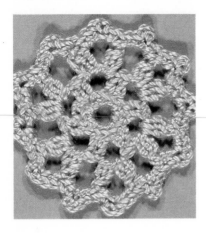

base ring: work 7 ch, join with sl.st.
1st round: 1 ch, 12 dc/sc into ring, join with sl.st into first dc/sc, 3 ch.
2nd round: 1 tr/dc in next st, (3 ch, 1 tr/dc in each next 2 sts) five times, 3 ch, join with sl.st to top of 3 ch.
3rd round: sl.st along next tr/dc and next ch, 3 ch, tr/dc2tog in same 3 ch loop (half work 2 tr/dc and finish the 2 sts together), 4 ch, tr/dc3tog in same loop, (4 ch [tr/dc3tog, 4 ch, tr/dc3tog] in next loop) five times, 4 ch, join with sl.st to top of first cluster.
4th round: 1 ch, (2 dc/sc, 3 ch, 2 dc/sc in each loop) twelve times, join with sl.st to first dc/sc.

sts, 2 tr/dc in loop, 4 ch) three times, 2 tr/dc in loop, 1 tr/dc in each next 3 sts, 1 tr/dc in loop that began the sequence, join with sl.st to 3rd ch of 7 ch.
3rd round: sl.st in next ch, 7 ch, (2 tr/dc in loop, 1 tr/dc in each next seven sts, 2 tr/dc in loop, 4 ch) three times, 2 tr/dc in loop, 1 tr/dc in next 7 sts, 1 tr/dc in loop that began the sequence, join with sl.st to 3rd ch of 7 ch.
4th round: sl.st in next ch, 7 ch, (2 tr/dc in loop, 1 tr/dc in each next eleven sts, 2 tr/dc in loop, 4 ch) three times, 2 tr/dc in loop, 1 tr/dc in next 11 sts, 1 tr/dc in loop that began the sequence, join with sl.st to 3rd ch of 7 ch.

base ring: work 4 ch, join with sl.st.
1st round: 4 ch, (1 tr/dc, 1 ch) eleven times into ring, join with sl.st to 3rd ch of 4 ch.
2nd round: 3 ch, tr/dc2tog in same place (half work 2 tr/dc and finish the 2 sts together), (3 ch, tr/dc3tog in ch loop) eleven times, 3 ch, join with sl.st to top of first cluster.
3rd round: sl.st in first ch, 1 ch, 1 dc/sc in loop, (5 ch, 1 dc/sc in next loop) eleven times, 2 ch, join with 1 tr/dc in first dc/sc.
4th round: 1 ch, 1 dc/sc in same place (5 ch, 1 dc/sc in next loop, 1 ch, [5 tr/dc, 3 ch, 5 tr/dc] in next loop, 1 ch, 1 dc/sc in next loop) four times but omitting the final dc/sc in the last group worked and joining the work with a sl.st in first dc/sc.

base ring: work 4 ch, join with sl.st.
1st round: 5 ch, (3 tr/dc in ring, 2 ch) three times, 2 tr/dc in ring, join with sl.st to 3rd ch of 5 ch.
2nd round: sl.st in next ch, 7 ch, (2 tr/dc in loop, 1 tr/dc in each next 3

base ring: work 8 ch, join with sl.st.
1st round: 3 ch, a 4 tr popcorn in ring, (5 ch, a 5 tr/dc popcorn in ring) three times, 5 ch, sl.st to top of popcorn.
2nd round: 3 ch, ([2 tr/dc, 2 ch, a 5 tr/dc popcorn, 2 ch, 2 tr/dc] in 5 ch sp, 1 tr/dc in popcorn) three times, (2 tr/dc, 2 ch, a 5 tr/dc popcorn, 2 ch, 2 tr/dc) in last 5 ch sp, sl.st to top of 3 ch.
3rd round: 3 ch, 1 tr/dc in each next 2 sts, (2 tr/dc in 2 ch sp, 2 ch, a 5 tr/dc popcorn, 2 ch, 2 tr/dc in 2 ch sp, 1 tr/dc in next 5 sts) three times, 2 tr/dc in 2 ch sp, 2 ch, a 5 tr/dc popcorn, 2 ch, 2 tr/dc in 2 ch sp, 1 tr/dc in each last 2 sts, sl.st to top of 3 ch.
4th round: 3 ch, 1 tr/dc in each next 4 sts, (2 tr/dc in 2 ch sp, 2 ch, a 5 tr/dc popcorn, 2 ch, 2 tr/dc in 2 ch sp, 1 tr/dc in each next 9 sts) three times, 2 tr/dc in 2 ch sp, 2 ch, a 5 tr/dc popcorn, 2 ch, 2 tr/dc in 2 ch sp, 1 tr/dc in each last 4 sts, sl.st to top of 3 ch.

base ring: work 6 ch, join with sl.st.
1st round: 2 ch, 1 tr/dc in ring, (1 ch, 4 tr/dc in ring) three times, 1 ch, 2 tr/dc in ring.
2nd round: sl.st to first 1 ch sp, 2 ch, (2 tr/dc, 2 ch, 3 tr/dc) in same sp, (1 ch, 3 tr/dc, 2 ch, 3 tr/dc) in next three 1 ch spaces, 1 ch, sl.st to top of 2 ch.
3rd round: sl.st to first 2 ch sp, 3 ch, (3 d.tr/tr, 3 ch, 4 d.tr/tr) in same sp, (2 ch, 4 d.tr/tr in 1 ch sp, 2 ch, [4 d.tr/tr, 3 ch, 4 d.tr/tr] in 2 ch sp) 3 times, 2 ch, 4 d.tr/tr in last 2 ch sp, 2 ch, sl.st to top of 3 ch.
4th round: sl.st to first 2 ch sp, 3 ch, (3 d.tr/tr, 3 ch, 4 d.tr/tr) in same sp,

([2ch, 4 d.tr/tr in 2 ch sp] twice, [4 d.tr/tr, 3 ch, 4 d.tr/tr in 3 ch sp]) three times, (2 ch, 4 d.tr/tr in 2 ch sp) twice, sl.st to top of 3 ch.
5th round: 1 dc/sc in each st and 3 dc/sc in each 3 ch space to end, sl.st to first dc/sc.

base ring: work 6 ch, join with sl.st.
1st round: 3 ch, tr/dc2tog in ring, (3 ch, tr/dc3tog in ring) seven times, 3 ch, sl.st to top of first cluster.
2nd round: sl.st to centre of first 3 ch sp, 1 ch, 1 dc/sc in same place, (5 ch, 1 dc/sc in next sp) seven times, 2 ch, 1 tr/dc in first dc/sc.
3rd round: (5 ch, [tr/dc3tog, 3 ch, tr/dc3tog in next sp], 5 ch, 1 dc/sc in next space) three times, 5 ch, (tr/dc3tog, 3 ch, tr/dc3tog) in next sp, 2 ch, 1 tr/dc into tr/dc.
4th round: (5 ch, 1 dc/sc in next sp, 5 ch, [1 dc/sc, 5 ch, 1 dc/sc] in corner 3 ch sp, 5 ch, 1 dc/sc in next 5 ch sp) four times, sl.st to first ch.

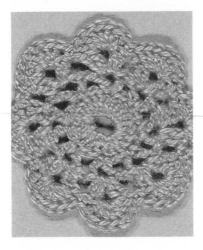

base ring: work 6 ch, join with sl.st.
1st round: 2 ch, 23 tr/dc in ch, sl.st to top of 2 ch.
2nd round: 4 ch, 1 tr/dc in same place, 1 ch, (miss 2 sts, [1 tr/dc, 2 ch, 1 tr/dc] in next st, 1 ch) seven times, sl.st to second ch of 4 ch.
3rd round: 2 ch, (1 tr/dc, 2 ch, 2 tr/dc) in 2 ch sp, (1 ch, [2 tr/dc, 2 ch, 2 tr/dc] in next 2 ch sp) seven times, 1 ch, sl.st to top of 2 ch.
4th round: ([7 tr/dc in 2 ch sp] eight times, 1 dc/sc in 1 ch sp) eight times, sl.st to first st.

next 5 sts, 2 ch, 1 tr/dc in next st, 2 ch) three times, sl.st to top of 3 ch.

base ring: work 6 ch, join with sl.st.
1st round: 3 ch, 15 tr/dc in ring, sl.st to top of 3 ch.
2nd round: 3 ch, 2 tr/dc in same st, (2 ch, miss 1 st, 1 tr/dc in next st, 2 ch, miss 1 st, 3 tr/dc in next st) three times, 2 ch, miss 1 st, 1 tr/dc in next st, 2 ch, sl.st to top of 3 ch.
3rd round: 3 ch, 5 tr/dc in centre st, 1 tr/dc in next st, 2 ch, 1 tr/dc in next tr/dc, 2 ch, (1 tr/dc in next st, 5 tr/dc in centre st, 1 tr/dc in last st, 2 ch, 1 tr/dc in next st, 2 ch) three times, sl.st to top of 3 ch.
4th round: 3 ch, 1 tr/dc in each next 2 sts, 5 tr/dc in centre st, 1 tr/dc in each next 3 sts, 2 ch, 1 tr/dc in next st, 2 ch, (1 tr/dc in each next 3 sts, 5 tr/dc in centre st, 1 tr/dc in each next 3 sts, 2 ch, 1 tr/dc, 2 ch) three times, sl.st to top of 3 ch.
5th round: 3 ch, 1 tr/dc in each next 4 sts, 5 tr/dc in centre st, 1 tr/dc in each last 5 sts, 2 ch, 1 tr/dc in next st, 2 ch, (1 tr/dc in each next 5 sts, 5 tr/dc in centre st, 1 tr/dc in each

base ring: work 8 ch, join with sl.st.
1st round: 1 ch, 12 dc/sc in ring, sl.st to first dc.
2nd round: 6 ch, miss 1 st, (1 d.tr/tr in next st, 2 ch) eleven times, sl.st to third ch of 6 ch.
3rd round: 5 ch, ([1 dc/sc in next sp, 2 ch] twice, [3 tr/dc, 2 ch, 3 tr/dc] in next sp, 2 ch) [1 dc/sc in next sp, 2 ch] twice) three times, 3 tr/dc, 2 ch, 2 tr/dc in last sp, sl.st to third ch of 5 ch.
4th round: 1 ch, ([1 dc/sc in next sp, 2 ch] three times, [3 tr/dc, 2 ch, 3 tr/dc] in corner sp, 2 ch) four times, sl.st to first dc.
5th round: 1 ch, ([1 dc/sc in first st, 2 dc/sc in 2 ch sp] three times, 1 dc/sc in next each 3 sts, 3 dc/sc in corner sp, 1 dc/sc in next each 3 sts, 2 dc/sc in 2 ch sp) four times, join with sl.st to first dc/sc.

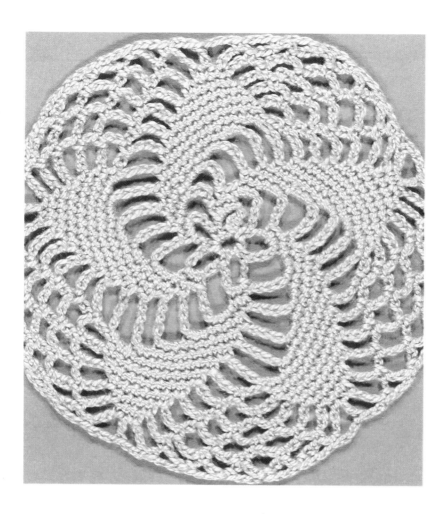

base ring: work 5 ch, join with sl.st.
1st round: (6 ch, 1 dc/sc in ring) five times.
NB it is helpful to mark the last dc/sc of each round with contrast thread.
2nd round: (6 ch, 3 dc/sc in 6 ch loop) five times.
3rd round: (6 ch, 3 dc/sc in 6 ch loop, 1 dc/sc in each next 2 dc/sc) five times.
4th round: (6 ch, 3 dc/sc in 6 ch loop. 1 dc/sc in all but last dc/sc of group) five times.
5th to 7th rounds: as 4th round ending with 5 sections, each of 13 dc/sc.
8th round: (5 ch, 1 dc/sc in centre of loop, 5 ch, miss 1 dc/sc, 1 dc/sc in all but last dc/sc) five times.
9th round: ([5 ch, 1 dc/sc in next loop] twice, 5 ch, miss 1 dc/sc, 1 dc/sc in all but last dc/sc) five times.
10th round: ([5 ch, 1 dc/sc in next loop] three times, 5 ch, miss 1 dc/sc, 1 dc/sc in all but last dc/sc) five times.
11th round: ([5 ch, 1 dc/sc in next loop] four times, 5 ch, miss 1 dc/sc, 1 dc/sc in all but last dc/sc) five times.
12th round: ([5 ch, 1 dc/sc in next loop] five times, 5 ch, miss 1 dc/sc, 1 dc/sc in all but last dc/sc) five times.
13th round: 5 ch, 1 dc/sc in next loop, ([3 ch, 1 dc/sc in next loop] five times, 3 ch, 1 tr/dc in second of next 3 dc/sc, 3 ch, 1 dc/sc in next loop) five times but omitting dc/sc at end of last repeat, sl.st to first dc/sc.

MEDALLIONS AND QUILT SQUARES

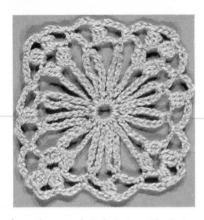

base ring: work 6 ch, join with sl.st.
1st round: 1 ch, (1 dc/sc in ring, 15 ch) twelve times, sl.st to first dc.sc.
2nd round: sl.st to centre of first 15 ch loop, (3 ch, tr/dc2tog, 4 ch, tr/dc3tog in same loop), ([4 ch, 1 dc/sc in next loop] twice, 4 ch, [tr/dc3tog, 4 ch, tr/dc3tog in next loop]) three times, (4 ch, 1 dc/sc in next loop) twice, 4 ch, sl.st to first cluster.
3rd round: sl.st to next sp, 3 ch, tr/dc2tog in same sp, 4 ch, tr/dc3tog in same space, (4 ch, 1 dc/sc in next sp, 4 ch, tr/dc3tog in next sp, 4 ch, 1 dc/sc in next sp, 4 ch, [tr/dc3tog, 4 ch, tr/dc3tog] in next sp) three times, 4 ch, 1 dc/sc in next sp, 4 ch, tr/dc3tog in next sp, 4 ch, 1 dc/sc in last st, 4 ch, join with sl.st to first cluster.

times, 3 ch, sl.st to top of 3 ch.
4th round: 3 ch, 1 tr/dc in each next 4 tr/dc, (3 ch, 1 dc/sc in 3 ch sp, 3 ch, 1 tr/dc in each next 5 tr/dc) five times, 3 ch, 1 dc/sc in last sp, 3 ch, join with sl.st to top of 3 ch.
5th round: 3 ch, half work 1 tr/dc in each next 4 tr/dc and finish tog. ([5 ch, 1 dc/sc in next sp] twice, 5 ch, half work 1 tr/dc in each next 5 tr/dc and finish tog) five times, (5 ch, 1 dc/sc in next sp) twice, 5 ch, sl.st to first cluster.
6th round: sl.st into each next 3 ch, 1 ch, 1 dc/sc in same place, (5 ch, 1 dc/sc in next 5 ch sp) seventeen times, 5 ch, sl.st to first dc/sc.
7th round: sl.st into each next 3 ch, 1 ch, 1 dc/sc in same ch, (5 ch, 1 dc/sc in next 5 ch sp, 3 ch, [5 tr/dc, 3 ch, 5 tr/dc] in next sp, 3 ch, 1 dc/sc in next sp) five times, 5 ch, 1 dc/sc in next 5 ch sp, 3 ch, [5 tr/dc, 3 ch, 5 tr/dc] in next sp, 3 ch, sl.st to first dc/sc.

base ring: work 6 ch, join with sl.st.
1st round: (4 tr/dc, 1 ch in ring) four times, sl.st to second ch of 6 ch.
2nd round: (4 tr/dc, 1 ch, 4 tr/dc, 1 ch in each 1 ch sp) four times, sl.st to ch.
3rd round: ([4 tr/dc, 1 ch, 4 tr/dc, 1 ch] in corner sp, [4 tr/dc, 1 ch] in each 1 ch sp to next corner) four times, sl.st to ch.
4th round: ([4 tr/dc, 1 ch, 4 tr/dc] in corner loop, 4 tr/dc in each 1 ch sp) four times, sl.st to ch.

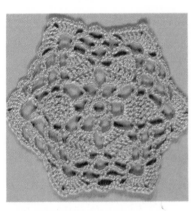

base ring: work 6 ch, join with sl.st.
1st round: 1 ch, 12 dc/sc in ring, sl.st to first dc/sc.
2nd round: 1 ch, 1 dc/sc in same place as ch, (7 ch, miss 1 st, 1 dc/sc in next st) five times, 3 ch, miss 1 dc/sc, 1 d.tr/tr in top of first dc/sc.
3rd round: 3 ch, 4 tr/dc round d.tr/tr, (3 ch, 5 tr/dc in 7 ch sp) five

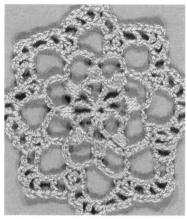

base ring: work 6 ch, join with sl.st.
1st round: 6 ch, (1 d.tr/tr in ring, 2 ch) 7 times, sl.st to 4th ch of 6ch.
2nd round: 2 ch, h.tr/h.dc4tog in next sp, (7 ch, h.tr/h.dc5tog in next sp) seven times, 7 ch, sl.st. to first cluster.
3rd round: sl.st in each next 3 ch, 1 ch, 3 dc/sc in same sp, (9 ch, 3 dc/sc in next sp) seven times, 8 ch, 1 dc/sc in first dc/sc.
4th round: 3 ch, tr/dc2tog into next dc and next ch (missing dc/sc between), (2 ch, miss 1 ch, 1 tr/dc in next ch, 2 ch, miss 1 ch, [1 tr/dc, 3 ch, 1 tr/dc] in next ch, 2 ch, miss 1 ch, 1 tr/dc in next ch, 2 ch, miss 1 ch, [tr/dc3tog in next ch, second dc/sc and next ch]) seven times, 2 ch, miss 1 ch, 1 tr/dc in next ch, 2 ch, miss 1 ch, [1 tr/dc, 3 ch, 1 tr/dc] in next ch, 2 ch, miss 1 ch, 1 tr/dc in next ch, 2 ch, sl.st to top of first cluster.

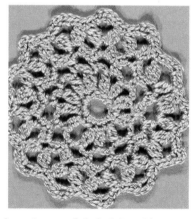

base ring: work 8 ch, join with a sl.st.
1st round: 1 ch, 12 dc/sc in ring, join with a sl.st to first dc/sc.
2nd round: 3 ch, 1 tr/dc in same

place as 3 ch, (3 ch, tr/dc2tog) in next st eleven times, (half work 2 tr/dc and finish the 2 sts together), 4 ch, join with a sl.st to first cluster.
3rd round: sl.st in each next 2 ch, 1 ch, 1 dc/sc in same place as 1 ch, (4 ch, 1 dc/sc in next loop) eleven times, 4 ch, sl.st to first dc/sc.
4th round: 1 ch, (2 dc/sc, 3 ch, 2 dc/sc in 4 ch loop) twelve times, join with a sl.st to first cluster.
5th round: 3 ch, tr/dc2tog in loop, 4 ch, tr/dc3tog in same loop, (tr/dc3tog, 4 ch, tr/dc3tog in next loop) eleven times, join with sl.st to first cluster.
6th round: 1 ch, 1 dc/sc in same place as 1 ch, (2 dc/sc, 3 ch, 2 dc/sc) in next loop, 1 dc/sc between two clusters) eleven times, (2 dc/sc, 3 ch, 2 dc/sc) in last loop, join with sl.st to first dc/sc.

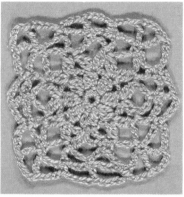

base ring: work 4 ch, join with sl.st.
1st round: 1 ch, 8 dc/sc in ring, sl.st to first dc/sc.
2nd round: 3 ch, tr/dc2tog in first st, (3 ch, tr/dc3tog in next st) seven times, 3 ch, sl.st to top of cluster.
3rd round: 3 ch, 1 tr/dc in first st, (miss 3 ch, [tr/dc2tog, 5 ch, tr/dc2tog] in next cluster) seven times, tr/dc2tog in last cluster, 5 ch, sl.st to top of 3 ch.
4th round: sl.st to next cluster, 7 ch, (1 dc/sc in 5 ch sp, 4 ch, miss 1 cluster, 1 tr/dc in next cluster, 4 ch) seven times, 1 dc/sc in next sp, 4 ch, sl.st. to 3rd ch of 7 ch.
5th round: 1 ch, 1 dc/sc in same place as ch, (4 ch, miss 4 ch, [1 d.tr/tr, 4 ch, 1 d.tr/tr] in next dc/sc, 4 ch, miss 4 ch, 1 dc/sc in next tr/dc, 4 ch, miss 4 ch, 1 h.tr/h.dc in next dc/sc, 4 ch, miss 4 ch, 1 dc/sc in next tr/dc) four times ending last repeat by omitting last dc/sc and joining with sl.st to first dc/sc.

MEDALLIONS AND QUILT SQUARES

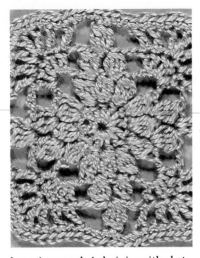

base ring: work 4 ch, join with sl.st.
1st round: 3 ch, 11 tr/dc in ring, join
with sl.st to top of 3 ch.
2nd round: 3 ch, h.tr/h.dc3tog in
same place as 3 ch, (1 ch, h.tr/
h.dc4tog in next st) twice, (5 ch,
[h.tr/h.dc4tog in next st, 1 ch twice,
1 h.tr/h.dc4tog in next st]) three
times, 4 ch, sl.st to top of cluster.
h.dc3tog in same sp, 1 ch, h.tr/
h.dc4tog in next sp, (2 ch, 5 tr/dc in
5 ch sp, 2 ch, h.tr/h.dc4tog in next
sp, 1 ch, h.tr/h.dc4tog in next sp) 3
times, 2 ch, 5 tr/dc in 5 ch sp, 2 ch,
sl.st to top of cluster.
4th round: sl.st to next sp, 3 ch, h.tr/
h.dc3tog in same sp, 3 ch, (1 tr/dc
in next st, 1 ch, 1 tr/dc in next st, 1
ch, [1 tr/dc, 1 ch, 1 tr/dc, 1 ch, 1 tr/
dc] in next st, 1 ch, 1 tr/dc in next st,
1 ch, 1 tr/dc in next st, 3 ch, 1 h.tr/
h.dc4tog in 1 ch sp, 3 ch) four
times, sl.st to top of cluster.
5th round: 1 ch, 1 dc/sc in each st
and ch working 3 dc/sc in centre st
of corner groups, sl.st to first dc/sc.

base ring: work 8 ch, join with sl.st.
1st round: 1 ch, (1 dc/sc in ring, 3 ch,
1 d.tr/tr in ring, 3 ch) eight times,
sl.st to first st.
2nd round: sl.st into each next 3 ch
and into first d.tr/tr, (12 ch, 1 tr/dc
in ninth ch from hook, 3 ch, sl.st to
top of next d.tr/tr) eight times.
3rd round: sl.st into each next 4 ch, 3
ch, ([1 h.tr/h.dc, 7 dc/sc, 1 h.tr/h.dc]
in next 8 ch loop, 1 tr/dc in next tr/
dc, miss last 3 ch of next and first 3
ch of following section, 1 tr/dc in
next ch) six times, [1 h.tr/dc, 7 dc, 1
h.tr/dc in last 8 ch loop, 1 tr/dc in

next tr/dc, miss last 3 ch of next and
first 3 ch of following section, sl.st
to top of 3 ch.
4th round: 1 ch, 1 dc/sc inserting
hook under sl.st which joined 3rd
round, ([3 ch, miss 1 h.tr/h.dc and 1
dc/sc, 1 dc/sc in next dc/sc, 3 ch,
miss 1 dc/sc, [1 dc/sc, 4 ch, 1 dc/sc]
in next dc/sc, 3 ch, miss 1 dc/sc, 1
dc/sc in next dc/sc, 3 ch, miss [1 dc/
sc, 1 h.tr/h.dc, 1 tr/dc], 1 dc/sc
between the 2 tr/dc, miss 1 tr/dc)
seven times, 3 ch, miss 1 h.tr/h.dc in
1 dc/sc, 1 dc/sc in next dc/sc, 3 ch,
miss 1 dc/sc, [1 dc/sc, 4 ch, 1 dc/sc]
in next dc/sc, 3 ch, miss 1 dc/sc, 1
dc/sc in next dc/sc. 3 ch, miss [1 dc/
sc, 1 h.tr/h.dc, 1 tr/dc, sl.st to first
dc/sc.

base ring: work 6 ch, join with sl.st.
(central rose motif).
1st round: 4 ch, 1 dc/sc in second ch,
(4 ch, 1 dc/sc in next ch) five times,
4 ch, join with sl.st to 4 ch.
2nd round: (1 dc/sc, 4 tr/dc, 1 dc/sc)
in each loop six times.
3rd round: (back of work) 3 ch, 1 dc/
sc in next dc/sc of 2nd round, (3 ch,
1 dc/sc in back of second dc/sc of
each group of round 2) five times,
to make 6 loops.
4th round: (1 dc/sc, 6 tr/dc, 1 dc/sc)
in each loop.
5th round: (back of work) 4 ch, 1 dc/
sc in back of work as for round 3 to
make 6 loops.
6th round: (1 dc/sc, 7 tr/dc, 1 dc/sc)
in each loop.
7th round: (back of work) 5 ch 1 dc/
sc in back of work as for round 3 to
make 6 loops.
8th round: (1 dc/sc, 8 tr/dc, 1 dc/sc)
in each loop.

9th round: (back of work) 5 ch worked loosely, 1 dc/sc in back of work as for round 3 to make 6 loops.

10th round: (1 dc/sc, 9 tr/dc, 1 dc/sc) in each loop.

11th round: (back of work) 6 ch, 1 dc/sc in back of work as for round 3 to make 6 loops.

row 12: (1 dc/sc, 10 tr/dc, 1 dc/sc) in each loop.

This completes the rose motif.

Leaf section

first mark positions for leaves by marking positions for 8 leaves evenly spaced then work 5 ch, 1 dc/sc at back of rose to form 8 loops.

For each leaf spray, work * 1 dc/sc in loop, 8 ch, 1 dc/sc in second st from hook, 5 tr/dc in next 5 sts, 1 dc/sc in lst st*, 9 ch, 1 dc/sc in second st from hook, 5 tr/dc in next 5 sts, 1 dc/sc in second st from hook, 5 tr/dc, 1 dc/sc, 1 dc/sc in lower part of first leaf, work from * to * once more for third leaf then 3

ch, 1 dc/sc into next loop, 3 ch, begin next leaf spray from *. When four sprays are down, fasten off. Join thread again at tip of a middle leaf

1st round: 3 dc/sc in this leaf, (8 ch, 1 dc/sc in next leaf, 8 ch, 1 dc/sc in next leaf, 8 ch, 3 dc/sc in corner leaf) repeat until last corner is reached and sl.st last ch to dc/sc.

2nd round: 1 dc/sc in each ch, each dc/sc and 3 dc/sc in centre corner st.

3rd & 4th rounds: as 2nd round.

5th round: * (1 tr/dc in centre corner st, 1 ch, 1 tr/dc in same st), 1 ch, miss 1 ch, 1 tr/dc in next st until second corner is reached; repeat from * to end of work.

6th round: * 1 dc/sc in first tr/dc of corner, 3 dc/sc in 1 ch sp, 1 dc/sc in second tr/dc of corner, (5 ch, 1 dc/sc in st nearest hook, 3 tr/dc in next 3 sts, miss 1 tr/dc of border, 1 dc/sc in next tr/dc) until second corner is reached; repeat from * to end of work.

MEDALLIONS AND QUILT SQUARES

base ring: work 12 ch, join with sl.st.

1st round: 1 ch, 18 dc/sc into ring, join with sl.st to first dc/sc.

2nd round: 1 ch, starting at same st as 1 ch (1 dc/sc, 3 ch, miss 2 sts) six times, join with sl.st to first dc/sc.

3rd round: 1 ch, (1 dc/sc, 3 ch, 5 tr/dc, 3 ch, 1 dc/sc) in each loop six times, join with sl.st to first dc/sc.

4th round: 1 ch, (1 dc/sc worked between 2 dc/sc group, 5 ch behind 5 tr/dc group of previous round) six times, join with sl.st to first dc/sc.

5th round: 1 ch, (1 dc/sc, 3 ch, 7 tr/dc, 3 ch, 1 dc/sc) in 5 ch loop six times, join with sl.st to first dc/sc.

6th round: 1 ch, (1 dc/sc between 2 dc/sc, 6 ch behind 7 tr/dc group of previous round) six times, join with sl.st to first dc/sc.

7th round: sl.st to next ch, 3 ch, (4 tr/dc, 2 ch, 1 tr/dc) in first loop, 6 tr/dc in next loop, (2 tr/dc, 2 ch, 4 tr/dc) in next loop, (5 tr/dc, 2 ch, 1 tr/dc) in next loop, 6 tr/dc in next loop, (2 tr/dc, 2 ch, 4 tr/dc) in last loop, join with sl.st to top of 3 ch.

8th round: 3 ch, 1 tr/dc in each next 4 sts, (3 tr/dc, 2 ch, 3 tr/dc) in 2 ch space, (1 tr/dc in each next 9 sts, [3 tr/dc, 2 ch, 3 tr/dc] in 2 ch space), three times, 1 tr/dc in each last 4 sts, join with sl.st to top of 3 ch.

9th round: 1 ch, 1 dc/sc in same st, (1 dc/sc in next st, 3 ch picot closed with sl.st in same st) twice, 1 dc/sc in each next 3 sts, [3 ch picot in same st, 1 dc/sc in next st] twice, [1 dc/sc, 7 ch, 1 dc/sc] in 2 ch loop, [1 dc/sc in next st, 3 ch picot in same st] twice, 1 dc/sc in each next 3 sts, [3 ch picot in same st, 1 dc/sc in next st] twice, 1 dc/sc in each next 2 sts) four times ending the last repeat with 1 dc/sc in each next 3 sts, [3 ch picot, 1 dc/sc in next st] twice, 1 dc/sc in last st, join with sl.st to first dc/sc of round.

10th round: sl.st to top of 3 ch picot, 1 dc/sc in same loop, 5 ch, 1 dc/sc in first of next picot group, 5 ch, (1 dc/sc, 5 ch, 1 dc/sc) in 7 ch loop, ([5 ch, 1 dc/sc in second picot of group] twice, [5 ch, 1 dc/sc in first picot of group] twice, 5 ch, [1 dc/sc, 5 ch, 1 dc/sc in 7 ch loop]) three times, (5 ch, 1 dc/sc in second picot of group) twice, 5 ch, join with sl.st to first dc/sc.

base ring: work 6 ch, join with sl.st.

1st round: 1 ch, 16 dc/sc in ring, sl.st to first dc/sc.

2nd round: 6 ch, miss 2 sts (1 tr/dc in next st, 3 ch, miss 1 st) seven times, sl.st to third ch of 6 ch.

3rd round: 1 ch, (1 dc/sc, 1 h.tr/h.dc, 5 tr/dc, 1 h.tr/h.dc, 1 dc/sc in 3 ch sp) eight times, sl.st to first dc/sc.

4th round: 1 ch, (1 dc/sc between 2 dc/sc, 6 ch behind 9 st group) eight times, sl.st to first dc/sc.

5th round: 1 ch, (1 dc/sc, 1 h.tr/h.dc, 6 tr/dc, 1 h.tr/h.dc, 1 dc/sc in 6 ch sp) eight times, sl.st to first dc/sc.

6th round: sl.st to second tr/dc of group, 1 ch, 1 dc/sc in same place as ch, 6 ch, miss 2 tr/dc, 1 dc/sc in next tr/dc, (6 ch, 1 dc/sc in second tr/dc of next group, 6 ch, miss 2 tr/dc, 1 dc/sc in next tr/dc) seven times, 3 ch, 1 tr/dc in first dc/sc.

7th round: 3 ch, 3 tr/dc over the 1 tr/dc, (4 ch, [1 dc/sc in 6 ch sp, 6 ch] twice, 1 dc/sc in 6 ch sp, 4 ch, [4 tr/dc, 4 ch, 4 tr/dc] in next 6 ch sp) three times, 4 ch, (1 dc/sc in next 6 ch sp, 6 ch) twice, 1 dc/sc in next 6 ch sp, 4 ch, 4 tr/dc in last space, 4 ch, sl.st to top of 3 ch.

base ring: work 6 ch, join with sl.st.
1st round: 4 ch, (1 tr/dc in ring, 1 ch) eleven times, join with sl.st to third ch of 4 ch.
2nd round: sl.st to next ch, 3 ch, tr/dc3tog in same sp, (2 ch, tr/dc4tog in next sp, 3 ch, 1 d.tr/tr in next tr/dc, 3 ch, tr/dc4tog in next sp, 2 ch, tr/dc4tog in next sp) four times but omitting the last tr/dc4tog in final sequence, sl.st to top of first cluster.
3rd round: 1 ch, 1 dc/sc in same sp, (2 ch, miss next 2 ch sp, 4 tr/dc in 3 ch sp, 2 ch, 1 d.tr/tr in d.tr/tr, 3 ch, hook into top of d.tr/tr and sl.st, 2 ch, 4 tr/dc in next 3 ch sp, 2 ch, miss next 2 ch sp, 1 dc/sc in next cluster) four times but omitting the last dc/sc in final sequence, sl.st to first dc/sc.

into ring, 1 ch, 1 h.tr/h.dc in top of first cluster, 3 ch.
2nd round: tr2tog in loop made by h.tr/h.dc, (3 ch, [tr/dc3tog, 3 ch, tr/dc3tog] in next space) five times, 3 ch, tr/dc3tog in last space, 1 ch, 1 h.tr/h.dc in top of last cluster, 3 ch.
3rd round: tr/dc2tog in loop made by h.tr/h.dc, (3 ch, [tr/dc3tog, 3 ch, tr/dc3tog] in next space, 3 ch, tr/dc3tog in next space) five times then (3 ch, [tr/dc3tog, 3 ch, tr/dc3tog] in last space) 1 ch, 1 h.tr/h.dc in top of first cluster, 3 ch.
4th round: 1 tr/dc in loop made by h.tr/h.dc, (3 tr/dc in next space, [3 tr/dc, 2 ch, 3 tr/dc] in next space, 3 tr/dc in next space) five times, then 3 tr/dc in next space, (3 tr/dc, 2 ch, 3 tr/dc) in next space, 1 tr/dc in last space, join with sl.st to top of third ch.
5th round: 1 ch, 1 dc/sc in same place, 1 dc/sc in each st and each ch joining at end of round with a sl.st in first dc/sc.

base ring: work 6 ch, join with sl. st.
1st round: 3 ch, tr/dc2tog (half work 2 tr/dc and finish the 2 sts together) into ring, (3 ch, tr/dc3tog) 5 times

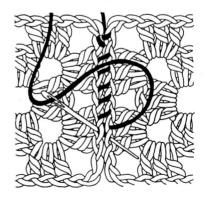

Techniques

Getting Started

Tools and Yarns

Standard crochet hooks are made from aluminium, plastic or bone, from 15cm to 20cm in various lengths and between 2mm to 25mm in diameter. Some have handles which some crocheters find easier to use. Steel crochet hook for finer work are available in sizes from 0.60mm to 2.50mm.

Tunisian crochet hooks are longer, usually about 30cms with a knob at one end and a hook at the other, in sizes from 2mm upwards. Many of the yarns currently used for knitting are equally suited to crochet work though boucle and nubby yarns can cause problems especially when several stitches have to be worked together. The size, the twist and the finish of yarns must be considered when choosing a yarn and the yarn must be appropriate for the design to be worked. A tightly twisted yarn gives a firm finish while a long haired yarn will give a soft, fluffy finish. Fine yarns are best suited to delicate lace work while thick heavy yarns work best with bolder designs.

Practically all crochet work begins with a chain foundation.

1

Making a chain

To work a chain, first make a slip loop [fig 1]. Hold the yarn in the left hand and make a loop with the right hand. Hold the loop in place between the thumb and forefinger of the left hand. Take hold of the crochet hook in the right hand and insert it through the loop and under the yarn.

2

With the right hand catch the long end of yarn, [fig 2]. If you find it more comfortable hold the crochet hook between thumb and middle finger resting the forefinger near

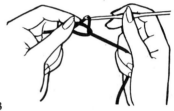

3

the tip of the hook. Draw the loop through and leaving the hook in the yarn, pull the short end to close the loop round the hook, [fig 3].

4

Loop the yarn round the little finger, across the palm and behind the forefinger of the left hand. Pull the yarn gently so that it lies round the fingers firmly, [fig 4]. Catch the

5

knot of the loop between the thumb and forefinger, [fig 5]. Pass the hook under the yarn and catch the yarn with the hook. This is called 'yarn over hook' (yoh). Draw

6

the yarn through the loop on the hook to make one chain, [fig 6]. Continue in this way until the foundation chain is the desired length. The last loop on the hook is NOT counted as a stitch.

Basic Stitches

Chain (ch)

This is the foundation of crochet work. With yarn in position and the loop on the hook as shown in fig 5 and 6, pass the hook under the yarn held in the left hand and catch yarn with hook [fig 7], draw yarn

7

through loop on hook, repeat this action until chain is the desired length [fig 8].

8

Slip Stitch
(sc or sl.st/sc or ss)

Put the hook into the stitch to left of the hook, yarn over hook and draw through a loop, draw this loop through loop on the hook [fig 9]. When a number of chains have

9

to be joined into a circle, the circle is closed with a slip stitch [fig 10].

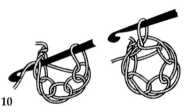

10

Double Crochet/Single Crochet
(dc)   (sc)

Begin with 1 chain for turning then put the hook into the second stitch

11

to left of hook, yarn over hook, [fig 11] draw through a loop, (2 loops on hook), [fig 12], yarn over hook

12

and draw through 2 loops on hook, (1 loop remains on hook), [fig 13].

13

Continue working each stitch this way omitting the turning chain.

TECHNIQUES

Half Treble/Half Double Crochet
(h.tr)   (h.dc)

Begin with 2 chains for turning then yarn over hook [fig 14], put hook into third stitch to left of hook, yarn over hook and draw through a loop, (3 loops on hook), yarn over hook, [fig 15] draw yarn through all loops on hook, (1 loop remains on hook), [fig 16]. Continue working each stitch this way

18

through 2 loops on hook, yarn over hook, [fig 19] and draw yarn

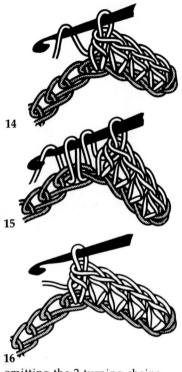

14

15

16

19

through remaining 2 loops, (1 loop remains on hook), [fig 20]. Continue working each stitch this way · omitting the 3 turning chains.

omitting the 2 turning chains.
Treble/Double Crochet
(tr)   (dc)

Begin with 3 chains for turning then, yarn over hook, [fig 17], put

20

Double Treble/Treble
(d.tr)   (tr)

Begin with 4 chains for turning then yarn over hook twice, put hook into fifth stitch to left of hook, yarn over hook and draw through a loop, (4 loops on hook), [fig 21],

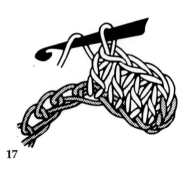

17

hook into fourth stitch to left of hook, yarn over hook and draw through a loop, (3 loops on hook), yarn over hook, [fig 18] and draw

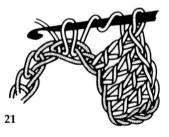

21

yarn over hook and draw through 2 loops on hook, yarn over hook and draw through next 2 loops on hook, yarn over hook and draw through remaining 2 loops, (1 loop remains on hook). Continue working each stitch this way omitting the 4 turning chains.

Triple Treble/Double Treble
(t.tr)   (d.tr)

Begin with 5 chains for turning then yarn over hook three times,

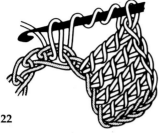

22

put hook into sixth stitch to left of hook yarn over hook and draw through a loop, (5 loops on hoop), [fig 22], (yarn over hook and draw through next 2 loops) four times, (1 loop remains on hook). Continue working each stitch this way omitting the 5 turning chains.

Quadruple Treble/Triple Treble
(q.tr)   (t.tr)

Begin with 6 chains for turning then yarn over hook four times, put hook into seventh stitch to left of hook, yarn over hook and draw through a loop, (6 loops on hook),

23

[fig 23], (yarn over hook and draw through next 2 loops) five times, (1 loop remains on hook). Continue working each stitch this way omitting the 6 turning chains.

Basic Stitches for Filet Crochet

Filet crochet designs are worked on a mesh usually made from a combination of treble/double crochet and chain stitches. The ground mesh is made by working 1 tr/dc, 1 ch, miss 1 st, and repeating this to end of work or by working 1 tr/dc, 2 ch, miss 2 sts for a wider

mesh. The spaces are filled by working 1 tr/dc in 1 ch space, 2 tr/dc in 2 ch spaces, a multiple of 2+1, 3+1 respectively. Start the ground

24

25

mesh with 4 turning ch (this forms the first tr/dc and 1 ch space) or 5 turning ch (this forms the first tr/dc and 2 ch space), [figs 24 and 25].

The instructions for filet crochet designs are most often given in the form of a chart where the squares to be filled in are shown in the form of a *, a x or a ● while the mesh ground is shown as an open square. This has the happy result that many embroidery and tapestry patterns can be worked in filet crochet. When a chart is being used it must be remembered that you are always looking at the right side of the work so even number rows must be read from left to right.

Although filet crochet is formed from two basic stitches there are two other constructions that should be noted. These are bars and lacets worked over 2 squares of the mesh. A bar is formed by working 5 chain stitches, missing 5 chains or a lacet then working 1 tr/dc into next st. A lacet is made by working 3 chain stitches, missing 2 stitches, 1 dc/sc in next stitch, 3 chain, miss 2 stitches, 1 tr/dc in the next stitch, [fig 26].

26

Basic Method for Tunisian Crochet

Tunisian crochet patterns are worked rather differently to standard crochet. A special hook is needed, longer than the usual crochet hook and looking more like a knitting needle with a knob at one end, a hook at the other. Once the foundation chain has been worked, all the stitches are worked AND KEPT ON THE HOOK to the end of the row. Then the stitches are worked back until there is just one stitch on the hook. Many Tunisian crochet patterns start with the same two starting rows. These come from the first two rows of Standard/Simple Tunisian stitch.

Standard/Simple Tunisian Stitch.

Start with a foundation chain with the number of stitches required.
row 1 (outward): put hook into second chain from hook, yarn over hook, draw loop through and leave on hook, * hook into next ch, yarn over hook, draw loop through and leave on hook; repeat from * to end of row.
row 2 (return): without turning the work, yarn over hook, draw through a loop, * yarn over hook and draw through 2 loops on hook; repeat from * to end of work, 1 turning ch.
row 3 (outward): miss first loop, * put hook into next loop, yarn over

27

hook and draw through a loop; repeat from * to end of work.
row 4 (return): as row 2 (return). [fig 27].

Decorative Stitches

Picots
Picots are made from 3, 4 or 5 chain stitches according to the size of picot required. The final chain is joined to the work by working a dc/sc into the first chain [fig 28].

28

Puffs
The illustration shows a line of puff stitches worked on a multiple of 2. To make a puff, yarn over hook, put hook into stitch to be worked and draw yarn up 1cm (⅜ins), (yarn over hook, hook into same stitch and draw yarn up) three times, yarn over hook and draw through all loops [fig 29]. An extra chain

29

30

stitch can be worked to close the puff more firmly.
Clusters
These are usually worked with tr/dc or d.tr/tr stitches. Two or more stitches are worked in the same stitch leaving the loop of each on

31

the hook then the cluster is finished by taking the yarn over the hook and drawing it through all loops, [figs 30, 31]. An extra chain can be worked to close them firmly. Clusters can also be worked over more than one stitch, [fig 32].

32

Popcorns

Work one chain, then the stated number of stitches, (in fig 33, 5 tr/

33

dc). Take the final loop of the last stitch worked from the hook and put the hook into the one chain before the group of stitches, then into the dropped loop and draw the yarn through.

Bullion Stitch

Yarn over hook the required number of times, usually up to 10 times, hook into stitch, yarn over hook and draw loop through, yarn over hook and draw through all loops on hook, (one at a time if this is easier), finish by working a chain to close the stitch.

Spikes

These are made by taking the hook below the row previously worked. A loop is drawn through and up to the height of the current row and the stitch is then finished normally. A spiked cluster is made by drawing loops through a sequence of sts, yarn over hook and drawing through all loops, 1 ch to close the cluster. If a sequence of spiked clusters is to be worked, the next cluster is made by first putting the hook into the loop which closed the previous cluster then working the number of spikes required.

Relief Stitches

These are worked by taking the hook round the stem of a stitch.

A relief front tr/dc (r.f.tr/dc) is made by wrapping the yarn over the hook, taking the hook from the front and from right to left round the stitch to be worked and then completing the stitch normally.

A relief back tr/dc (r.b.tr/dc) is made by wrapping the yarn over the hook, taking the hook from the back and from right to left round the stitch to be worked and then completed normally.

Crossed Stitches

One method is to miss a stitch, work the given stitch in the next st and then the given stitch in the missed st. Another method makes a crossed stitch which is separate from its pair. Again, miss 1 stitch, work the given stitch in the next st and with the hook behind the stitch just worked, put it into the missed stitch and work the given stitch.

X and Y Stitches

These are worked on the longer crochet stitches without actually crossing them.

Using a double treble/treble stitch, yarn over hook twice and put hook into stitch, yarn over hook and draw a loop through, yarn over hook and draw through 2 loops (3 loops on hook), yarn over hook and put hook into given stitch, yarn over hook, draw loop through, yarn over hook and draw through 2 loops (two 'legs' made), (yarn over hook and draw through 2 loops) three times, (λ) shape made. Work number of chains required to begin to work the second arm. Yarn over hook, put hook into the centre of the λ and draw loop through, (yarn over hook and draw through 2 loops) twice. This completes the X shape.

Methods of Working Crochet

Crochet can be worked in rows or in rounds.

When working in rows it is necessary to work extra chain stitches to bring the hook and yarn up to the level of the next row to be worked. The work is turned, as in knitting, to start the next row. When this forms the first stitch of the next row it is important not to work into the first stitch of the new row. The number of chains required to make the turning chain depends on the stitch being or, sometimes, on the yarn being used. If the side edge looks 'pulled' try using 1 chain more. Otherwise unless a different number is given in the pattern instructions, the table below lists the number of turning chains required.

UK	USA
double crochet	1 single crochet
half treble	2 half double crochet
treble	3 double crochet
double treble	4 treble
triple treble	5 double treble
quadruple treble	6 triple treble

Crochet worked in rows is turned by means of these turning chains at the end of each row until the required length has been worked. Crochet worked in rounds is joined by a slip stitch worked into the last stitch with the yarn pulled through the last stitch and loop on hook, leaving one loop on hook. The same method applies when work-

ing circular motifs. The initial chain is joined with a slip stitch and the next round is worked into this circle; each round is completed by means of a slip stitch into the first stitch of the round.

Hook Sizes

A point to watch when working any patterns published prior to 1970 is the difference between earlier hook sizes and today's international hook sizes. Always consult the conversion chart on page 191 to establish the correct hook for these earlier patterns. See also the following section on Tension.

Tension

As with knitting, tension is often the one step overlooked, but it is vitally important to obtain the correct tension given in pattern instructions to get the desired measurements.

Checking tension

Work a small square in the main pattern and with the hook size given, to a measurement of at least 10cms (4ins) square, more if the stated tension is for 10cms (4ins). Put the sample on to a flat surface and mark out the tension width of the pattern with pins [fig 34].

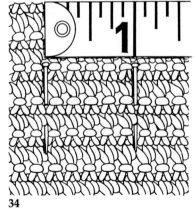

34

Count the number of stitches and rows carefully and if the tension is correct then the design can safely be begun. If there is ANY doubt, then work another sample using a smaller size hook if there are fewer stitches to the given tension, a larger size hook if there are more stitches than given.

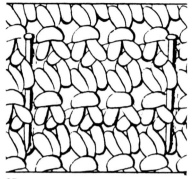

35

Contemporary crochet patterns pose few problems but any one fortunate to find patterns published prior to 1970 should consult the hook conversion chart on page 191. Fig 35 shows a stitch worked on an old size 2 hook giving four stitches to the inch and fig 36, the

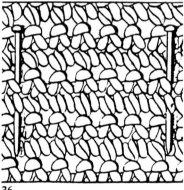

36

same pattern worked on today's size 2 hook giving six stitches to the inch. This tension difference would substantially alter the measurements.

Working with more than one Colour

With right side of work facing

When changing colours during a row of tr/dc, before drawing the

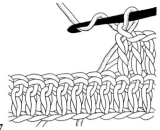

37

yarn through the last two loops on the hook, take the new colour and put it over the hook, leaving the main colour at the back of the work, then draw through the last two loops with the new colour. If the area of contrast colour is small the main colour can be left at the back of the work but if it is made of several stitches it is best to carry the main colour over the contrast yarn and then to the back of the work, then put the contrast yarn over the hook and complete the stitch [fig 37]. Where a lot of colours are being used it is a good idea to use a bobbin for each colour to avoid a tangle of yarns.

These are useful too when a solid block of one contrast colour is being worked. In each case, the yarns must be twisted together at the change of colour to avoid holes.

With wrong side of work facing

When changing colours during a row of tr/dc, keep the last two loops on the hook, bring the main colour to the front of work, put the contrast yarn over the hook and finish working the stitch. Where several stitches form the pattern then carry the main colour over the contrast yarn, then work the stitch in the contrast yarn.

NOTE if working in h.tr/h.dc, change the yarn before drawing through the three loops on the hook; if working in dc/sc, before drawing through the two loops on the hook.

Reading Pattern Instructions

Pattern instructions will give the number of chains to be worked to form the foundation chain. These will be given as a multiple of x; any number of odd or even stitches.

Any number of odd or even stitches is self explanatory. Where the term, a multiple of x, is used, the number given is the number of stitches required to work that particular stitch which is then repeated for as many times as required to achieve the final measurement. If the pattern states, for example, a multiple of 4+1, then the number of stitches must be divisible by four plus one further stitch. In this book, the instructions also give the number of turning chains required for the first or base row.

As with knitting patterns, crochet instructions also use asterisks (*) to show which part of the instructions should be repeated to the end of the row. A typical example would be:

row 2: work (1 h.tr/h.dc, 1 tr/dc) into first stitch, * miss next 2 sts, work (1 dc/sc, 1 h.tr/h.dc, 1 tr/dc) in next st; repeat from * to last 3 sts, miss 2 sts, 1 dc/sc in last st, 1 turning ch.

Where more than one stitch is to be worked into a single stitch, this is indicated by the use of brackets and where this instruction is to be repeated, the number of times this has to be done is given after the end bracket. The * indicates the section of the instructions to be repeated and the end of that section is marked with either ; or another *. Any instructions required for the ending of the row follow this section, ending with the number of turning chains required for the next row. Some books place the number of changing chains at the beginning of the next row and in many designs, they act as the first stitch of that row.

Shaping

All shaping is worked by adding to or taking away a number of stitches from a row. It must be remembered that the average row in crochet is much deeper than in knitting so, when shaping a garment, care must be taken not to decrease or increase

in such a way as to leave an uneven edge which could spoil the look of the finished garment. Most reliable patterns give shaping instructions for decreasing by omitting the first and last stitches on a row and increasing, by working twice into the first and last stitches on a row. This, however, can produce an uneven edge which is awkward to seam when making up. There are better methods which give a neater finish.

Shaping in Pattern

The number of stitches cast on for each garment piece is calculated to fit the pattern exactly. As soon as any shaping is required, the beginning and ends of pattern rows will change. Patterns made from basic stitches pose few problems as it can be seen how to work each stitch from the stitches worked before. With more elaborate patterns, it is best to study how the stitch works then increase or decrease accordingly.

A row counter helps to keep a count of rows so that you know exactly which pattern row is being worked and when the next piece of shaping is due.

Decreasing

To decrease a number of stitches
Work the required number of rows, omitting the turning chain at the end of the last row. On the next row, work the number of stitches to be cast off in slip stitch, then work the turning chain (to count as the first stitch of this row), miss the first stitch from the hook and work in pattern to the end of the row. [fig 38]

If groups of stitches are to be cast off at each end of the row, work as given above, then work in pattern to the required number of stitches from the end of the row, work the turning chain and turn. If stitches

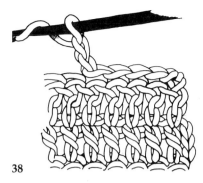

38

are to be cast off on the following row, omit the turning ch at the end of the row.

To decrease a stitch

Unless a pattern is being used where individual decreasing instructions are given, work the turning chain to count as the first stitch in the usual way, miss the second stitch from the hook, work in pattern to the last 2 stitches, miss the next stitch and work the last stitch, then work the turning chain. If a long stitch, such as double treble or triple treble (treble or double treble) is being worked, an alternative method of decreasing avoids a gap. In this method the turning chain forms the first stitch then the second stitch is worked in the normal way but omitting the last stage (ie 2 loops remain on hook), work the third stitch also omitting

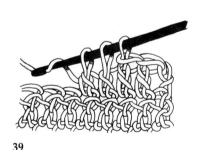

39

the last stage, (ie now 3 loops remain on hook), yarn over hook, draw loop through all loops on hook leaving one loop on hook. [fig 39]

In this way the second and third stitches become one stitch only at

the top of the stitch thus giving the correct number of stitches for the following row but filling what would otherwise be a space at the base of the stitches. The same method can be used at the end of a row, taking the second and third from last stitch together and working the last stitch in the usual way.

Increasing

To increase a number of stitches

Work the required number of rows omitting the turning chain at the end of the last row. Work a turning chain for the required number of stitches to be cast on plus those for the turning chain, turn. Count the turning chain as the first stitch, work in pattern across the other chain stitches then to end of row.

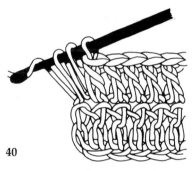

40

To increase a stitch

Work the turning chain to count as the first stitch then work two stitches in the second stitch or stipulated stitch. At end of row work two stitches in the last but one stitch, work the last stitch in the usual way and work the turning chain to count as the first stitch of the next row, [figs 40, 41].

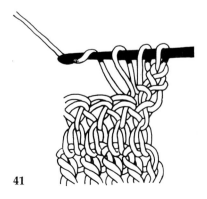

41

Buttonholes

These are worked as either vertical or horizontal buttonholes.

Vertical buttonholes

At the point where the buttonhole is to be worked divide the work in two and work each side separately. When the required depth has been worked, continue the work across both sections.

Horizontal buttonholes

When working in double/single crochet, these are made by missing 2 or more stitches and working the equivalent number of chains. On the next row, double/single crochet stitches are worked over the chain stitches, [fig 42]. As half treble/half double crochet stitches are deeper, to avoid too large a hole, work thus:

At the beginning of the buttonhole put the hook from top to bottom under the middle thread of the stitch just completed, yoh, draw a loop through, yoh and draw through 2 loops. This replaces the first ch. Then continue with * 1 ch, hook under left thread of previous st, yoh and draw through a loop *. Repeat from * to * for the required width of the buttonhole. Finish the buttonhole by putting hook again under the thread to the left of the last stitch, yoh, draw a loop through, miss the required number of stitches in previous row to correspond to the number of stitches worked for the buttonhole, put hook in next stitch, yoh and draw a loop through, yoh and draw through the 3 loops on hook.

When working in treble/double crochet the method is the same except that the hook for the first stitch is put under the first diagonal thread half way down the last treble/double crochet. Complete by drawing through a loop under the last diagonal thread, missing the required number of stitches in previous row, hook into next stitch, yoh, draw a loop through, yoh and draw through 2 loops, yoh and draw through remaining 2 loops. Continue in pattern.

Buttons

To make crochet covered buttons is simple. The foundation can be round button moulds, an inexpensive button, a ring to be covered with crochet.

Round buttons

Work 3 ch and join with a slip stitch.

1st round: 6 dc/sc in circle, join with a slip stitch to first st.

2nd round: 2 dc/sc in each st of previous round, join with a slip stitch to first stitch.

3rd round: 1 dc/sc into each st, join with a slip stitch into first stitch. Repeat 3rd round until foundation ring or button is covered.

Last round: * miss 1 dc/sc, 1 dc/sc in next st; repeat from * to end, join with a slip stitch into first stitch.

Slip crochet cover over button and draw together underneath leaving an end of yarn for sewing on the button.

Ring buttons

Work a round of dc/sc closely all round the ring, join with a slip stitch to first st. Across the back of the ring, work strands of yarn diagonally and sew to garment through the centre of these strands.

Seams

Use a blunt ended wool needle and the original yarn for sewing together. If the yarn is not suitable for sewing use a 3 ply yarn in the same shade. On a garment made from an even pattern such as double crochet, half treble or treble crochet (single crochet, half double

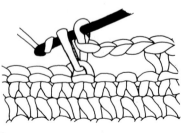

42

crochet, double crochet) seams may be joined by a single row of double (single) crochet, great care being taken to ensure that the seam is the same length as the finished garment and that it has not been stretched or pulled too tightly. Woven flat seams and back stitch seams may be used where they prove suitable. More open patterns will require the use of a woven flat seam to bring the two edges together without a ridge forming.

Woven flat seam

With the right sides of the work facing each other, place your finger between the two pieces to be joined, insert the needle from the front, through both pieces below the corresponding 'pips', pull the yarn through and insert the needle from the back through both pieces the length of a small running stitch and pull the yarn through. The seam will then be drawn together and will be flat and very neat when pressed. [Fig 43]

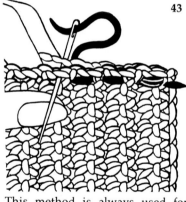

43

This method is always used for baby garments, ribbing and underclothes.

Back stitch seam

This method is firm, yet elastic, keeps the garment in shape and will not break if roughly treated.

Place the two pieces to be joined, right sides together, and join in the sewing yarn by making three small running stitches over each other, one stitch in from the edge. Put the needle back into the beginning of the running stitch and pull the yarn through, insert the needle from the back through the fabric and beyond the first running stitch, the length of another small stitch, and pull the yarn through. [fig 44]

Repeat this along the seam keeping stitches neat and even and one stitch in from the edge of both pieces of fabric and taking great care not to split the worked stitches.

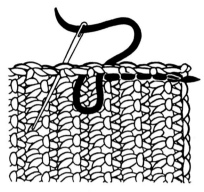

44

Decorative seam

Lapped seams can be used on yokes and square set sleeves when a firm fabric stitch has been worked. Place the parts to be joined, right sides together, with the underneath part projecting a half inch (1.25cm) beyond the upper part. Backstitch along edge, turn to the right side and backstitch a half inch (1.25cm) from the first seam through both thicknesses of fabric, taking care to keep the line of stitching even and straight.

Pattern instructions will say in what order seams should be worked.

Shoulder seams

Backstitch firmly one stitch in from the edge, taking the stitching across the steps of shaping in a straight line. Press on the wrong side. For heavy garments, reinforce these seams with ribbon or tape.

Set in sleeves

Mark centre top of sleeve and pin in position to shoulder seam, then pin the cast off stitches to cast off underarm stitches of body. Keeping the sleeve smooth on either side of the shoulder seam, work a fine back stitch round the curves as near to the edge as possible.

Side and sleeve seams

Join with back stitch in one complete seam as near to the edge as possible.

Sewing on collars

Place right side of collar to wrong side of neck, matching centre backs

TECHNIQUES

and taking care not to stretch the neckline. Join with a firm back stitch as near the edge as possible.

Sewn-on bands

For bands worked separately use a woven flat seam to join to garment matching row for row.

Sewn-on pockets or any applied band or decoration

Use a slip stitch, taking care to keep the line absolutely straight. A good way to ensure a straight sewing line is to thread a fine knitting needle, pointed at both ends, under every alternate stitch of the line to be followed and catch one

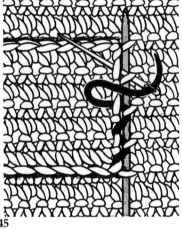

45

stitch from the edge of the piece to be sewn on and one stitch from the needle alternately, using matching yarn [fig 45].

Skirt waist

Cut elastic to size required and join into a circle. Mark the waistline of the skirt and the elastic into quarter sections and pin the elastic into position on the wrong side taking

46

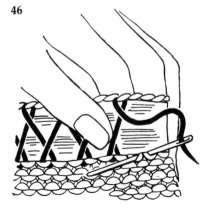

care to distribute the work evenly. Hold the work over the fingers of the left hand and with the elastic slightly stretched, work a herring-bone stitch, catching the elastic above and below [fig 46].

Ribbon facings

Where possible, lightly press the part to be faced taking care not to stretch the edge. Choose a soft ribbon. When facing buttonhole bands the ribbon should be wide enough to cover the strip with a quarter to half inch/.60 to 1.25cm to spare on either side and a half inch/1.25cm hem top and bottom. Take great care not to stretch the crochet when measuring the ribbon lengths and cut the facing for buttonhole and button bands at the same time so that they match exactly. Fold in the turnings, pin ribbon to the wrong side, easing the crochet evenly, while checking that the buttonholes are evenly spaced.

With matching thread, slip stitch with the smallest possible stitches along all edges. Cut buttonholes against the straight grain of the ribbon remembering to make them wide enough for the buttons. Oversew the ribbon and crochet together to avoid fraying, then neaten by working buttonhole stitch with the original yarn [fig 47].

47

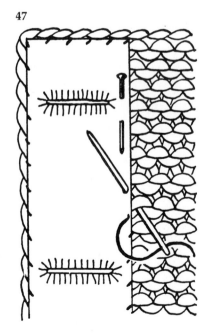

Grosgrain ribbon can be shaped to fit a curved edge by pressing with a hot iron and gently stretching one edge until the desired curve is

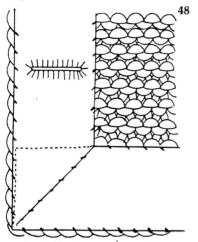

48

made. When facing with ribbon on two edges at right angles, seam outside edge in place first, then fold ribbon in a mitred corner before seaming inside edge [fig 48].

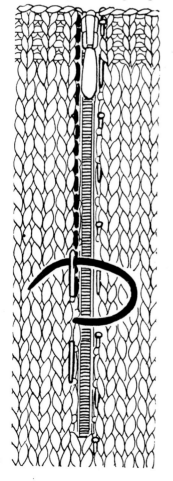

49

Sewing in zip fasteners
Pin in the zip to the opening taking great care not to stretch the crochet. Sew in the zip using backstitch, keeping the grain of the crochet straight. Except on very heavy garments, it is better to use nylon zips because of their lightness and flexibility [fig 49].

Adapting Patterns to Crochet

One of the reasons for a book about crochet stitches is to give the inventive crocheter a wider choice of designs. Crochet is worked to tension just as for knitting: crochet stitch patterns can be just as attractive as those found in knitting stitch books. As any knitwear designer would confirm, successful designs are a combination of a good garment shape, a suitable stitch pattern and the right weight of yarn. A little experimentation with yarn and stitch pattern will show the type of garment to which they are best suited.

Suitable knitting patterns can then be converted to crochet. The first stage is to chart out the measurements given in the instructions on to graph paper and a small calculator is very helpful in doing this. If full measurements are not given in the instructions then take measurements at

a) the first row after the rib welt
b) the point at which any increases are made for the body of the design
c) the width at the armhole
d) the length from edge to armhole
e) the length from armhole to shoulder seam
f) the width of the shoulder seam
g) the length of the sleeve seam
h) any neckline shaping
work either in cms or ins; as in cooking, the conversion is not precise.

Take the number of stitches quoted in the instructions and divide these by the number of a) stitches then b) tension quoted, ie, there are 100 stitches and a tension of 10 sts over 10cms (4ins). This will give a measurement of 100cms (40ins) which will include any ease that was built into the design. Do the same calculation with the rows if the knitting instructions do not give length measurements.

Put these measurements on graph paper using either one square as a row/stitch or on larger graph squares, 1 inch per square. Then take the tension of the crochet stitch pattern you plan to use and work this in reverse. As an example a bust measurement of 91cms (36ins) is required plus the appropriate amount of ease in wear.

For this example an ease factor of 10cms (4ins) is assumed giving a finished measurement of 102cms (40ins). The stitch pattern to be used works on a multiple of 10+1 to a tension of 16 sts over 10cms (4ins) and the design has a separate front and back of equal width.

The 102cms (40ins) is then divided by 2 to give a separate front and back. Divide the 51cms (20ins) by 10cms (4ins) to estimate the number of stitches that will be required.

51 (20) divided by 10cm (4ins) = 5.1 (5)

5.1 (5) multiplied by 16 (the number of stitches of the stated tension) = 81.6 (80) stitches

The stitch pattern requires a multiple of 10+1. The number of stitches is then adjusted so that the pattern fits nicely over the work, giving a final stitch requirement of 81 sts each for front and back.

The tension square worked for the stitch to be used will also show the number of rows required to get either 5 or 10cms (2 or 4ins). This is then used to get the length required. The same principle applies to the other measurements, a) through to h) listed above.

Many crochet stitch patterns make a firm, almost cloth like, material and these can be used in conjunction with commercial paper patterns. Take the measurements of the pattern pieces, the tension of the stitch pattern and work each piece to the size of the paper pattern piece. Then assemble according to the instructions. It is best to avoid any heavily darted or elaborately shaped patterns but a simple dart as for a skirt can be worked with a sequence of simple decreases.

Yarns

Yarns given in patterns do not always stay in the spinners' ranges and so it is often necessary to find a substitute yarn. There is little problem with standard 4 ply (USA lightweight) or double knitting qualities (USA medium weight) but others can cause real difficulties. It is important to try to keep to the original yarn type and then to experiment to find the correct hook size and tension. You may have to try one or two hook sizes above or below the stated size before the correct tension becomes possible. Or, if you are happy with the yarn and the look of the tension square but it isn't the same as the original, it is quite simple to rewrite the pattern to the new tension.

With any yarn substitution comes the problem of estimating just how much yarn will be required.

When working to published instructions and where the tension remains the same, then it is a simple matter to multiply the number of balls by their length and then divide that figure by the length per ball of the substitute yarn. Some pattern instructions give the yardage/metreage per ball of yarn and it is often given on yarn ball bands and in spinners' yarn books; otherwise a telephone call or letter to the spinner should provide the information.

Where the tension differs from the original or it is not possible to find out the length of the original yarn, there are several ways of estimating the amount of substitute yarn that will be required.

The simplest is to find a similar pattern and note the amount of yarn used. Another is to measure off a length of the planned substitute yarn and work as many stitches as possible on this length. Divide the yardage/metreage of the substitute yarn by the length used then multiply this figure by the number of stitches. This gives the number of stitches that each ball will make. Then take the measurements of the design. Estimate the number of rows that will be needed and multiply these by the number of stitches per row. Divide this figure by the number of stitches each ball will work. This gives the number of balls of yarn that will be required. An alternative is to work a full ball of the substitute and then make a sketch of the garment with its measurements, measure the piece that has been worked and estimate from that how much yarn will be required.

Hints on Working Crochet

After casting on the foundation chain and working the first row, it can be infuriating to find that you have miscounted and there are too few chains in the base chain to finish correctly. One way to overcome this is to ensure that a long tail of yarn is left when making the initial slip knot so that, if necessary, you can use this to make good the missing number of chains.

Although a standard chart for turning chains is given on page 154, the number of chains needed can alter, dependent on the hook size and type of yarn and stitch being used so, at times, fewer or more chains may be needed.

When the turning chain counts as the first stitch of a row, take care to ensure that a stitch is worked at the end of the row into the top of the turning chain of the previous row. When the turning chain does not count as a first stitch then remember to work the first stitch and not to work the stitch into the top of the turning chain.

It is helpful to occasionally count the number of stitches being worked to ensure that none have been lost.

Joining in yarn in the middle of a row is easily done. Just before the join needs to be made, put the hook into a stitch, loop the new yarn over and pull yarn through then continue with the new yarn. Alternatively, if the pattern being worked is a solid design, the new yarn can be laid across the top of the work, stitches worked over it,

the work continued in the new yarn with the remnant of the previous yarn being laid along the top of the work and stitches worked over it. If pieces have to be sewn together at the finish of the work, and if the yarn is suitable for seaming, leave a generous amount of yarn after fastening off which can be used to sew the seams.

Foundation chains can tend to draw in the bottom of the work. A way to avoid this is to work the base chain with a hook one size larger or with doubled yarn.

A rather more solid foundation chain can be worked instead of the simple chain. After making the first loop, work 2 ch, hook into first loop, * yoh, draw a loop through, yoh and draw it through the 2 loops on hook; repeat from * to end putting the hook each time into the thread at left.

Newcomers to crochet will find it easier to begin if they start with a large hook and thick yarn.

Left handed crocheters can use standard diagrams by following the right handed image in reverse. Just prop the book open with the appropriate page facing towards the mirror.

The approved way to crochet is illustrated on page 148. However, some would be crocheters find this difficult and for them it is often easier to wind the yarn round the right hand, hold the hook in the right hand and work the stitch using the right hand. The left hand is used to hold the work. Heresy, but it works.

Neater edges are obtained if the first stitch is missed on each row, the appropriate turning ch taking its place and at the end, 1 stitch is worked into the turning ch.

To establish if you are looking at the right or wrong side of the work, look for the end of yarn at the beginning of the foundation chain. It will be at the left hand edge when the right side is facing provided that the first row worked was a right side row.

As a move to making crochet patterns internationally understood, some books and magazines are beginning to use symbols as well as words for the instructions. A chart showing these is on page 190.

INSTRUCTIONS

Cap Sleeved Sweater with Deep V Back

MATERIALS
Pingouin Charmille
7(8:9) 1¾oz/50g balls
each approx 132yds/120m
colour white
Pingouin Coton Mercerisé 5
2(3:3) 3½oz/100g balls
each approx 385yds/350m
colour white
crochet hook size 7mm/K or size to
give recommended tension/gauge
pair knitting needles size 5.50mm
TENSION/GAUGE
9 tr/dc and 6 rows to 4ins/10cms
using 2 strands of yarn and 7mm/K
hook. Check tension/gauge before
commencing work
SIZES
32(36:38) ins
81(91:96) cm
Directions are for smallest sizes
with larger sizes in parentheses
Finished Measurements
at underarm
35½(39:41) ins
89(98:102) cm
length
24¾(25¼:25¾) ins
61.5(64:65) cm
sleeve width at upper arm
13(16:17) ins
38(41:43) cm
NOTE
1. use 2 strands of yarn
2. rib bands are knitted with 3
strands of yarn
3. to decrease 1 st, (yoh, draw up a
loop in next st, yoh and draw
through 2 loops on hook) twice,
yoh, and draw through all 3 loops
on hook

FRONT
With Charmille, chain 42(46:48)
and begin pattern as follows:
Row 1: work 1 tr/dc in fourth ch

and all subsequent ch to end of
row, 3 turning ch. (40:44:46) sts.
Row 2: miss first st, 1 tr/dc in every
st to end of row, 1 tr/dc in turning
ch, 3 turning ch.
Repeat row 2 for pattern and work
until front measures 13½ins/34cm
from beginning or 2½ins/6cm less
than desired length to underarm.
Cap Sleeves
Next row: ch 6(8:10), 1 tr/dc in 4th
ch from hook, 1 tr/dc in each ch and
st to end of row. With another 2
strands of yarn, ch 4(6:8), with first
2 strands of yarn, work 1 tr/dc in
each ch. (48:56:62) sts.
Fasten off second 2 strands of yarn.
Work even until sleeve measures
7½(8, 8½) ins/19(20.5:21.5) cm.
Left Neck and Shoulder Shaping
Next row: sl.st across first 5(6:7) sts
then work in pattern across next
10(12:13) sts, turn.
Next row: work in pattern across
first 5(6:6) sts. Fasten off.
Right Neck and Shoulder Shaping
With right side facing, miss centre
18(20:22) sts, join 2 strands of yarn,
3 ch, work in pattern across next
10(12:13) sts, turn. Work as for left
neck and shoulder reversing
shaping.

BACK
Work as for front until back
measures 8½ins/21.5cms from
beginning.
V Neck Shaping
Next row: work in pattern across
20(22:23) sts, join another 2 strands
of yarn, work in pattern across rem
20(22:23) sts. Working both sides in
pattern at same time, work 1 row
even. Dec 1 st at each neck edge on
every other row 9(10:11) times and
AT SAME TIME when front
measures same as back to underarm, work cap sleeves as for front.
Cont to work as for front until
sleeve measures 7½(8:8½) ins/
19(20.5:21.5) cms – 15(18:20) sts on
each side. Shape shoulders as for
front.

NECKBAND
With Coton Mercerisé 5 cast on 137
(141:145) sts and work 1 row in k1,
pl rib. Continue in rib and dec 1 st
at each end of every other row until
work measures 2ins/5cm from beg.

Inc 1 st at each end of every other row until work measures 4ins/10cm. Cast off loosely in rib.

SLEEVE BANDS
With knitting needles cast on 47 (49:51) sts and work in k1, p1 rib for 4ins/10cm. Cast off loosely in rib.

FINISHING
Sew shoulder and top sleeve seams. For bottom bands, with right side facing, pick up and k 69(71:75) sts evenly across bottom edge. Work k1, p1 rib for 2½ins/6cms then cast off loosely in rib. Sew side and sleeve seams. Sew mitred edges of neckband together. Sew one edge of neckband to neck edge, centering mitred edge at centre V. Fold neckband in half to wrong side and sew. Sew one edge of sleeve band to sleeve edge. Fold sleeve band in half to wrong side and sew.

Sleeveless Top with Ridged Collar and Hem

MATERIALS
Pingouin Fil d'Ecosse 4
12(14:16:18) 50g balls
each approx 110yds/100m
colour white
OR
Lane Borgosesia Cotone Del Borgo
12(14:16:18) 50g balls
each approx 101yds/93m
colour white
crochet hooks 3.50mm/E, 4mm/F, 4.50mm/G or size to obtain given tension/gauge
1¼yd/1m of ⅛ins/3mm oval elastic
TENSION/GAUGE
18 dc/sc to 4ins/10cms over border st using 3.50mm/E hook.
17½ dc/sc to 4ins/10cms over dc/sc using 4.50mm/G hook.
Check tension/gauge before commencing work.
SIZES
32(34:36:38) ins
81(86:91:96) cm
Directions are for smallest size with larger sizes in parentheses.
Finished Measurements
at underarm
36(38:40:42) ins
90(95:101:105) cm
length
22½(23½:24½:24½) ins
57(60:62:62) cm

NOTE
1. back and front are worked in one tubular piece to armholes.
2. sl.st ribs are added to border and collar when garment is complete.

BODY
With 3.50mm/E hook chain 171 (179:189:197) for lower edge, join with sl.st to form ring.
Round 1: work 1 dc/sc in 2nd ch from hook and all subsequent ch to end of row (170:178:188:196) sts. Do not join or ch 1 at beg of each round. Mark beginning of round.
Round 2: 1 dc/sc in each st.
Round 3: working in back loops only, 1 dc/sc in every st.
Repeat rounds 2 and 3 until work measures 5ins/12.5cm from beg. Change to 4.50mm/G hook and on next round dec 12 dc/sc evenly around (158:166:176:184) sts until work measures 15(15½:16:16) ins/38(39:40.5:40.5) cm from beginning.
Front Armhole Shaping
Next row: ch 1, sl.st in first 4(4:5:5) dc/sc, ch 1, 1 dc/sc in each next 71(75:78:82) dc/sc for front, leave rem sts unworked, turn.
Next row: ch 1, 1 dc/sc in every dc/sc of previous row, turn.
Next row: working in dc/sc, dec 1 dc/sc at each end of row, turn.
Repeat last 2 rows 4 times more

INSTRUCTIONS

(61:65:68:72) sts. Work straight until armhole measures 3½(4: 4½:4½) ins/9(10:11.5:11.5) cm.

Left Front Shoulder Strap

Next row: ch 1, inc 1 dc/sc in first dc/sc (armhole edge), 1 dc/sc in each of next 21(23:24:25) dc/sc, leave rem sts unworked, turn. (23:25:26:27) dc/sc for left shoulder strap.

Next row: ch 1, draw a loop through each of next 3 dc/sc, yoh and draw through all 4 loops on hook (2 dc/sc dec at neck edge), 1 dc/sc in each dc/sc to end, turn.

Dec 2 dc/sc on every row at neck edge 4 times more and AT SAME TIME, inc 1 dc/sc at armhole edge on every 6th row 2 times more and cont to dec 1 dc/sc at neck edge on every row 8(10:10:10) times then on every other row 3 times. Work 1(0:0:0) row straight on 4(4:5:6) dc/sc. Fasten off.

Right Front Shoulder Strap

With right side facing, miss centre 17(17:18:20) dc/sc, join yarn to next dc/sc with a sl.st, ch 1, 1 dc/sc in each next 21(23:24:25) dc/sc, inc 1 dc/sc in last dc/sc (23:25:26:27) sts. Cont as for left shoulder strap reversing all shaping.

Back Armhole Shaping

With right side facing, miss 8(8:10: 10) dc/sc from edge of front, join yarn to next dc/sc with a sl.st, ch 1, 1 dc/sc in each next 71(75:78:82) dc/sc for back, turn.

Next row: ch 1, 1 dc/sc in each dc/sc of previous row, turn.

Next row: working in dc/sc, dec 1 dc/sc at each end of row, turn.

Repeat last 2 rows 4 times more (61:65:68:72) sts. Work straight until armholes measure 3½(4:4½: 4½) ins/9(10:11.5:11.5) cm. Inc 1 dc/sc at each end of next row and every 6th row 2 times more and AT SAME TIME, when armhole measures 4(4½:5:5) ins/10(11.5: 12.5:12.5) cm shape neck and work shoulder straps as for front.

FINISHING

With right sides together and 3.50mm/E hook, sl.st shoulders together. With right side facing work 92(96:100:100) dc/c evenly around each armhole edge.

COLLAR

With wrong side of sweater facing and 3.50mm/E hook, work 142(150: 160:168) dc/sc evenly around neck edge.

Round 1: working through back loops only, 1 dc/sc in each st. DO NOT JOIN OR CH 1 AT BEG OF ROUNDS. Mark beg of rounds.

Round 2: working in dc/sc through both loops inc 20 dc/sc evenly around (162:170:180:188) sts.

Round 3: working through back loops only, 1 dc/sc in each st.

Rounds 4 & 5: as rounds 2 & 3 (182:190:200:208) sts

Rounds 6 & 7: as rounds 2 & 3 (202:210:220:228) sts

Rounds 8 & 9: as rounds 2 & 3 (222:230:240:248) sts

Round 10: 1 dc/sc in each st through both loops

Round 11: as round 3

Rounds 12–24: rep rounds 10 & 11

Round 25: sl.st in each dc/sc.

Fasten off.

Sl.St. Ribs

With right side facing and with 4mm/F hook, beg at lower edge of garment, fold garment along first row of free back loops and work sl.st loosely in each free back loop around (be sure not to pull sl.sts too tightly or work will pucker). Fasten off at end of round. Work sl.st rib in each round of back loops along lower edge and around collar. Cut elastic to desired length for top of collar. Secure and fasten into a circle. Working from right side over elastic, with 3.50mm/E hook work 1 dc/sc in each free loop of dc/sc at base of collar.

Press lightly with warm iron.

Two Piece Dress

MATERIALS
Lister DK Crepe
Top
8(8:9) 40g balls
each approx 144yds/130m
colour white (MC main colour)
6(7:8) 40g balls
colour navy (CC contrast colour)
Skirt
9(10:11) 40g balls
colour white (MC main colour)
OR
Bernat Saluki
Top
7(7:8) 50g balls
each approx 150yds/137m
colour white (MC main colour)
5(6:7) 50g balls
colour navy (CC contrast colour)
Skirt
8(9:10) 50g balls
colour white (MC main colour)
crochet hook 5mm/H
3mm/2USA circular knitting needle
29ins/73.5cm
7 ⅝ins/1.5cm buttons

1yd/1m ½ins/13mm elastic for skirt
TENSION/GAUGE
16 tr/dc and 16 h.tr/h.dc to 4ins/
10cms using 5mm/H hook; 12 rows
tr/dc and 12 rows h.tr/h.dc to 5ins/
12.5cm using 5mm/H hook. Check
tension/gauge before commencing
work.
SIZES
32(34:36) ins
81(91:96) cm
Directions are for smallest sizes
with large sizes in parentheses
Finished Measurements
Top
at underarm
33½(35½:37½) ins
.84(98:94) cm
length
23½(24:24½) ins
59.5(61:62) cm
Skirt
Finished waist measurement
28(30:32) ins
71(76:81) cm
length
26½ins/67cm

NOTE
1. always change colours on last st
of row before, working off last 2
loops of last st with new colour.
2. all bands are knitted on later.
3. if skirt is lengthened, more yarn
will be needed.

BACK
Chain 69(73:77) loosely in CC.
Base row: work 1 tr/dc in 4th ch
from hook and all subsequent ch to
end of row (67:71:75 sts counting
turning ch), 3 turning ch.
Row 1: miss first st, 1 tr/dc in every
st to end of row, 1 tr/dc in turning
ch, 3 turning ch.
Repeat row 1 for pattern
Stripe pattern
1 row CC, 3 rows MC, 2 rows CC.
Work even in pattern for 12½ins/
32cm or 2ins/5cm less than desired
length to underarm ending with a
MC stripe.
Underarm Shaping
Keeping to pattern st and stripe
pattern, inc 2 sts at each end of
every row 3 times (working 2 sts in
same st for inc), then 1 st at each
end of every row once (81:85:89)
sts.
Sleeves
Next row: keeping in pattern, ch
66(66:70) loosely, 1 tr/dc in 4th ch
from hook, 1 tr/dc in each ch, cont

INSTRUCTIONS

across 81(85:89) back sts, do not fasten off, with a second strand, ch 64(64:68) loosely, with first strand work 1 tr/dc in each ch to end (209:213:225) sts. Fasten off second strand. Work even until sleeve measures 5(5½:6)ins/12.5(14:15)cm

Top Sleeve and Shoulder Shaping

Next row: keeping in pattern, sl.st across 12(12:15) sts then work to within last 12(12:15) sts and turn.

Following row: sl.st across 18 sts, work to within last 18 sts, turn.

Next row: sl.st across 11(11:12) sts, work to within last 11(11:12) sts, turn.

Following row: sl.st across 15 sts, work to within last 15 sts, turn.

Next row: sl.st across 11(11:12) sts, work to within last 11(11:12) sts, turn.

Following row: sl.st across 5(6:6) sts, work to within last 5(6:6) sts, turn.

Next row: sl.st across 4 sts, work next 5 sts and fasten off. Miss centre 47(49:51) sts, join yarn, work 5 sts, fasten off.

FRONT

Work as·for back until first row of sleeve is completed.

Right Sleeve and Neck Shaping

Next row: (wrong side) 1 tr/dc in each next 81(82:87) sts, turn.

Work even in pattern until sleeve measures same as back to top of sleeve.

Work top of sleeve and shoulder shaping as for one sleeve of back.

Left Sleeve and Neck Shaping

Next row: (wrong side) with wrong side facing, miss next 5 sts from right neck edge, join yarn with a sl.st in next st, 1 tr/dc in next st, cont across rem 123(126:133) sts.

Work even in pattern for 6 more rows ending at sleeve edge.

Next row: Work to last 42(44:46) sts, turn. Cont to work on these 81(82:87) sts until sleeve measures same as back to top of sleeve. Work top of sleeve and shoulder shaping as for one sleeve of back.

FINISHING

Bottom Bands

With right side facing, circular needle and MC, pick up and k 79(83:87) sts evenly across bottom edge. Work back and forth in k1, p1 rib for 2ins/5cm or desired length. Cast off loosely in rib. Sew top of

sleeves and shoulder seams in corresponding colours.

Cuffs

With right side facing, circular needle and MC, pick up and k 55(57:61) sts evenly across sleeve edge. Work back and front in k1, p1 rib for 2ins/5cm or desired length. Cast off loosely in rib. Sew undersleeve and side seams in corresponding colours.

Neckband

With right side facing, circular needle and MC, pick up and k 45(47:49) sts from side edge of right neck to shoulder seam, pick up and k 55(57:59) sts across back neck to shoulder seam, place a marker, pick up and k 31(33:35) sts to bottom of left neck edge, place a st marker, pick up and k 44(46:48) sts across bottom edge (175:183:191) sts. Work back and forth in k1, p1 rib for 1¼ins/3cm, dec 1 st before and after corner marker on every other row. Cast off loosely in rib. Sew placket edge to neckband. Sew on 2 buttons.

SKIRT

Front

Begin at top edge using MC and ch 62(66:70) loosely.

Base row: 1 h.tr/h.dc in 3rd ch from hook and all subsequent ch to end of row (61:65:69) sts counting the turning ch, turn.

Row 1: ch 2, miss first st, 1 h.tr/h.dc in every st, 1 h.tr/h.dc in turning ch. ** rep row 1 for pattern st.

Inc 1 st at each end (working 2 sts in same st for inc) on every other row 4 times. Work even for 4 rows. Inc 1 st at each end of next row. Work even for 4 rows. Inc 1 st at each end of next row ** (73:77:81) sts. Work even until front measures 25½ins/64.5cm from beginning or desired length ending with a wrong side row.

Hem

Next row: ch 2, work 1 h.tr/h.dc in back loops only of each st to end of row.

Following row: ch 2, 1 h.tr/h.dc in both loops of every st to end of row.

Repeat last row once more. Fasten off.

Back

With MC ch 68(72:76). Rep row 1 as for front (67:71:75) sts. Work as front between ** and ** (79:83:87) sts. Complete as for front.

FINISHING
Sew right side seam.
Placket
With right side facing, circular needle and MC, pick up and k 161 sts along left front edge. Work back and forth in k1, p1 rib for 1¼ins/3cm. Cast off loosely in rib. Sew placket to left side seam. Turn hem to wrong side and sew in place.
Waistband
With right side facing, hook and MC, join yarn at left side seam then work in dc/sc along waist edge taking in to 28(30:32) ins/71(76:81) cm or desired waist size, turn. Work in dc/sc for 2ins/5cm. Fasten off. Sew waistband seam. Fold waistband in half to wrong side and sew in place leaving a 1ins 2.5cm opening. Cut elastic to desired length. Draw elastic through waistband and sew ends of elastic together. Sew opening closed. Sew on 5 buttons along placket. DO NOT PRESS.

Striped Vest

MATERIALS
Scheepjeswool Granada
5(5:6:6) 1¾oz/50g balls
each approx 110yds/100m
colour sea green (main colour MC)
1(1:2:2) 1¾oz/50g balls
colour teal (contrast colour CC)
crochet hook 5mm/H or size to obtain recommended tension
TENSION/GAUGE
15 dc/sc and 21 rows to 4ins/10cm over stripe pattern using 5mm/H hook.
Check tension/gauge
before commencing work.
SIZES
32(34:36:38) ins
81(86:91:96) cm
Finished Measurements
at underarm
33(35:37:39½) ins
83(88:93:98) cm
length
19¼(19½:19½:19¾) ins
48(49:49:49.5) cm

BACK
With MC, chain 63(67:71:75).
Row 1: (right side) 1 dc/sc in 2nd ch from hook and all subsequent ch to end of row, turn. (62:66:70:74) sts.
Row 2: Ch 1, 1 dc/sc in every st to end of row.
Rows 3–6: as row 2
Row 7: Change to CC and work as row 2
Continue in dc/sc in stripe pattern working 6 rows in MC and 1 row in CC, until back measures 12ins/30cm from beginning or desired length to armhole.
Armhole Shaping
Next row: keeping to stripe pattern work 1 sl.st in each first 2 (3:4:5) sts, ch 1, 1 dc/sc in each next 58 (60:62:64) sts, turn. Continuing in stripe pattern, dec 1 st at each end of every other row 10 times in all. (38:40:42:44) sts remain. Fasten off.

FRONT
Work as for back to armhole.
Neck and Armhole Shaping
Next row: keeping to stripe pattern, work 1 sl.st in each first 2 (3:4:5) sts, ch 1, 1 dc/sc in each next 29 (30:31:32) sts, turn. Continuing in stripe pattern, dec 1 st at neck edge on every row 17(18:19:20) times in all and AT SAME TIME as shaping neck, dec 1 st at armhole edge on every other row 10 times in all. 2 sts remain.
With MC work straight on 2 remaining sts until strap measures 6½(7:7:7½) ins 16(18:18:19) cm. Fasten off.
Work second side in same way as first side reversing shaping.

INSTRUCTIONS

FINISHING

Sew side seams. Adjust straps to fit and sew to back neckline flush with edges of armholes. Press seams lightly with warm iron. With MC, work 1 row of dc/sc evenly around armholes and neck edge including straps.

Loose Fitting Jacket

MATERIALS

Stanley Berroco Dji-Dji
each ball approx 110yds/100m.
4(4:5) 50g balls
colour Royal Mist (A)
1(1:2) 50g balls
colour Peacock Mist (B)
3(3:4) 50g balls
colour Lilac Mist (C)
3(3:3) 50g balls
colour Bronze Mist (D)
Stanley Berroco Tiffany
each ball approx 110yds/100m.
4(4:5) 50g balls
colour Almond (E)
2(2:3) 50g balls
colour Plum (F)
plus of any double knitting/worsted
weight yarn
8oz/230g each of
Teal (G) and Plum (H)
4oz/120g of Magenta (I)
OR
Laines Anny Blatt Mohair et Soie
colours to choice; each ball 70yds/65m
colours A 7(7:8) 50g balls, B 2(2:4) 50g balls, C 5(6:7) 50g balls, D 5(5:5) 50g balls
Laines Anny Blatt 4
colours to choice, quantities as for

Tiffany, colours E–F
each ball approx 130yds/120m
double knitting yarn, colours to choice: same quantities for colours G–I
crochet hooks 5.50mm/I and 6mm/J or size to obtain the recommended tension
6 1ins/2.5cm buttons

TENSION/GAUGE

3 tr/dc sts to 1ins/2.5cm
3 tr/dc rows to 2ins/5cm using 6mm/J10 hook. Check tension/gauge before commencing work.

SIZES

small (6–8) medium (10–12) large (14–16). Directions are for smallest size with larger sizes in parentheses.

**Finished Measurements
at underarm**
approx 37½(39½:41½) ins
approx 95(100:105) cm
width across back at underarm
approx 17(18:19½) ins
approx 43(46:49.5) cm
sleeve width at upper arm
approx 14½(15:16) ins
approx 37(38:40.5) cm

NOTE

jacket is worked from the neck down in one piece

BODY

With 6mm/J hook and one strand each of A and G held together, ch 56(62:68).

Row 1: work 1 tr/dc in 4th ch from hook and in each next 8(10:12) ch (Left Front), in next ch work (2 tr/dc, 1 ch, 2 tr/dc [double inc]), 1 tr/dc in each next 6(8:10) ch (Left Sleeve), work double inc in next ch, 1 tr/dc in each next 16(18:20) ch (Back), a double inc in next ch, 1 tr/dc in next 6(8:10) ch (Right Sleeve), double inc in next ch, 1 tr/dc in last 9(11:13) ch (Right Front). (62:72:82) sts counting the turning ch, 3 turning ch.

Row 2: miss first st, * 1 tr/dc in each st to next 1 ch space and in that space work (1 tr/dc, 1 ch, 1 tr/dc [single inc]); repeat from * three times more, 1 tr/dc in each st to end of row, 1 tr/dc in turning ch, 3 turning ch.

Row 3: miss first st, * 1 tr/dc in each st to next 1 ch space, 1 double inc in space; repeat from * three times more, 1 tr/dc in each st to end of row, 1 tr/dc in turning ch, 3 turning ch.

Repeat rows 2 and 3 twice but using a strand each of B and G for first 2 rows, 1 row using a strand each of B and H, 1 row using a strand each of H and C.

Row 8: miss first st, with C and H 1 tr/dc in each next 2 sts, * with 2 strands of E, 1 tr/dc in each next 3 sts, with C and H, 1 tr/dc in each next 3 sts; repeat from * to end of row working incs as in row 2, 1 turning ch.

Row 9: with F and I, 1 dc/sc in every st working incs as in row 3, 1 turning ch.

Row 10: (Picot Row) With F and I, 1 dc/sc in first 2 sts, * 3 ch, sl.st in first ch (picot), 1 dc/sc in each next 2 sts; repeat from * to end of row working incs as in row 2 but not working the picots over incs, 1 turning ch.

Row 11: with 2 strands of E, * 1 dc/sc in each st to next picot, work 1 long dc/sc in st after picot (insert hook 2 rows below, pull up a loop and complete dc/sc); repeat from * to end of row working incs as in row 3, 3 turning ch.

Row 12: with C and I, 1 tr/dc in every st working incs as in row 2, 1 turning ch. (190:200:210) sts.

Join Body

Row 13: with 2 strands of E, 1 dc/sc in first 27(29:31) sts, 1 dc/sc in 1 ch space (Left Front), miss next 42(44:46) sts (Sleeve) 1 dc/sc in next 52(54:56) sts (Back), miss next 42(44:46) sts (Sleeve), 1 dc/sc in next 1 ch space, 1 dc/sc in every st to end of row (Right Front), 1 turning ch.

Row 14: with 2 strands of E, 1 dc/sc in first 11(13:15) sts, inc 1 st, work to underarm, 1 dc/sc in each st of Back inc 3 sts evenly spaced across, 1 dc/sc in each st of Front inc 1 st in 12th (14th:16th) st from end, 1 dc/sc in each next st, 1 turning ch.

Row 15: with 2 strands of D, 1 dc/sc in first 2 sts, * 1 long dc/sc in next

st, 1 dc/sc in each next 2 sts; repeat from * to end of row, 1 turning ch.

Row 16: with 2 strands of D, 1 dc/sc in first 19 sts, 1 h.tr/h.dc in next 10(12:14) sts, 1 tr/dc in each st of Back, 1 h.tr/h.dc in next 10(12:14) sts, 1 dc/sc in each next st to end of row (this prevents Back from pulling up), 3 turning ch.

Row 17: with A and G, 1 tr/dc in every st to end of row.

Row 18: with one strand of D, 1 dc/sc in first 2 sts, * (yoh, draw up a loop, yoh and draw through 2 loops) five times in next st, yoh and draw through 6 loops, 1 ch [popcorn made], 1 dc/sc in each next 2 sts; repeat from * to end of row.

Row 19: with 2 strands of E, 1 dc/sc in each st to st before next popcorn, 1 long dc/sc in next st, * 1 dc/sc in 1 ch of popcorn, 1 dc/sc in next st, 1 long dc/sc in next st; repeat from * to end of row.

Row 20: with 2 strands of E, 1 dc/sc in every st to end of row.

Row 21: with C and H, 1 tr/dc in every st to end of row.

Row 22: with F and I work a picot row omitting incs.

Rows 23–31: as rows 11–19

Next row: with 2 strands of E, 1 dc/sc in first 9(11:13) sts, 12 ch, miss next 12 sts (pocket opening), 1 dc/sc in every st to last 22(24:26) sts, 12 ch, miss next 12 sts, 1 dc/sc in every st to end of row.

Next row: repeat row 21 working a tr/dc in each dc/sc and ch.

Next row: repeat row 22, 1 turning ch.

Next row: 1 dc/sc in every st to end of row.

Next row: repeat row 8, 1 turning ch.

Next row: with C and F, repeat row 16, 3 turning ch.

Next row: 1 tr/dc in every st to end of row, 1 turning ch.

Change to smaller hook

Next row: 1 dc/sc in every st to end of row, 1 turning ch.

next row: 1 dc/sc in every st, dec 1 st in every fifth st, to end of row, 3 turning ch.

Next row: 1 tr/dc in every st to end of row, 3 turning ch.

Next row: miss first st, * yoh, put hook from front to back around stem of next tr/dc, draw up a loop (yoh and draw through 2 loops) twice [r.b.tr/dc]; repeat from * to

INSTRUCTIONS

end of row, 3 turning ch.
Next row: miss first st, * yoh, put hook from front to back to front around stem of next tr/dc (yoh and draw through 2 loops) twice [f.b.tr/dc]; repeat from * to end of row, 3 turning ch.
Repeat these last 2 rows once more, ending last row with 1 turning ch.
Last row: 1 dc/sc in every st to end of row. Fasten off.

SLEEVES

Join yarn and work across 44(46: 48) sts of sleeve (including underarm joining). Work pattern same as Body to last picot row.
Next row: with B and H, 1 tr/dc in every st to end of row.
Next 2 rows: with B and G, 1 tr/dc in every st to end of row
Next 2 rows: with D and G, 1 tr/dc in every st to end of row.
change to smaller hook.
remainder of sleeve is worked with 2 strands of A as follows.
Next row: 1 dc/sc in every st to end of row, 1 turning ch.
Next row: 1 dc/sc in every st, dec 1 st in every fourth st to end of row, 1 turning ch.
Next row: 1 dc/sc in every st and end of row, 1 turning ch.
Next row: dec 1 st in every other st, 1 dc/sc in every st to end of row, 1 turning ch.
Next row: 1 dc/sc in every st to end of row, 3 turning ch.
Next row: 1 tr/dc in every st to end of row.
Next row: work r.f.tr/dc across row.
Next row: work r.b.tr/dc across row.
Next row: work r.f.tr/dc across row.
Next row: 1 dc/sc in every st to end of row. Fasten off.

COLLAR

With larger hook and 1 strand each of A and G, work 1 row of dc/sc around neck edge working decs over incs, 1 turning ch.
Next row: 1 dc/sc in first 6 sts, 1 h.tr/dc in each st (working dec as before) to last 6 sts, 1 dc/sc in these sts, 2 turning ch.
Next row: 1 tr/dc in each st to end of row, 2 turning ch.
Next row: work r.b.tr/dc in each st, 1 tr/dc in turning ch, 2 turning ch.
Next row: work f.r.tr/dc in each st, 2 turning ch.
Repeat these last 2 rows once more ending with 1 turning ch.

Next row: 1 r.b.dc/sc in first 7 sts, r.b.tr/dc in every st to last 7 sts, r.b.dc/sc in each last 7 sts, 1 dc/sc in turning, ch, 1 turning ch.
Last row: 1 dc/sc in every st to end of row. Fasten off.

Pocket Linings (make 2)

With smaller hook and 1 strand of E, ch 21. Work 2 rows in dc/sc then continue in dc/sc as follows:
3 rows using C, 2 rows using F, 8 rows using C. Fasten off.
Sew top of pocket linings to top of pocket openings of Front. Sew other 3 sides to inside of Fronts matching stripes.

FINISHING

With larger hook and 1 strand each of A and G, join yarn from right side to top of left front collar. Dc/sc along left front edge to C and H row, drop A and G (do not fasten off), join C and H and continue in dc/sc to lower edge, 1 turning ch.
Work dc/sc in each st, changing colours as before, to base of collar. Turn work to right side and work a row of backward dc/sc (from left to right) along side to collar. Fasten off.
Join A and G to base of collar and work 2 more rows of dc/sc along left front edge only (not collar), matching colours as before.
On right front edge, from right side work a row of dc/sc along front edge to top of collar, changing colours as on Left Front. DO NOT TURN WORK
Work a row of backward dc/sc (corded edge) along side of collar and right front edge matching colours. Fasten off. Weave in all ends.
Place markers on left front edge for 6 buttons, first marker 1½ins/4cm from lower edge, last marker at top edge, other markers spaced evenly between.

Button Loops

Make button loops on right front edge opposite markers, making the top 2 loops with A and G, rem loops with C and F as follows:
with smaller hook, join yarn behind corded edge, draw up a loop and ch 10 very tightly, sl.st over corded edge, 1 ch, cut yarn and pull loop through.
Weave in all ends.
Block collar, cuffs and bottom band to prevent curling.

Sleeveless Pullover

MATERIALS
Stanley Berroco Dji Dji
2(2:3:3) 50g balls
light purple heather colour A
2(2:3:3) 50g balls
viola heather colour B
1(1:2:2) 50g balls
light blue/violet heather colour C
2(2:3:3) 50g ball
royal blue heather colour D
2(2:3:3) 50g balls
gold/red heather colour E
each ball approx 100m/110yds
Stanley Berroco Cambridge Tweed
2(2:3:3) 50g balls
nut colour F
OR
Laines Anny Blatt Mohair et Soie
each ball approx 70yds/65m
colours A,B,D,E 4(4:5:5) 50g balls
colour C 2(2:3:3) 50g balls
tweed yarn to choice 2(2:3:3) 50g
balls
crochet hook 6mm/J10
1 pair 4mm (US 6) knitting needles
or size to get given tension/gauge

TENSION/GAUGE
12 dc/sc and 13 rows to 10cm (4ins)
using A and crochet hook 6mm/J,
18 sts to 10cm (4ins) using F and
4mm (6) knitting needles
Check tension/gauge before commencing work.

SIZES
32(34:36:38) ins
81(86:91:96) cm
Directions are for smallest sizes
with larger sizes in parentheses
**Finished measurements
at underarm**
36(37½:40:41½) ins
90(93:100:103) cm
length
23½(23½:24:24) ins
60(60:61:61) cm

NOTE
1. When changing colours, always
draw new colour through last 2
loops of previous colour.
2. When working with 2 colours,
carry yarn not in use along top of
previous row, working over it with
second colour.

BACK
With A ch 55(57:61:63).
Row 1: (wrong side) With A, work
1 dc/sc in second ch from hook, 1
dc/sc in each next 6(7:9;10) ch
drawing B through last 2 loops of
last dc/sc, * with B, work 1 dc/sc in
each next 8 ch drawing A through
last 2 loops of last st, with A, work 1
dc/sc in each next 8 ch drawing B
through last 2 loops of last st;
repeat from * once then with B,
work 1 dc/sc in each next 8 ch, with
A work 1 dc/sc in each last 7
(8:10:11) ch, turn. (54:56:60:62) sts.
Row 2: With A, 1 ch, 1 dc/sc in each
next 7(8:10:11) sts, * with B, work 1
dc/sc in each next 8 sts, with A, 1
dc/sc in each next 8 sts; repeat from
* once then with B, work 1 dc/sc in
each next 8 sts, with A, work 1 dc/
sc in each last 7(8:10:11) sts, turn.
Rows 3–9: repeat row 2
Row 10: With C, 1 ch, 1 dc/sc in
each st to end of row, turn.
Row 11: With D, 1 ch, work 1 dc/sc
in each first 7(8:10:11) sts, * with E,
1 dc/sc in each next 8 sts, with D, 1
dc/sc in each next 8 sts; repeat from
* once then with E, work 1 dc/sc in
each next 8 sts, with D work 1 dc/sc
in each last 7(8:10:11) sts, turn.
Rows 12–14: repeat row 11
Row 15: repeat row 10
Rows 16–17: repeat row 11
Rows 18–22: repeat rows 10–14
Row 23: repeat row 10
Rows 24–32: repeat row 2
Repeat rows 10–23 for pattern.
Continue straight in pattern until
back measures 34cm (13½ins) from

INSTRUCTIONS

beg or desired length to armhole ending with a wrong side row. Fasten off.

Armhole Shaping

Next row: Keeping to pattern with right side facing, rejoin yarn to fourth dc/sc with a sl.st and work a dc/sc in this st, work across row to last 3 sts, leave these unworked, turn. (48:50:54:56) sts.

Work one row in pattern.

Continue in pattern, dec 1 st at each end of every row 4(4:5:5) times. 40(42:44:46) sts.

Work straight until armhole measures 9(9:9½:9½) ins 23(23: 24:24) cm. Fasten off.

FRONT

With B chain 55(57:61:63).

Row 1: (wrong side) With B, work 1 dc/sc in second ch from hook, 1 dc/sc in each of next 6(7:9:10) ch, * with A, work 1 dc/sc in each next 8 ch, with B, work 1 dc/sc in each next 8 sts; repeat from * once with A, 1 dc/sc in each next 8 sts then with B work 1 dc/sc in each last 7(8:10:11) sts, turn.

Row 2: with B, 1 ch, work 1 dc/sc in each first 7(8:10:11) ch, * with A, work 1 dc/sc in each next 8 sts, with B, work 1 dc/sc in each next 8 sts; repeat from * once then with A work 1 dc/sc in each next 8 sts, with B, work 1 dc/sc in each last 7(8:10: 11) sts, turn.

Continue in this way to work rows 3–32 and then repeat rows 10–32 as for back substituting A for B, B for A, E for D and D for E until there are the same number of rows as for back to armhole and ending with a wrong side row. Fasten off.

Armhole shaping

Shape armhole as for back. Then work straight until armhole measures 5(5:5½:5½) ins 12.5(12.5: 14:14) cm ending with a wrong side row.

Neck shaping

Next row: work in pattern across first 16(17:18:19) sts, turn. Continue in pattern, dec 1 st at neck edge on every row 5 times. (11:12:13:14) sts. Work until front measures same as back to shoulder. Fasten off.

With right side facing and keeping to pattern, miss centre 8 sts and rejoin yarn to next st, work across 16(17:18:19) sts, turn. Work left side of neck as for right side, reversing shaping. Fasten off.

FINISHING

Back Band

With right side facing and 4mm (6) knitting needles and F, pick up and k 75(79:85:89) sts evenly along lower edge of back. Work 5 rows in st.st. With C, k 2 rows. With F, work 5 more rows in st.st. Cast off loosely.

Front Band

Work as for back band.

Armbands

Sew shoulder seams. With right side facing and 4mm (6) knitting needles and F pick up and k 92 (92:97:97) sts evenly along armhole edge.

Row 1: Purl

Row 2: Knit, dec 1 st at each end.

Rows 3–4: repeat rows 1–2

Row 5: Purl

Row 6: with C, knit, dec 1 st at each end.

Row 7: With C, knit.

Row 8: with F, knit, inc 1 st at each end.

Row 9: Purl

Rows 10–13: repeat rows 8–9 twice.

Cast off loosely.

COLLAR

With right side facing, 4mm (US 6) knitting needles and F, begin at centre front and pick up and k 28 sts along front neck to shoulder and 20 sts along back neck edge. 48 sts for half collar.

Rib row 1: (wrong side) * p1, k1; repeat from * to end of row.

Repeat this row until collar measures 3¼ins (8.5cm). Change to C and work 1 row in rib. Cast off loosely in rib. For second half of collar, with right side facing, 4mm (US 6) knitting needles and F, begin at centre back, pick up and k 20 sts along back neck edge to shoulder and 28 sts along front neck ege to centre front. 48 sts.

Rib row 1: (wrong side) * k1, p1; repeat from * to end of row.

Repeat this row and complete as for right side of collar.

Sew back collar seam. Sew side seams. Fold bands in half along the C stripe and sew to wrong side.

Blouson Jacket in Openwork Pattern

MATERIALS
Pingouin Fil d'Ecosse no 8
7 (7) 50g balls
each approx 285m/310yds
colour white
crochet hook 2.50mm/B
1 pair knitting needles 2mm (US 00)
or size to give recommended tension/gauge
6 buttons
flat elastic

TENSION/GAUGE
14 tr/dc and 14 rows to 10cm (4ins) using 2.50mm/B crochet hook and grid pattern

SIZES
32–34 and 36–38ins
81–86 and 91–96cm
Directions are for smallest sizes with larger sizes in parentheses

Finished Measurements

at underarm
37½ and 39½ins
95 and 100cm

length
26 and 26¾ins
66 and 68cm

Grid Pattern (worked over a chain base)
Row 1: work 1 tr/dc in fifth ch from hook, * 1 ch, miss 1 ch, 1 tr/dc in next ch; repeat from * to end of row, 3 turning ch.
Row 2: miss first st, * 1 tr/dc in next st, 1 ch; repeat from * to end of row ending with last tr/dc in second ch.
repeat row 2 throughout

BACK
Make a foundation ch of 143 (151) ch + 3 turning ch and work in grid pattern. (72:76) grids.
When work measures 16cm (6¼ins), dec 1 st at each end of row every 10cm (4ins) three times. (66: 70) tr/dc.
When work measures 47(46)cm/ 18½(18)ins, shape armholes.

Armhole shaping
Leave 4 tr/dc unworked at each end of row and continue straight on remaining 58 (62) tr/dc until work measures 67cm (26½ins).

Shape shoulders
Dec at each end of every row as follows: 7 tr/dc twice and 6 tr/dc once, 7 tr/dc three times AT THE SAME TIME after the first shoulder shaping leave the centre 18 (20) tr/dc unworked for neck.

RIGHT FRONT
make a foundation ch of 71 (75) ch + 3 turning ch and work in grid pattern. (36:38 tr/dc).
When work measures 16cm (6¼ins), dec 1 tr/dc at armhole edge (left hand side of work) every 10cm (4ins) three times. (33:35) tr/dc. When work measures 47(46)cm/ 18½(18)ins, shape armhole.

Armhole shaping
Leave 4 tr/dc unworked at armhole edge. (29:31) tr/dc. Continue straight on rem sts until work measures 58cm (22¾ins).

Shape neck (at right hand side of work)
Dec 1 tr/dc at beg of each alt row 9 (10) times. Continue straight until work measures 67cm (26½ins).

Shape shoulder
Dec 7 tr/dc once, 6 (7) tr/dc once, 7 tr/dc once at armhole edge.

LEFT FRONT
Work as for right front, reversing all shapings.

SLEEVES
With 2mm (00) knitting needles cast on 63 (65) sts and work 8 cm (3¼ins) in k1, p1 rib. Cast off very loosely.
With 2.50/B crochet hook work across the rib in grid pattern inc 45 (48) tr.dc evenly across row. Con-

tinue by inc 1 tr/dc at each end of every 7th row five times. (55:58) tr/dc.

When work measures 47cm (18½ ins) including the ribbing at cuff, change to dc/sc and work 78 (82) dc/sc for 3 cm (1¼ins). Fasten off.

POCKETS
Make a foundation ch of 37 ch + 3 turning ch. Work 19cm (7½ins) in grid pattern. 19 tr/dc. Fasten off.
Pocket Border
Work 3 rows of dc/sc all round pocket inc 1 dc/sc at each corner on every row.

FINISHING
Stitch shoulder seams. Sew in sleeves, sew side and sleeve seams.
Right Front Border
With 2mm (00) needles cast on 15 sts and work in k1, p1 rib working 6 buttonholes (4 sts wide and 5 sts in from outer edge), the first one 4.5cm (1¾ins) from lower edge, the others spaced 10cm (4ins) apart. When work measures 56cm (22ins), cast off.
Left Front Border
Work as for right front border omitting buttonholes.

COLLAR
Beginning at outer edge and using 2mm (00) needles, cast on 183 sts and work 6cm (2¼ins) in k1, p1 rib. Continue by dec at each end of every alt row as follows: 1 st five times, 2 sts six times.
Next cast off at each end of row as follows: * 7 sts once, 6 sts once; repeat from * twice more. Cast off rem 71 sts.

Stitch under the 2 rows of grids as a hem at lower edge of blouson. Stitch front borders in place (with buttonholes on right front). Sew on collar. Place pockets above the hem at lower edge of front and stitch along edge of front and stitch along edge of grid pattern leaving a flap of 6cm (2½ins) at the top of pocket. Thread through elastic through hem at lower edge. Sew on buttons.

Cluster Patterned Top

MATERIALS
Pingouin Fil d'Ecosse 8
3(3) 50g balls colour white
each approx 285m/310yds
crochet hook 2.50m/B
or size to give recommended tension/gauge
TENSION/GAUGE
8 arcs and 16 rows to 10cm (4ins) using 2.50mm/B crochet hook and pattern stitch

SIZES
32–34 and 36–38ins
81–86 and 91–96cm
Directions' are for smallest sizes with larger sizes in parentheses
Finished Measurements
at underarm
36 and 39ins
91 and 98cm
length
18½ins/47cm

Pattern Stitch (worked over a ch base)
Row 1: 6 ch to turn, * miss 3 ch, 1 dc/sc in next st, 5 ch; repeat from * to end of row.
Row 2: * (5 ch, 1 dc/sc in third ch of loop) three times, 2 ch, 4 tr/dc worked together in the dc/sc, 2 ch, 1 dc/sc in the third ch, 2 ch, 4 tr/dc worked together in the dc/sc, 2 ch, 1 dc/sc in the third ch; repeat from * to end of row ending with 2 arcs = (5 ch, 1 dc/sc) twice.
Row 3: * (5 ch, 1 dc/sc in third ch) twice, 5 ch, 1 dc/sc in st that joined the 4 tr/dc, 2 ch, 4 tr/dc worked

together into the dc/sc. 2 ch, 1 dc/sc in st that joined the 4 tr/dc, 5 ch, 1 dc/sc; repeat from * to end of row.

Row 4: * 5 ch, 1 dc/sc in third ch; repeat from * to end or row.

Row 5: 5 ch, 1 dc/sc in third ch, 2 ch, 4 tr/dc worked together, 2 ch, * (5 ch, 1 dc/sc in third ch) three times, 2 ch, 4 tr/dc worked together, 2 ch, 1 dc/sc, 2 ch, 4 tr/dc worked together, 2 ch, 1 dc/sc; repeat from * to end of row.

Row 6: 5 ch, 1 dc/sc in st that joined the 4 tr/dc, * 2 ch, 4 tr/dc worked together in the dc/sc, 2 ch, 1 dc/sc in st that joined the 4 tr/dc then: (5 ch, 1 dc/sc) twice; repeat from * to end of row.

Row 7: as row 4

Row 8: repeat from row 2

To work 4 tr/dc together:
* yoh, put hook into a st, yoh, draw through a loop, yoh, draw through 2 loops; repeat from * three more times in the same st, yoh, draw through the 5 loops left on hook, 1 ch to close.

BACK

Make a foundation ch of 144 (152) ch + 6 turning ch. Work in pattern stitch (37/39 arcs) dec 1 arc at each end of row every 10cm (4ins) twice. When work measures 33cm (13ins) and after working a complete motif, work 5 rows of dc/sc, working 4 dc/sc in each arc on first row.

FRONT

Make a foundation ch of 160 (168) ch + 6 turning ch. Work in pattern stitch (41/43 arcs) dec 1 arc at each end of row every 12cm (4¾ins) twice. (37:39 arcs)

When work measures 33cm (13ins) shape armholes.

Armhole Shaping

Dec 1 arc at each end of every third row twice and then on every alt row 7 times AT THE SAME TIME when work measures 40cm (15¾ins) shape neck.

Neck Shaping

Leave the centre 5 arcs unworked and continue each side separately, dec at neck edge on every row as follows:
2 arcs twice, 1 arc three (four) times.
Complete other side to match reversing all shapings.

FINISHING

Armhole borders:
Work 54 dc/sc along the sloped armhole edges. Work a further 4 rows dec 1 dc/sc at each end of row.

Neck Border:
Make 80 ch on each side of neck for the straps. Work in dc/sc along the 80 ch of one side then work 95 dc/sc along front neck, then work along the 80 ch of the other side. Work 5 rows of dc/sc over all these sts, dec 4 sts evenly around neck curve on each row. Tie the straps at back neck. Stitch side seams. Work 1 row of dc/sc around lower edge of top.

Make a cord of double yarn.
Make a chain then work 1 row of sl.st along this chain.
Thread this cord through the first row of arcs at lower edge and tie at front.

Heart Patterned Filet Sweater

MATERIALS

Pingouin Cotton Perle no 5
11 (12) 50g balls colour white
each approx 200m/220yds
crochet hook 2mm/B
1 pair knitting needles 2.50mm (US 2)
set of 4 knitting needles 2.50mm (US 2)

SIZES

32–34 and 36–38ins
81–86 and 91–96cms

INSTRUCTIONS

Finished Measurements
at underarm
39½ and 41ins
100 and 104cm
length
25 and 25½ins
TENSION/GAUGE
17 grids and 17 rows to 10cm (4ins) using a 2mm crochet hook and grid pattern

Grid Pattern (worked on a ch base)
Row 1: work 1 tr/dc in fourth ch from hook, * 1 ch, miss 1 ch, 1 tr/dc in the next st; repeat from * to end of row, 3 turning ch.
Row 2: miss first st, * 1 tr/dc in next st, 1 ch, 1 tr/dc in next st; repeat from * to end of row, 3 turning ch. Repeat row 2
Grid Pattern (with motifs)
Work this from the chart. One open square represents 1 tr/dc, 1 ch, 1 tr/dc. To work the filled squares, after the tr/dc into the first tr/dc, work 2 tr/dc together thus:
yoh, put hook into ch or st, draw one loop through, yoh, draw yarn through 2 loops, yoh, hook into same st, draw one loop through, yoh, draw yarn through 2 loops, yoh, draw yarn through all 3 loops.

then dec 1 grid at beg of following 5 rows.
Repeat from * until 27 (29) decs have been worked. When work measures 57cm (22½ins) 27 grids remain. Fasten off.

FRONT
Work as for back until work measures 35 (34) cm 13¾ (13¼) ins.
Shape armholes
Leave 2 grids unworked at each end of row then dec in same way as for back until 24 (26) decs have been worked AT THE SAME TIME when work measures 50cm (19¾ ins), shape neck.
Neck Shaping
Leave the centre 11 grids unworked and continue each side separately. Dec 3 grids at neck edge on foll row and 2 grids unworked on following 4 alt rows. Complete second side to match, reversing all shapings.

RIGHT SLEEVE
Make a foundation ch of 114 (122) ch + 3 turning ch. Work 5 rows in grid pattern (57:61 grids) then continue by following the chart and beginning with 10 (12) grids then 1

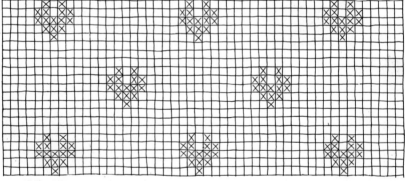

BACK
Make a foundation ch of 170 (178) + 3 turning ch and work 1 row in grid pattern. (85:89) grids. Then continue in grid pattern with motifs following the chart beginning with 6 (8) grids then 1 motif, to end of row. When work measures 35 (34) cm 13¾ (13¼) ins, shape armholes
Armhole shaping
Leave 1 grid unworked at each end of next row then decrease:
* 1 grid at beg of following 2 rows. Work 1 row straight then dec 1 grid at beg of next 3 rows. Work 1 row

motif to end of row. Continue by inc 1 grid at each end of every 10th row five times. (67:71) grids. When work measures 42cm (16½ins) shape armholes.

Armhole shaping
Leave 2 grids unworked at each end of next row then cont by working the same decs as for back at left hand side of work (back edge) and at the same time work the same decs as for front at the right hand side of work (front edge).

Complete work by leaving 5 grids unworked at beg of next row at front edge then 2 grids at same edge on following 3 alt rows then 1 grid on following alt row.

Work left sleeve as for right reversing all shapings.

Rib for lower edge

With 2.50mm (2) knitting needles, pick up and k 142 (146) sts evenly along lower edge of back. Work 7cm (2¾ins) in k2, p2 rib. Cast off. Work in same way at lower edge of front.

FINISHING

Stitch back raglan seams and one front raglan seam.

Neck Border

With a set of 4 2.50mm needles, pick up and k 200 sts evenly around neck. Work 2cm (¾ins) in rows of k2, p2 rib. Cast off.

Stitch the second front raglan seam and neck border seam. Stitch side and sleeve seams. Fold the last 3 rows of grids at lower edge of sleeves to wrong side of work and stitch in place. Thread elastic through these hems.

Loose Fitting Pullover in Tunisian Crochet

Note: not the original yarn but substitute will give a similar effect

MATERIALS

Pingouin Pingofrance or Confort each ball is approx 140yds/125m
4(5:5:6) 50g balls
colour black (MC main colour)
3(3:4:5) 50g balls colour white (A)
3(3:4:5) 50g balls colour grey (B)
3(3:4:5) 50g balls colour black/white (C)
Tunisian crochet hook 5mm/H
standard hooks 3mm/D, 5mm/H
stitch holder

TENSION/GAUGE

18 sts and 17 rows to 4ins/10cm using 5mm/H Tunisian crochet hook
16 sts and 15 rows to 4ins/10cm over h.tr/h.dc using 5mm/H crochet hook.

Check tension/gauge before commencing work.

SIZE

32(34:36:38) ins
81(86:91:96) cm

Finished Measurements at underarm
38(40:42:44) ins
96(100:105:109) cm

length
20¼(21¼:21¼:22¼) ins
52(54:54:57) cm

sleeve width at upper arm
16(17:17:18) ins
40(42.5:42.5:45) cm

TUNISIAN PATTERN STITCH

Make a chain of desired length.

Row 1: (outward) insert hook under top loop only of second ch from hook, forming a loop on hook, draw up a loop under top strand of each ch to end of work. There will be the same number of loops on hook as number of ch.

Row 1: (return) yoh, draw through first loop, * yoh, draw through 2 loops; repeat from * until 1 loop remains, 1 ch.

Row 2: (outward) Keeping all loops on hook, insert hook under second vertical bar from hook, yoh and draw up a loop, * draw up a loop in each vertical bar to last bar, insert hook under 2 (front and back) strands of last st, draw up a loop (this will give a firm edge)

Row 2: (return) as row 1 (return).

To inc at beg (outward) row: ch 1, pull up a loop under first vertical bar (inc made), work to end.

INSTRUCTIONS

To inc at end of row: at beg of previous (return) row, yoh and draw through first loop, ch 1, work to end. At end of following (first (outward) row, pull up a loop in extra ch 1 (inc made).

To cast off: at beg of first (outward row), draw up a loop under vertical bar as usual and draw this loop through hook (sl.st worked). Cast off each st in this way. At end of first outward row, work to sts to be cast off, join another length of yarn and sl.st across sts in the same way.

BACK

With 5mm/H Tunisian crochet hook, and colour A ch 86(90:94:98), work row 1 (outward) of pattern st. * With B, work next 2 halves of patt st. With MC, work next 2 halves of patt st. With A work next 2 halves of patt st *. Repeat between * and * for stripe patt until back measures 8 (8½:8½:9) ins/20.5(21.5:21.5:23) cm from beg.

Sleeve Shaping

Inc 1 st each end every row 6 times, then every other row 4 times (106: 110:114:118) sts and back should measure approx 11¼ (11¾:11¾: 12¼) ins/29(30:30:31.5) cm from beg. Work straight in patt until straight edge of sleeve measures 9(9½:9½:10) ins/23(24:24:25.5) cm from last inc sts.

Shoulder shaping

Cast off at each end of every first (outward) row 6 sts 2(1:0:0) times, 7 sts 3(4:4:3) times, 8 sts 0(0:1:2) times. Cast off rem 40(42:42:44) sts for back of neck.

FRONT

Work as for back until straight edge of sleeve measures 6½(7:7:7½) ins/ 61.5(17.5:17.5:19) cm from last inc sts, end with a (return) row.

Neck Shaping

Next row: work until there are 45(46:48:49) sts on hook, sl.sts to a st holder, cast off centre 16(18:18: 20) sts for neck, work to end.

Working on right side sts only, cast off from neck edge every row 3 sts twice, 2 sts 3 times (33:34:36:37) sts. Work straight until same length as back to shoulder. Shape shoulder as for back. Work left side of front to correspond to right side. Sew side and shoulder seams.

SLEEVES

Note: sleeves are worked in rounds with a standard crochet hook.

With right side facing, standard 5mm/H hook and C, work 64(68: 68:72) h.tr/h.dc round armhole edge of front and back (approx 5 h.tr/h.dc worked in every 6 rows). Join and place marker for beg of round and sl. marker every round. Working through back loop only to form ridge on right side, cont in h.tr/h.dc and AT SAME TIME, dec 1 st at beg of round every 4th round 12(6:6:0) times, every 3rd round 4(12:12:20) times (48:50:50:52) sts and sleeve should measure approx 16ins/40cm from beg.

Cuff Edging

Change to 3mm/D hook and MC and work in rounds of sc/sl.st for 7 rounds. Turn work, work 1 round more of sc/sl.st on wrong side. Fasten off.

FINISHING

Lower Edging

With right side facing, 3mm/D and MC, work 172(180:188:196) sc/sl.st evenly round lower edge of back and front. Join and work in rounds of sc/sl.st for 8 rounds. Finish same as cuff edging.

Armhole edging

With right side facing, 3mm/D and MC, work 115(120:120:127) sc/sl.st around armhole edge where sleeve was joined. Join and work in rounds of sc/sl.st for 11 rounds. Finish same as for cuff edging.

Neckband

With right side facing, 3mm/D and MC, work 124(130:130:136) sc/sl.st evenly around neck edge. Join and work in rounds of sc/sl.st for 5 rounds. Finish same as for cuff edging.

Filet Work Crochet Collar

MATERIALS

Phildar Fil d'Ecosse no. 5
1 1⅓oz/40g ball
approx 152yd/140m
colour ecru
1.50mm/6 USA crochet hook
2mm/B crochet hook or size to give recommended tension/gauge
1 set hook and eye

TENSION/GAUGE

26 tr/dc and 16 rows to 4ins/10cm using 2mm/B hook. Check tension/gauge before commencing work.

SIZES

One size fits all

Finished measurements

Width around neck edge 16¼ins/41cm

depth 4ins/10cm

INSTRUCTIONS

With 1.50mm/6 hook ch 110 tightly for neck edge.

Row 1: with 2mm/B hook work 1 tr/dc in 4th ch from hook and all subsequent ch to end of row. (108 sts counting the ch 3 as 1 tr/dc). Turn.

Row 2: ch 3, work in tr/dc and inc 20 tr/dc evenly across row. (128 sts)

Row 3: ch 3, 1 tr/dc in first tr/dc (1 tr/dc inc), 1 tr/dc in each next 2 sts, 2 ch, *miss 2 sts, 1 tr/dc in each next 4 sts, 2 ch; repeat from * to last 5 sts, miss 2 sts, 1 tr/dc in each next 2 sts, 2 tr/dc in turning ch (1 tr/dc inc), turn.

Row 4: ch 3, inc 1 tr/dc, * ch 2, miss 2 sts, 1 tr/dc in next st, 2 tr/dc in 2 ch space, 1 tr/dc in next st; repeat from * ending with ch 2, miss 2 tr/dc, 2 tr/dc in turning ch, turn.

Row 5: ch 3, inc 1 tr/dc, 1 tr/dc in next st, * 3 tr/dc in 2 ch space, ch 2, miss 2 tr/dc, 1 tr/dc in each next 2 sts, ch 2, miss 2 ch space, 1 tr/dc in each next 2 sts, ch 2, miss 2 sts; repeat from * ending with 3 tr/dc in 2 ch space, ch 2, miss 2 sts, 1 tr/dc in each next 2 sts, 2 tr/dc in 2 ch space, 1 tr/dc in next st, 2 tr/dc in

turning ch, turn.

Row 6: ch 3, inc 1 tr/dc, 1 tr/dc in each next 6 sts, * ch 2, miss 2 ch space, 1 tr/dc in each next 3 sts, (ch 2, miss 2 ch space, 1 tr/dc in each next 2 sts) twice; repeat from * ending with ch 2, miss ch 2 space, 1 tr/dc in each next 5 sts, 2 tr/dc in turning ch. Turn.

Row 7: ch 3, inc 1 tr/dc, 1 tr/dc in each tr/dc and 2 tr/dc in each 2 ch space ending with 2 tr/dc in turning ch (149 sts). Turn.

Row 8: ch 3, inc 1 tr/dc, * ch 2, miss 2 sts, 1 tr/dc in each next 4 tr/dc; repeat from * to last 4 tr/dc, end with ch 2, miss 2 sts, 1 tr/dc in next st, 1 tr/dc in turning ch. Turn.

Row 9: ch 3, inc 1 tr/dc, 1 tr/dc in next st, * 2 tr/dc in next 2 ch space, ch 2, miss 2 tr/dc, 1 tr/dc in each next 2 sts; repeat from * ending with 2 tr/dc in last 2 ch space, 1 tr/dc in next st, 1 tr/dc in turning ch. Turn.

Row 10: ch 3, inc 1 tr/dc, 1 tr/dc in each next 3 sts, * ch 2, miss 2 sts, 2 tr/dc in 2 ch space, ch 2, 1 tr/dc in each next 2 sts; repeat from * ending with 1 tr/dc in each last 2 sts, 1 tr/dc in turning ch. Turn.

Row 11: ch 3, inc 1 tr/dc, ch 2, miss 2 sts, * 1 tr/dc in each next 2 sts, 2 tr/dc in 2 ch space, 1 tr/dc in each next 2sts, ch 2, miss 2 ch space; repeat from * ending with 1 tr/dc in each next 4 sts, 1 tr/dc in turning ch. Turn.

Row 12: ch 3, inc 1 tr/dc, * ch 2, miss 2 sts, 1 tr/dc in each next 2 sts, ch 2, miss 2 ch space, 1 tr/dc in each next 2 sts; repeat from * to end. Turn.

Row 13: ch 3, inc 1 tr/dc, 1 tr/dc in next st, * 2 tr/dc in next 2 ch space, ch 2, miss 2 sts, 2 tr/dc in 2 ch space, 1 tr/dc in each next 2 sts, ch 2, miss 2 ch space, 1 tr/dc in each next 2 sts; repeat from * ending with 2 tr/dc in 2 ch space, ch 2, miss 2 sts, 2 tr/dc in 2 ch space, 1 tr/dc in next st, 1 tr/dc in turning ch. Fasten off.

EDGING

With right side facing and 2mm/B hook, rejoin cotton to beg ch of collar, work 20 dc/sc in row along side edge, 3 dc/sc in corner, 1 dc/sc in each tr/dc, 2 dc/sc in each 2 ch space along lower edge, 3 dc/sc in corner, 20 dc/sc along side edge.

Fasten off. Rejoin yarn at beg of edge, * work 1 dc/sc in each next 3 dc/sc, ch 4, 1 dc/sc in same dc/sc (one picot made); repeat from * around edge. Press lightly. Sew on hook and eye at neck edge to fasten.

Bedspread

MATERIALS

Pingouin Corrida 4
95 50g balls
each approx 120yds/110m
colour white
crochet hook 4.50mm/G

SIZE

Bedspread measures approx 280cm × 180cm (110ins × 71ins) and it is made from 126 squares seamed together, each approx 20cm/8ins square

NOTE

1. Pineapple st
(yoh, hook into st or space, yoh and draw loop through) 4 times into the same st or space, yoh and draw through first 8 loops on hook, yoh and draw through last 2 loops on hook.

2. Crab st
dc/sc worked from left to right

INSTRUCTIONS

Base Round: work 5ch and join in a ring with a sl.st.

Round 1: 2 ch, 1 h.tr/h.dc, (2 ch, 2 h.tr/h.dc) 3 times, 2 ch, 1 sl.st into second ch, 1 sl.st into next space before h.tr/h.dc.

Round 2: 3 ch, * (1 h.tr/h.dc, 2 ch, 1 h.tr/h.dc) in 2 ch space, 1 ch, 1 h.tr/h.dc between 2 h.tr/h.dc, 1 ch; repeat to end ending with (1 h.tr/h.dc, 2 ch, 1 h.tr/h.dc in 2 ch space, 1 ch, 1 sl.st into second ch.

Round 3: sl.st into last 1 ch space of 3rd round, * (1 ch, 1 pineapple) into each next two 1 ch space, (1 h.tr/h.dc, 2 ch, 1 h.tr/h.dc) in 2 ch space; repeat to end ending with 1 ch, 1 sl.st into first ch.

Round 4: * (1 ch, 1 pineapple) into each next three 1 ch spaces, 1 ch, (1.h.tr/h.dc, 2 ch, 1 h.tr/h.dc) into 2 ch loop; repeat from * to end ending with 1 ch, 1 sl.st into beginning 1 ch.

Round 5: * (1 ch, 1 pineapple) into each next four 1 ch spaces, 1 ch, (1 h.tr/h.dc, 2 ch, 1 h.tr/h.dc) into 2 ch space; repeat from * to end ending with 1 ch, 1 sl.st into beginning 1 ch.

Row 6: * 1 ch, 2 dc/sc into first 1 ch space (before first pineapple), (1 ch, 1 pineapple) into each next three 1 ch space, 1 ch, 2 dc/sc into next 1 ch space, 1 ch, (1 h.tr/h.dc, 2 ch, 1 h.tr/dc) into 2 ch space; repeat from * to end ending with 1 ch, 1 sl.st into beginning 1 ch.

Round 7: * 1 ch, 2 dc/sc, 2 dc/sc into 1 ch loop (before first pineapple), 1 ch, (1 pineapple, 1 ch) into each next two 1 ch space, 2 dc/sc into next 1 ch space, 2 dc/sc, 1 ch, (1 h.tr/h.dc, 2 ch, 1 h.tr/h.dc) into 2 ch space; repeat from * to end ending with 1 sl.st into beginning 1 ch.

Round 8: * 1 ch, 4 dc/sc, 1 dc/sc into next 1 ch space, 1 ch, 1 pineapple into next 1 ch space, 1 ch, 1 dc/sc into next 1 ch space, 4 dc/sc, 1 ch, (1 h.tr/h.dc, 2 ch, 1 h.tr/h.dc) into 2 ch space; repeat from * to end ending with 1 sl.st into beginning 1 ch.

Round 9: 1 ch, * 1 dc/sc in first 1 ch space, 5 dc/sc, 2 dc/sc into each 1 ch space before and after pineapple of round 8, 5 dc/sc, 1 dc/sc into 1 ch space, (1 h.tr/h.dc, 2 ch, 1 h.tr/h.dc) into 2 ch space; repeat from * to end ending with 1 sl.st into beginning 1 ch.

Round 10: 1 ch, * 19 dc/sc, (1 h.tr/h.dc, 2 ch, 1 h.tr/h.dc) into 2 ch space; repeat from * working 2 dc/sc into st at each side of each corner group and end with 1 sl.st into beginning 1 ch.

Round 11: 1 ch, * 22 dc/sc, (1 h.tr/h.dc, 2 ch, 1 h.tr/h.dc) into 2 ch space; repeat from * working 2 dc/sc into st at each side of each corner group and end with 1 sl.st into beginning 1 ch.

Round 12: 1 ch, * 2 dc/sc into first st, (1 pineapple, 3 dc/sc) 5 times, 1 pineapple, 2 dc/sc into next st, (1 h.tr/h.dc, 2 ch, 1 h.tr/h.dc) in 2 ch space; repeat from * to end ending with 1 sl.st into beginning 1 ch.

Round 13: 1 ch, * 26 dc/sc, (1 h.tr/h.dc, 2 ch, 1 h.tr/h.dc) into 2 ch space; repeat from * ending with 1 sl.st into beginning 1 ch.

Fasten off.

FINISHING

Using a flat seam, join squares to form a rectangle 14 squares long by 9 squares wide.

Edging

Round 1: 1 dc/sc in every st but working 2 dc/sc in each corner.

Round 2: * 1 tr/dc, 1 ch, miss 1 st; repeat from * to end.

Round 3: as round 1

Round 4: crab stitch.

Crochet Terms

UK	USA
SLIP STITCH (SL.ST)	SLIP STITCH (SL.ST)
DOUBLE CROCHET (DC)	SINGLE CROCHET (SC)
HALF TREBLE (H.TR)	HALF DOUBLE CROCHET (H.DC)
TREBLE (TR)	DOUBLE CROCHET (DC)
DOUBLE TREBLE (D.TR)	TREBLE (TR)
TRIPLE TREBLE (TR.TR)	DOUBLE TREBLE (D.TR)
QUADRUPLE TREBLE (Q[UAD] TR)	TRIPLE TREBLE (TR.TR)
QUINTUPLE TREBLE (QT[UIN] TR)	QUADRUPLE TREBLE (Q[UAD] TR)
SEXTUPLE TREBLE (S[EXT] TR)	QUINTUPLE TREBLE (QT[UIN] TR)
CAST OFF	FASTEN OFF
MISS	SKIP
TENSION	GAUGE
WORK STRAIGHT	WORK EVEN
YARN OVER HOOK (YOH)	YARN OVER (YO)

Foreign Language Terms
French

Fourniture	Materials
fil(s)	yarn(s)
aiguilles (aig)	needles
bouton(s)	button(s)
crochet	crochet hook
pelotes (pel)	balls

Taille	Measurements
36, 38, 40, 42, 44 cm	31, 32, 34, 36, 38 ins
petit, moyenne, grand, patron	small, medium, large, X large
tour de poitrine	chest measurement
unique	one size
hauteur	long, length
hauteur totale	complete length

Points employes	Stitches used
bride (br)	treble (tr)
bride double (d-br)	double treble
chainette (ch)	chain
demi-bride (demi-br)	half treble
demi-maille	slip stitch
maille (m)	stitch
maille coulee	slip stitch
maille en l'air (ml) or (m.air)	chain
maille serrée (m.s)	double crochet
maille de tete	top of stitch
maille torse	twisted, crossed stitch
picot (pi)	picot
triple bride (triple-br)	triple treble

Explications	Instructions
à travers	through, across
ajoute	add
alternativement (alt)	alternately
anneau	ring
arceau (ar)	arch
arrêter	stop
arrière	back (loop)
augmenter (augm)	increase
avant	front (loop)
boucle (bl)	loop
brin	stem
carré ajoute	added square
carré plein	full square
carré vide	empty square

c'est-à-dire (c-a-d)	that is to say,
centimetre (cm)	centimetre
chaque/ chacune (ch)	each, every
chiffre	number
couleur (col)	colour
commencer	begin
continuer (cont)	continue
coquille	shell
couler une ou plusieurs boucles	draw through one or more loops
courbe	curve
crocheter (croch)	to crochet
croisee	crossed
depuis	since
dernier/ derniere	last
devant	in front of
diminuer (dim)	decrease
double (d)	double
e [ie 2e]	times [ie twice]
echantillon	pattern
egalement (egal)	equally, evenly
endroit (end)	front, right
ensemble (ens)	together
envers (env)	wrong side, back of work
environ	about
espace	space
etc	etc
éventuellement (ev)	eventually, finally
exactement (exact)	exactly
extérieur (exter)	exterior
fermer en rond	close a ring
feuille	cluster
figure (fig)	illustration
fois (fs)	times
fs ou x	number of times
gramme (g)	gram
graphique	diagram, chart
grille	grid
groupe (gr)	group
intérieur (int)	inside
jeté	yarn over hook
lisiere (lis)	selvedge
même	same
nouveau	new
numero (No)	number
par exemple (p.ex)	for example
piquer	hook into
point	stitch

précédement (preced)	previous(ly)
prenant	take
rabattre (rab)	cast off
ramener	return
rang (rg)	row
répéter (rep)	repeat
reprendre (repr)	repeat
respectivement (resp)	respectively
restant (rest)	remaining
sauter	miss (a stitch)
selon	according to
séparément (sep)	separately
signe de reprise *	start of repeat *
sous	under
supérieur (super)	above
suivant (suiv)	following
temps	times
terminer (term)	finish
tirer en boucle	draw through a loop
total (total)	total, all
toujours (touj)	always
tour (t)	round
tourner	turn
tous/toute/ toutes (ts/tte/ tts)	all
travail (trav)	work
triangle (tr)	shell with ch

German

Material	Materials
Faden	yarn, thread
garn	yarn
Häkelnadel	crochet hook
Knopt, Knöpfe	buttons
Stricknadeln	needles

Masse	Measurements
Grosse	size
36, 38, 40, 42	32, 34, 36, 38
Oberweite	actual chest measurement
Ganze Länge	total length

Grundmuster/ Strickmuster	Stitches used
Doppel- stäbchen (D-Stb)	double treble
dreifaches Stäbchen	triple treble
eineinhalb- fache Stäbchen (1½f–Stb)	1½ treble

Feste Masche (fM)	double crochet
Halbe Stäbchen (h.Stb)	half treble
Kettenmasche (KM)	chain
Kopfmasche	top of stitch
Kreuzstäbchen	crossed treble
Luftmasche (Lftn)	chain
Masche (M)	stitch
Muster	stitch
Picot (Pi)	picot
Stäbchen (Stb)	treble
Verkreuzte Masche	crossed stitch
Verdrehte Masche	crossed or twisted sts

Maschenprobe/ Häkelprobe	Tension
20 M und 25 R = 10cm im Quadrat	20 sts and 25 rows = 10 cm

Anleitungen	Instructions
Abbildung (Abb)	illustration
abnehmen (abn)	decrease
Abschluss	finishing
abwechselnd (abw)	alternate
alle	all
am	by, in
Anfangen	beginning
Anschlag (Anschl)	cast on
Anzahl (Anz)	number
Arbeit (Arb)	work
arbeiten (arb)	work, make
Ärmel	sleeve
auf	on
aufnehmen (aufn)	increase, pick up
aus	out of, through
Beginn	begin
beginnen	beginning, begin
beide	both
beidseitig (beids)	at each end/on both sides
beitragen	add
Bogen (Bo)	arch, sheet
dabei	yet at the same time/there by
dann	then
das heisst (dh)	which means,
dauern	last
dazwischen	in between
den	of the
doppelt (dopp)	double

FOREIGN LANGUAGE TERMS

German	English	German	English
Doppelstäbchen (D-Stb)	double treble	restliche (restl)	remaining
dritte	third	Reihe(n) (R)	row
durch	through	Rondelle	circle, ring
eine	one	Rücken	back
einmal	once	Rückseite (Rucks)	wrong side of work
einzig	only	Runde (Rd)	round, circular
ende	end	Schlinge (Schl)	loop
erste	first	Schulter	shoulder
Einstichstelle	look through	separat (sep)	separate(ly)
eventuell (evtl/ev)	if so	seite	side, page
fächer	shell	sind	are
Farbe	colour	Stäbchen (Stb)	stitch
fassen	fasten	stechen	hook into
folgende (folg)	follow	teilen	divide
für	for	Total (tot)	total
fortlaufende (fortl)	the very next	über	over
gerade	straight	Umschlag (U)	yoh
gleich(e)	alike, same	überspringen (überspr)	and continue
Gramm (g)	gramme	und so weiter (usw)	thus
hak	crochet hook	verlängert (verl)	lengthen
Häkelnadel	crochet hook	versetzt (vers)	move, put
hin	along, there	verteilt (vert)	distribute
hinter(e)	behind	vor	before
hoch	high	vordere	front
holen	catch	vorne	previous
immer	always	weiterarb	continue to work
jede, jeder	each, ever	weiterhin	from now on
kante	border, corner	wendemaschen	turning ch
Kästchen (Ka)	square	wiederholen (wdh)	repeat
Kreuzschlinge	crossed	Wiederholungszeichen *	*, repeat
lassen	leave	Zahl	number
links (li)	left	ziehen durch ein/eine oder mehr	draw through one or more loops
locker	loosely	zum Beispiel (zB)	for example
Mal	times	zum Wenden (ZW)	turn
Maschenglied	loop	Zus	together
mittel/mittleren	middle, centre	zusammen (zus)	together
Modell (Mod)	pattern	zwei	two
Motiv	pattern	zweite	second
Musterbogen (Musterbo)	pattern sheet	zweimal	twice
nach	after	zwischen	between
nacheinander	one after another		
näschst	nearer		
Nadel (N)	needle		
nähte	seam		
neu	new		
noch	beside		
nocheinmal	once more		
nochmals	( ) more times		
Nummer (nr)	number		
oben	at the top		
oder	or		
quadrant	square		
Randmasche (Rdm)	edge stitch		
rechts (re)	right		
respektiv (resp)	respectively		

Italian

Occorrente	Materials
bottone	buttons
ferre	needles
filati	yarn
gomitolo	ball
uncinetto	crochet hook

Misure	Measurements
taglia (tg)	size
42, 44, 46, 48	32, 34, 36, 38
altezza	length

Punti impiegati	Stitches used
maglia alta (m.alta)	treble
maglia alta doppia	double treble
maglia bassa (m.bassa)	double crochet
maglia di testa	stitch in top
mezzo maglia alto	half treble
mezzo maglia bassa	slip stitch
punto (p)	stitch
punto alto (p.a.)	treble
punto alto doppio (p.d)	double treble
punto basso (p.b.)	double crochet
punto bassissimo (p.bb)	slip stitch
punto catenella (p.cat)	chain
punto incrociata	crossed stitch
punto passato	slip stitch

Campione	Tension
20 p.e 25 f = un quadrato di 10cm di lato	20 sts and 25 = 10cm

Esecuzione	Instructions
alternative-mente (alt)	alternative
altezza (alt)	length
altri	another
ancora	again, more
anello	ring
archetto	arch
arco	arch
asole	loop
assieme (ass)	together
attesa (att)	required
aumentare (aum)	(to) increase
aumento (aum)	increase
aumentando	increasing
avviare (avv)	cast on
cambiare	change
catenella (cat)	chain
centemetre (cm)	centimetre
cerchio	ring
circa (ca)	round
chiudere (chiud)	fasten off
chiuderla	close it
chiuso	close, fasten

circolare	circular
colore (col)	colour
come segue (c.s.)	as follows, thus
continuare (cont)	continue
cucira	stitch, seam
cucite	stitch, seam
dalle	by the
davanti	front
dell'	of the
destra (des)	right
dietro	back
diminuire (dim)	to decrease
diminuzione (dim)	decrease
diritto (dir)	knit
disegno	design
diviso (div)	divide
e	and
eccetera (ecc)	etc
eseguire	work
e cosi via (ecvs)	in this way
eventualmente (event)	finally
fermare	fasten off
ferro/ferri (f)	row(s)
figura (fig)	pattern, diagram
fissare	arrange
foglia	leaf, cluster
formato	made
gettato (gett)	yoh
giro (G)	round
giungere	reach, fold
gomitolo (gom)	ball
grafico	chart
grammi (g)	grams
gruppi	group
incrociare (incr)	crossed
iniziare (iniz)	begin
inizio	first st (ch)
inseriti	enclose, insert
insieme (ins)	together
larghezza (largh)	width
laterale (lat)	side
lavorare (lav)	work
lavoro (lav)	work
lunghezza (lungh)	length
maglia (m)	stitch
modello (mod)	pattern
nel,nella	in the
nocciolina	cluster
numero (No)	number
ogni	each
pagina (pag)	page
pari	even number
passare	draw through/ slip
piccolo	small

FOREIGN LANGUAGE TERMS

piegare	turn		
pieno	filled		
pippiolino	picot		
piu	more, longer		
posteriore	back		
precedente (prec)	previous		
prendere (prend)	take		
quadratto	square		
qualche	any, some		
rimanente (rim)	remaining		
ripetere (rip)	repeat		
ripetere da * a *	repeat from * to *		
riprendere (ripr)	pick up		
rompere	break		
rovescio (rov)	wrong side		
saltare (salt)	miss a stitch		
segno di ripetizione (*)	repeat from *		
senso inverso	without turning		
senza	without		
seguente (seg)	following		
separatamente (separat)	separate(ly)		
sinistra (sin)	left		
solo	alone, only, one		
sospeso	leave unworked		
sottostante	below, under		
stesso	same, self		
successivo	following		
superiore (sup)	higher		
sulla	in the		
tanto	so, so long, so much		
tempi	times		
terminare (term)	finish		
terminando	finishing		
termine (term)	end		
totale (tot)	total		
ultima	last		
volta	time(s)		
voltare (volt)	time, turn		
vuoto	empty		

Spanish

Materiales	Materials
agujas (ag)	needles
boton	button
ganchillo	crochet hook
hilos	yarn

Medidas	Measurements
talla	size
40, 42, 44, 46	32, 34, 36, 38
alto, largo	length

Puntos empleados	Stitches used
media presilla	half treble
presilla doble	double treble
presilla sencilla	treble
punto (p)	stitch
punto de cabeza	in top of stitch
punto cadeneta	chain
punto cruzado	crossed stitch
punto deslizado	slip stitch
punto en al aire	chain
punto prieto de torcido	twisted, crossed stitch

Muestra de orientacion	Tension
20 p. y 25 v = un cuadro de 10cm tejido con las g del no 5	26 sts and 26 rows = 10cm using 5mm needles

Marcha de la labor	Instructions
a cada extremo	at each end
al cabo de	at the end of
al través de	through
abrochar	fasten
acabar	finish
alternativo	alternate(ly)
alto total (alt tot)	total length
anillo	loop
anterior	previous(ly)
antes	before
aquel tiempo	that time
arco	arch
armado	making up
arrollado	yoh
aumentar (aum)	to increase
aumento(s) (aum)	increase(s)
aun	still
bolsillo	pocket
borde	edge, border
bucle	loop
cadeneta	chain
cambiar	change
centro	centre
cerrar	close, finish
clave	key (to chart)
color	colour
completar	complete
con	with
continuar (cont)	continue
cosar	sew
crecido	yoh
cruzar	cross
cuello	collar
de cabo a rabo	from x to x
de (en) una sola vez	in one row, in one time
debajo	under
dejar en espera	leave unworked

delante	front	paras	fasten off
derecho	front or right side	precedente	previous
		previo	previously
deslizar	slip	proceder igual	work in same way
deslizer uno o varios bucles	draw through one or more loops	proseguir (pros)	continue
		recto	straight, without shaping
después	then, some		
détras	through back of loop	redondo	ring, round
		repetir (rep)	repeat
disminyendo	decrease	repetir de * a * (rep)	repeat from * to *
disminuir (dismin)	decrease		
		restante (rest)	remaining
dobladillo	hem	revés	wrong side
doble	double	sacar un lazo bucle	draw through a loop
dos	twice		
echar	yrn	saltar	miss
empezar	begin	seguir	continue
escote	neck, neckline	seperado	separate
espacio	space	siempre	always
espalda	back	siguiente (sig)	following, next
fino	fine	simultanea- mente	at the same time
ganchillo	crochet hook		
grueso	thick		
hacer	make	sin	without
hacer el lazo	make a loop	solo	one
hebra (h)	yarn or yoh	terminar	come to end, finish
hebra delante o atras	back or front of loop		
		todo	each, every, all
hilo	yarn	trabajar (trab)	work
hombro(s)	shoulder(s)	ultimo	last
igual	equal, the same	una vez	once
impar	odd (rows)	veces	times
invertir la explicación sentido inverso	reversing shaping or instructions	vuelta (v)	turn, turning
izquierdo	left hand edge		
juntos	join, together		
labor	work		
lado	side, edge		
levantar sin tejer	slip		
manga	sleeve		
mapa	chart		
menguar (meng)	decrease		
menguado	decrease		
mitad	half		
montar	cast on		
nuevo	new		
número de puntos divido de x mas x	number of stitches divis- ible by x plus x		
ojal	buttonhole		
omitir	miss		
orillo	selvedge		
otro	last		
ovillo	ball		
par	even (rows)		
para	from		

International Symbols

◯	chain		⋎⋏	five treble stitches worked in a single stitch
∩	slip stitch		⊕	picot of three chain
†	double crochet		⬭	two loop popcorn
⊤	half treble		⊕	three loop popcorn
⊤	treble		⊕	four loop popcorn
⊤	double treble		⊕	five loop popcorn
⊤	triple treble		◯	two loop puff stitch
⊤	quadruple treble		◍	three loop puff stitch
Ʇ	relief stitch worked at back		◍	four loop puff stitch
Ƭ	relief stitch worked at front		◍	five loop puff stitch
✕	crossed stitch		⊝	two loop cluster
⋎	two treble stitches worked in a single stitch		⊕	three loop cluster
⋓	three treble stitches worked in a single stitch		⊛	four loop cluster
⋎	four treble stitches worked in a single stitch		⊛	five loop cluster